Books written previously by the same author:

'Our Birth on Earth'

'When Scorpio Ruled the World'

'Heaven's Message—How to Read it Nowadays'

'Character Portraits of England's Plantagenet Kings'

Concise Character Portraits Of England's Tudor, Stuart and Protectorate Rulers: 1456-1714 A.D.

Chris Stubbs

Order this book online at www.trafford.com
or email orders@trafford.com

Most Trafford titles are also available at major online book retailers.

Printed in the United States of America.

ISBN: 978-1-4907-3528-3 (sc)
ISBN: 978-1-4907-3529-0 (e)

Library of Congress Control Number: 2014908092

Trafford rev. 05/08/2014

www.trafford.com

North America & international
toll-free: 1 888 232 4444 (USA & Canada)
fax: 812 355 4082

CONTENTS

The Tudor, Stuart and Protectorate Rulers

ACKNOWLEDGEMENTS

Once more, Lois Rodden's website: 'Astro.com' proved invaluable for abstracting much of the rated birth data.

Similarly, many thanks must continue to go to the staff of Wirral Libraries' Bromborough Branch for loaning the individual biographies referenced in the book. Also, my wife, Angela, made time available for writing it. I should also like to thank my daughter, Hilary, and her friends Alex Jones and Dan O'Leary, for their efforts to keep me up-to-date with computing. Invariably, Toby kept me company during the preparation of the whole book.

To all those who love Astrology

FOREWORD

Continuing from where we left off in the previous book, we have assembled the Character Portraits of the Tudor, Stuart and Protectorate rulers of England from 1456-1714 A.D. As before, these portraits have been derived by following the author's proposed and previously described method for sorting, combining and blending interpretations of indicators from the individual ruler's Epoch and Birth charts. Please note that none of the interpretations come from the author. All points from the interpretations have been included but duplication has been minimised. Importantly, the unpolished portraits are impartial and consist of relatively modern expressions for appreciation and comparison purposes. The word 'Concise' has been added to the title because the most speculative, the more mundane and the least relevant interpretations have been relegated to smaller print. However, the order throughout the portraits remains unchanged so that they are as complete, or otherwise, as the method used allows. Additionally, all the natal charts are collected in time order in Appendix 1 so that the Character Portraits can stand on their own. In case of interest, Appendix 2 gives some of the natal charts of those who nearly became England's rulers during the time-frame of the book. To conclude, Appendix 3 examines the Tudors and the Stuarts as separate groups to try and find particular hereditary traits among them.

Overall, the book attempts to stand as a showcase for Astrology; perhaps it can also serve as a reference source for History students of the English periods covered.

We start with King Henry VII . . . .

Henry VII

About the welcome given to Princess Catherine of Aragon: November, 1501:

*"Great and cordial rejoicings have taken place;
the whole people have taken part."*

in a letter to her parents, King Ferdinand and Queen Isabella.

Henry VII was King of England and Lord of Ireland from his seizing the crown on 22nd August, 1485 until his death on 21st April, 1509, as the first monarch of the House of Tudor.

Henry won the throne when he defeated Richard III at the Battle of Bosworth Field. He was the last king of England to win his throne on the field of battle. Henry cemented his claim by marrying Elizabeth of York, daughter of Edward IV and niece of Richard III. Henry was successful in restoring the power and stability of the English monarchy after the political upheavals of the civil wars known as the Wars of the Roses. He founded a long-lasting dynasty and, after a reign of nearly 24 years, was succeeded peacefully by his son, Henry VIII.

Although Henry can be credited with the restoration of political stability in England, and a number of commendable administrative, economic and diplomatic initiatives, the latter part of his reign was characterised by a financial rapacity, which stretched the bounds of legality. The capriciousness and lack of due process, which indebted many in England, were soon ended upon Henry VII's death after a commission revealed widespread abuses. Simple "greed", in large part, underscored the means by which royal control had been over-asserted in Henry's final years.

Henry was the only child of Edmund Tudor (1st Earl of Richmond) and half-brother of Henry VI through their mother, Catherine de Valois, daughter of Charles VI of France, widow of Henry V and subsequently wife of Owen Tudor, Henry's paternal grandfather. His mother, Lady Margaret Beaufort, was a great-granddaughter of John of Gaunt, the third son of Edward III, and aged just fourteen at the time of Henry's birth. His father, Edmund Tudor, died in captivity three months before Henry's birth. Henry was born at Pembroke Castle, Wales, on the 6th February, 1457 NS at five-to three in the morning (see Appendix 1, Figure 2). His Epoch (see Appendix 1, Figure 1) occurred on the 3rd May, 1456 NS at twenty-five-to-three in the morning.

Character Portrait

Introduction: Henry's well-integrated nature, being both objective and subjective, comprised several different parts, i.e. the honourable, the wilful, the softened assertive, the studious and the receptive, all interspersed with good and bad points. In short, he was complicated, intelligent, capable and very versatile.

General: As a generous, honourable character that inspired respect, Henry's only drawback was a tendency to be self-righteous and priggish. Pleasurable activities often exerted a great attraction for him, particularly those involving travel or outdoor life. He liked to be "spoilt". Self-expansion was shown in a kind, protective and sympathetic way. Although a kind, courteous and benevolent person, he could not pass by an offence easily, but would, nevertheless, soon be reconciled. He had aspiration, a love of science and of religion that improved his charitable nature somewhat.

Henry was truly the original commander of his life. Self-willed, revolutionary, self-insistent, disruptive, awkward, brusque and precipitate, his ideals were carried into actuality by an unusual power of leadership in practical, scientific and spiritual ways. He had self-confidence, faith in his own ideas, pride and passion, desire to rule, managing ability and dramatic instinct. His strong will made him highly independent, inventive, determined, authoritative, all with spiritual energy, as well as ability to read character. His obsession became megalomania with a compelling need to achieve fully-creative self-expression.

At the same time, Henry could have been assertive, aggressive, vigorous and courageous. He had energy for personal affairs. He was good at starting new enterprises and quick and stirring in action. Confident, argumentative, indignant yet with a constant flow of ideas, Henry had to be first. He was hopeful and optimistic but undertook more than he could accomplish. His determination greatly inclined him to go to extremes. Thus he had a tendency to impulsive action, hasty speech and when provoked said a great deal more than probably was thought, or meant. He tried to make adjustments to difficulties and to by-pass them but rarely without nervous stress. Yet all of these foregoing, fiery characteristics were softened and so seemed less offensive.

Most of the time, Henry had a good disposition. He was well-balanced and understanding with an harmonious temperament that contained much perseverance, carefulness and a liking for study. He was teachable, honest, trustworthy and sensitive but occasionally hasty. He was capable of deep concentration, ambition, tenacity, endurance, defiance, self-discipline and self-denial. There was a tendency to overvalue the practical and inclinations to be harsh, suspicious and avaricious.

There was an unassuming part to Henry's nature that was somewhat retiring, yet agreeable and sociable. He had a strongly artistic side with a particular interest in music. He was inclined to beauty and ease but too irresponsibly and lazily. He had imagination, refinement, sentiment, much charitable feeling and sympathy. Successful interests were possible in psychic, mystical and maritime matters. Strongly intuitive, his dreams and visions could have been precognitive. He may even have been mediumistic, through which he sought fulfilment, mental penetration, inspiration, prophesy and adventure. Unfortunately he suffered from varying moods leading to dual experiences of a contrasting nature so that he was torn between two different emotions, e.g. between inspiration on the one hand and secretiveness coupled with keen receptivity on the other. As a result, selfishness, jealousy, conventionality and the material side of life would have been cultivated. He tended towards the intangible and so to a lack of concreteness. Although he overvalued the practical, in a more refined way he was impractical in that he would concentrate on visions of the future rather than on those of the present. On this basis, all financial matters should, for safety, have been placed into more realistic hands.

Mentality: Henry tended to act at all times under a consideration of opposing views, or of sensitiveness to contrasting and antagonistic possibilities. Thus, he existed mainly in a world of conflicts. He appeared to be indecisive but his final choices and decisions would have been well-considered. He had a gift for seeing to the bottom of problems by digging deeply into analysis, which he used a little impulsively. Though constructive in a narrow, one-track way, order would have become rigid discipline and dreary planning. Mental loneliness could have resulted, often through fear and apprehension. A resulting lack of poise would then have led to brusque speech and writing.

Henry would have been learning how to allow his higher mind to understand and correct his former mistakes. Later on, he would have found himself doing all that he knew he should have done when he was younger, as his younger years did not fulfil him as much as they did his superiors.

Henry was brought into contact with the earlier formed parts of his higher mind in that he seemed to have already developed a mature sense of wisdom (more so than knowledge). Doubting himself caused him to look harder for his understandings than he really had to; but this was only until he learnt that all the effort he put in to try to think out solutions to problems was merely a part of his learning how to stop thinking. At once, he began to notice that the answers were always there.

Generally, Henry had a good, commonsense mentality and nervous force. He must have had to develop his intellectual skills so that he didn't have to rely on feelings and hunches. Usually, his mind worked fluently, quickly and with versatility. Talking, writing and speaking would have been easy. Communication took place by reading, writing and correspondence, as well as in educational matters. There was much seriousness about questions of faith and belief.

At times, Henry anxiously assimilated new philosophy and spiritual awareness with a desire to ingest all that he could. There was a reaching for all that was 'worth' to his higher being. Henry was a seeker of the first order and continued a mission throughout his life. He kept forming substance within his philosophical and spiritual beliefs, thereby transforming his collections of opinions into a very real sense of knowing. More deeply, he was developing his spiritual consciousness. He may well have experienced holy knowledge from the Bible, creating in him a powerful desire to use such understandings in his life. Eventually, he would have found self-respect before his God. He had begun this journey by trying to grasp every higher thought in the hope that sheer possession of much knowledge he would find what he was looking for. In the end, most of his learning came to him by much more natural means. His great awareness seemed to be coming from a different source than normal because the ways in which he expressed himself were rather unique. Thus, he had a great love for the ideas of "God" but not for the official format of any specific religious tradition. Fighting against rules, he knew the inner rules that would do him the most good.

Sometimes he lost his conscious train of thought because he was so interested in everything that he had difficulty narrowing his field of focus. He was learning how to become spiritually independent. He had to develop his understanding of life regardless of what was socially acceptable to the rest of his world and had to be able to stand on what he knew worked for him. Often this would have led him to experience much criticism from his friends and peers. It may even have endangered his marital ties. Still, his ultimate truth had to come from his unique sense of identity rather than come from any need to compromise what he knew for the sake of personal acceptability.

His intellect was profound but he still considered it necessary to test public opinion before taking any action that might have reflected on his credibility. Importantly, being well-informed meant that he had to learn as much as he could about many subjects. Fortunately, learning came easily to him and he rarely forgot what he had learned. Because of this he always made a worthwhile contribution to discussion, often amazing people with his wealth of information.

Henry constantly questioned the values of others. He sought to understand the deepest mysteries. Little in life went by him without him studying it clinically. His drive, however, was not only physical but mental and worldly orientated as well. Whether he expressed it physically or transformed it to mental regions this drive was powering all he sought to understand in the world. Aggressively, he created continued destruction in old, traditional habit patterns so that finally, he could go through a rebirth within himself on the deepest of levels. He was so linked with the values of others, that whether he liked it or not, he was strongly influenced by mass consciousness. The more he grew discontented with the world around him, the more he began to fathom the mysteries within himself.

Henry's desire to control and limit would have been freed to a certain extent, and his scope widened somewhat. His need for freedom would have become so strong that he had used every possible opportunity to achieve it. He knew that knowledge was the key to freedom and gaining it would have made it possible for him to achieve his goals. Freedom of thought and action would have been achieved through long study, determination and application. Gravity and dignity would have increased with age.

However, the danger was that his mind became over-widened so that it lost grasp, leading to carelessness, woolly thinking and indiscretion. His judgement would have become poor. Optimism followed by depression alternated. The general idea for Henry was to work hard during the optimistic times using every opportunity. On the other hand, he had to do his best to resist depression whenever it arose.

Intuitional and inspirational Henry had the ability to prophesy and to foresee the future. He had been born with natural, mediumistic talents that, if properly developed, could have led to a life of continued, worldly realisation. He could have had a strong, psychic tendency along with the desire to use it in the most honourable ways. Ideals and imaginative intuitions would have been kept in bounds and given shape and form that would have become useful in practice. Any limitation may have been felt through maze-like worries that would have tended to clear up in the long run through endurance and quiet keeping out of the limelight. Henry was highly introspective with a tendency to confuse his emotions with his rational thinking.

Henry went through emotional and mental conflict at the same time. His memories were often exaggerated as he tried to correct all the past situations in which he had not fully expressed himself. Also, he tended to repeat his experiences as if by repetition alone he became more secure in the correctness of how he had handled himself in the past. All his higher mind knowledge was now tested as he was asked to live it out at his emotional level. Thus, he had to have learned to believe faithfully and act upon his own truths.

Henry had a very strong sexual nature. To him sexuality represented the most unfathomable question of all. There was a great deal of semi-conscious sexual visualisation based on what he felt he needed from life. Still, in this area, in the world of business and in that of finance, he needed direction to keep himself from becoming too confused.

Henry was capable of absorbing impressions from his environment. Usually, he thought that all the feelings he experienced were his own and that ultimately they demanded some type of action or solution on his part but he was not truly obliged to accomplish this personally. He was highly sensitive, particularly to music and the arts, and had great difficulty dealing with the harshness of life, to which he was overly open. To balance himself, he made the mistake that he had to balance all that was around him. This made him more interested in other people's business than was actually good for him. He may have become so frustrated at trying to balance the world around him that, finally, he resorted to escapism to keep from recognising that his own personal difficulties were coming from problems that needed no solutions.

However, Henry did have a tremendous amount of insight into the mirror of himself, i.e. that part of his identity that he saw through the eyes of others. He could have learned to integrate better with his society through this kind of vision. Simultaneously, he would have been further removed from his basic essence because he would have sought to experience himself through others. He could have reached happiness by not reaching for it but by finding it within as a more or less permanent state of contentment with his own individual life experience as a small part of the overall worldly plan.

Lifestyle: Henry was restless, eager and when stimulated his aggressive nature sprang into action. It was the thrill of competition that made him accept challenges. He tended to thrive on sensationalism and conflict and put life-giving spirit into whatever affairs were of momentary concern. He would act a little impulsively in a wholly unashamed self-interest and found a complete emotional placing of himself, which wasn't disturbed by any inner complications, in any chosen reality. Thus, he was able to devote his attention completely to any given current task. Yet all this positivity was softened.

Henry's obsession was megalomania with a compelling need to achieve fully-creative self-expression. Henry was concerned with the overthrow of power for the purpose of transformation. He questioned the validity of the "establishment". Because of his desire for a world that he could have been proud to live in, he was perfectly willing to tear apart all that was built before him on foundations that he did not see as meaningful. He saw the world shift in values as a personal crusade in which he was to play some intrinsic part. Personally, he questioned his identity in terms of what he himself was doing to make his world more meaningful. Thus, he tried to project a sense of secure strength built on honest foundations to a world that so sorely needed it. He felt an obligation to overcome all that had ever made mankind weak. Thus, he spent his entire life with one goal in mind: to develop power first over himself, and then by example, over the fake structures in society that needed more creative and honourable foundations.

However, Henry's strong desire for new experiences was frustrated by emotional sensitivity and by his child-like need for protection, which, together, made him act out his life within his emotional self rather than through the world around him. Henry was most comfortable trying to augment his past, child-like qualities. He went through life with a type of innocence believing himself to be unsophisticated. He had a difficult adult life because living in his present tended to pull him out of a time period that probably represented more freedom than his current reality. His concept of truth had always been more emotional than mental. And so he tended not to respond well to reason but tried instead to develop all his awareness from his emotions. This tended to underline his child-like qualities. In other words, his freedom-loving nature had to be lived out within the confines of traditional principles. Unfortunately, no-one could solve this dilemma for him. For if he was truly to reach the power he knew he could have had, then he would have had to have found its source within himself.

Experiencing constant turmoil between the unique and the conventional, Henry would have identified from moment to moment with whatever gave him the strongest feeling of individual power. He could have become overly aggressive, losing control of himself whenever his ideas were threatened. He was power hungry and so was constantly discontented with whatever he had. Even if he had searched for spiritual answers, he would have grown overly zealous, too possessive and much too prideful of whatever awareness he had reached. Inwardly discontented, he would have poured out the residue of his unhappiness both telepathically and unconsciously onto everybody around him.

Henry's life had been built on past principles. There was a particular and uncompromising direction to his life-effort. He was interested in a cause but showed less concern over end-results and with no real desire to conserve either himself or his resources. Yet he was capable of unique achievement through a development of unsuspected events in his life but was also apt to waste energy through his improper alignment with various external situations. He dipped deeply into life and poured forth the gathered results of his gathered experiences with unremitting zeal. His moods and ways could have been changeful in an acceptable way since he liked new phases in life.

Henry's true nature would not have emerged until mid-life having found that conventionality was too restrictive. Highly independent, he could not have been led by the advice of others. He would rather have been his own disciplinarian than follow those who didn't really know what was best for him. Henry tended to represent man's need to withdraw from whatever traditions appeared to have outlived their usefulness. In many ways, he seemed to grow younger as he aged. Things became lighter, which once would have been burdensome for him.

Relationships

<u>Others:</u> Henry was genial, warm and affable. He always tried to be pleasant because he truly enjoyed people. He was guided by a high sense of ethics and moral behaviour, for which the public had learned to respect him. He became an instructor and inspirer of others. Realising that he was always eager to share what he knew, the public sought his help in solving problems. They knew that he could show them how to achieve the means for survival better. People knew that he could have been trusted to handle their affairs or to provide them with services. He won the approval of those around him by conceding to their desires if he could. His flair for saying the right thing at the right time endeared him to others. Still others would have been attracted to his resourcefulness and dedication. On the other hand, he reacted very strongly to older people in terms of whether or not he was capable of fulfilling their expectations of him. Additionally, some people could intimidate him fairly easily and make him believe that he owed them help with their problems. He tended to put other people's needs before his own but this only delayed satisfying his

own needs. He was extremely sensitive and so vulnerable to people's suggestions that he was obliged to help them. He felt that since he understood others' situations, he was more responsible to them. Sometimes he tried to give when he should have been receiving. But giving material gifts was not the best way to win people's approval. Instead, his willingness to help others when they needed it would have earned their appreciation. Thus, with a little self-control, he could have become very effective in winning people's support for his ideas. Indeed, he knew how to dramatise them to arouse people's genuine interest in him and in his ambitions.

Henry experienced disorientation in his relationship with others. Probably, he carried an unconscious chip on his shoulder, which became apparent in relationships that were highly argumentative, particularly when he was willing to experience a relationship at all. Basically, there was a mistrust of people so that he was constantly on guard against the possibility of being hurt. Indeed, it was this mistrust that caused him to initiate hostile feelings in others that, in turn, confirmed his original belief.

Henry's life was one continual lesson for his ego so that, one day, he could have aligned himself in a balanced perspective with the effects he caused in others. Unless he could have done this, he would have unconsciously experienced in himself every negative reaction he had caused in others.

It was painful for Henry not to know the answers to questions that people asked him. This only intensified his determination to be informed at all times. He had a highly developed sense of, and a keen insight into, other people's values. He liked to reform other people, and past experience had led him to believe that he had the wisdom that qualified him to do this. He was interested in knowing what other people were like beyond and behind their facades but he was reluctant to show his own colours. Openness clashed with his need for secrecy. He was also interested in what motivated people in their dealings with him (more importantly, however, was what motivated him!) He had a gift for anticipating other people's moves in their dealings with him. He was suspicious of those who sought his talents and feared that they would have exploited him for their own benefit. Although he may have been suspicious of people's motives, the chances were that he didn't resist them very much.

Henry had to watch a tendency to judge others because he could have alienated himself by doing this. Basically, however, he did try to be fair in his inner appraisal of people. The problem was that occasionally he tended to judge others because they did not meet the expectations that he had set for them. In this case, his introspection tended to be expressed rather than withheld!

Henry was always questioning the validity of other people's knowledge, while standing very firm about what he himself knew. Overall, he developed the fruits of a deep study of people and of the world. However, he had to learn to understand that the deepest truths he sought would only have come when he was not interpreting them on a personal level.

Usually, Henry set the stage for an encounter by first organising his ideas. People had no difficulty following his train of thought because he made proposals with ingenious sensitivity. His logic almost always impressed his listeners. If he had been sincerely concerned about people's welfare and had been urged by a spiritual desire to help them, then all would have been well.

Henry had a tendency to advance himself through ruthless behaviour towards others. He rarely allowed himself to be led by others and hardly ever asked for outside advice. As a result, he could have become a very bigoted, self-centred person, who didn't like his ideas being questioned by others. Thus, he could have lived his entire life totally off the track, missing the point, hearing everyone of his friends, neighbours and relatives telling him the same thing, yet never listening. He refused to conform to norms established by those he saw unconsciously as being of lesser value than himself. People tip-toed around him in fear of triggering him off, while he continued his mental game of shattering everybody's ego except his own.

Henry would have liked to serve as he was highly conscious of the needs of others but, at the same time, he tended to hold back. He found it so difficult to take care of his own affairs that he wouldn't volunteer to assist others. He kept his impressions to himself, often seeming to be in a state of suspended animation, until he sensed the need for his service. If he could have accepted the responsibility of working for some others' needs, he would have gained their admiration and respect. Certainly, he would have improved his public image by making occasional sacrifices to help others, who were truly in need.

Friends: Henry's fear of making a poor showing among opponents caused him to choose his friends carefully. Because he wasn't sure that he could stand securely on his own, he associated with people who were mature, willing to make a substantial contribution to the relationship so that it would have endured and didn't make demands. Prosperity with another in friendship was favoured. Enlisting the help of friends in his programs could have provided him with extra energy and enthusiasm. He mustn't have been afraid to accept offers of help from friends, who felt he needed it. The chances were that he had already been a friend to those in need himself. Hence, he would have benefitted from friends and patrons—or even from charity—if and when this had been needed.

Family: There was an uneasy expression of affections and a lack of harmony in Henry's home. His relationship with his mother would not have been easy. Probably, his brothers and sisters (although he had none) would have sought him out when they needed advice. Additionally, his moody or quarrelsome nature would have made for a lack of peace at home. Probably, he identified with his father (although he had died before he was born) in seeking the kind of success that would have fulfilled his expectations. His mother (and uncle) had conditioned him to question his qualifications for success unless his plans had their approval. However, if he had waited for their approval, he would never have established his own goals.

Warmth and affection entered into relationships of affection as expressed to young people in a family. Henry had a tendency to try to make others a part of his own family and to close in the outer world around it. He hoped that his children would become educated and so would go on to fulfil their own identities. He had expectations for his children and he urged them to achieve even when they lacked his enthusiasm. His creative ideas may have been his 'children' but with his real family, he hoped that they would have agreed with his ambitions for them. However, if they didn't, then he would have had to have been prepared to concede to their desires.

Probably, Henry's dilemma was to cope with the demands of his career and yet still satisfy his family's needs. Possibly, he would have felt guilty about not doing everything he should have, in both areas. Perhaps, he was taught that his most urgent priority should have been to his family.

Lover: The tendency was that Henry's relations with women were not easy. Although good looking with an attractive personality, he tended to have lacked amusement and social life. This sense of lack intensified his shyness and prevented an easy response to what could have brought happiness. As a result, he became conditioned to being happy alone. Consequently, he had much to learn about the give and take of intimate relationships. However, Henry would have had a strong interest in the opposite sex with a desire for domination. His ability to love and enjoy sexual life (and all things of beauty, the easy and the pleasant) was strong and robust but at the expense of delicacy and of sloppy emotion. His strong love nature made him demonstrative and ardent in affection, falling in love and readily expressing his sympathetic, sensitive and kind-hearted nature. There tended to be too many love affairs in his personal life, in which his capacity to receive impressions added to his gentle charm but which was overdone. He was naturally thoughtful where affection in a sexual relationship was concerned, in which warmth and enthusiasm entered readily but the idea of settling down with any one individual was, at first, discomforting. His desire for partnership had become overdone with a great deal of sexual restlessness and now, as well, a lack of ability to be happy alone. It was the quantity of sexual experiences that he desired, but his needs, although he may have thought them to be physical, were decidedly mental. Accordingly, there was the possibility for dangerous attachments but the chances were that he would have met his mate at school.

In choosing a lover, Henry was selective, preferring someone who was mature and willing to make a substantial contribution to their relationship so that it would have endured. Probably, he would have selected someone who was career-minded, or, at least, professionally trained in some career. Unless his partner was completely in agreement with his career aims, it would have been better for him to delay marriage until he had become established professionally. His mate should have understood that his career would have made many demands on his time.

There was prosperity through marriage. However, it was difficult for Henry to be married as the side of himself that he saw in his spouse's eyes was usually what he was least capable of accepting. He was a very difficult person to live with as he continually tested the loyalty, sincerity and honour of those around him. Probably, he indulged in private sexual fantasies.

Career

Early: Henry's destiny lay mainly in the hands of others as well as depending on prevailing circumstances. His fate was rarely under his own control. However, he was spurred to achievement despite obstacles. Some impelling force (plus his mother's and uncle's influences) behind him seemed to push him onward towards good or ill, unconsciously. Partnerships, marriage and legacies would have had a major financial impact, mainly for good, but occasionally bad. He would have had optimism, good fortune, good position and a lucky and successful journey through life involving good opportunities and helpful people but with a tendency to squander gains, to be extravagant and to trust to luck too easily. At the same time, he would have also met misfortunes, hardships and heavy, personal responsibilities.

Henry's parents gave him the training he needed to achieve his objectives by using his creativity. He knew that, in the long run, he would have stood strong on his own merits.

Henry realised that the best way to take full advantage of his creativity was to be educated. A formal education would have revealed the realities of life to him and prepared him for occasional setbacks. With his education he would have become ready to make a contribution that would have established his value to the world and to have satisfied an important social need. He came to value education as the first essential step towards achievement. He knew that it was the only way to exploit his creativity wisely. Although he was well-read and learnt easily, a good education was essential to his success. He had the energy, now all he needed was training and education. To meet the challenge of competition, this was what he needed. He mustn't have become embarrassed because his competitors were better informed, or to have been intimidated because of his lack of training. Although it was fun to ask questions, it was the answers that mattered.

Henry tended to have a "do-nothing" attitude about making an important investment in his future goals. Sometimes he felt that the world owed him a living and that he didn't have to apply himself if he didn't want to. But he wouldn't have felt fulfilled until he had overcome his fear and hesitation and asserted himself to get what he wanted out of life. Although he had been encouraged to think for himself, he may have failed to capitalise fully on his ideas and on his ability to solve problems. However, once he had developed his talents, he would have had many opportunities to grow. Yet it wasn't easy for him to be realistic about making his own life. On the one hand, secretly, he doubted that he would ever have achieved his goals in life. Though generally optimistic about his ability to succeed, he sometimes experienced deep anxiety because of early parental training that made him feel inadequate without their approval. However, on the other hand, he didn't doubt that he could have accomplished nearly anything he wanted. His faith was limitless and his devotion to any task was so complete that he could have "moved mountains"!

Becoming responsible for his own decisions became a necessary part of maturing for Henry. When he had learned to do this successfully, he would have grown increasingly confident and better able to handle future problems, which was urgent if he wanted to establish himself in the world. Becoming self-sufficient would have provided pressure for him to take advantage of his creativity, and to use it more resourcefully. He had to have learned to stand on his own before he could have hoped to achieve any accomplishments. How independent he became depended on how far he was able to accept another person's authority over him. Resisting authority only impeded his progress and showed his incompetence. He had to be able to face the challenge of competition, which would have given him the opportunity to taste success and feel the glow of accomplishment. After he had experienced success, he would have become addicted to it, and so he would have overcome a major hurdle in his life.

Henry's aspirations were higher than his inherent abilities so that promise outran performance. Although he preferred activity that brought him before the public, he was not sure that he could stand the abuses that he would have met when dealing with those in authority. He was easily unsettled by disharmony and so felt that this was a heavy price to pay. His wealth of ideas alone was not enough to guarantee success; he had to be willing to work to promote them. If he could have accepted responsibility for finding a way to earn a good living, the financial rewards would have given him security and compensated him for any emotional anxiety. Additionally, he could not have afforded to turndown any chances for advancement. In business and commerce he had to have worked for himself. He was good at starting new enterprises. He might have gone about his business with hardly a thought of making any greater commitment to life than that of succeeding in his own personal goals. Someday, however, he would have felt compelled to make a greater commitment that could have made an impression on society. Sometimes, it may have been difficult for him to determine what had the greater priority—his own needs or other people's—but he must not have lost his own identity through helping others. However, he must have realised also that others' needs had a high priority and that his own personal desires, at times, would have had to come second.

Vocation: Henry was suited for some relatively quiet occupation requiring little ambition than one involving publicity, responsibility or conflict. A career involving contact with the public was recommended for he had a talent for mixing with people and a sensitivity that endeared him to others. He might have applied his talent in public relations or in teaching. He may also have been good for occupations involving athletes, horses, imaginative pursuits for cultivating the mind, or for the church. Public relations, education, or hotel management would have allowed him to use his talents in ways that would have given him the success he wanted. He may have had to extend himself at the beginning but if he had persisted then it would have become almost effortless and very enjoyable. Hence, Henry should have sought a career before the public, so that the reaction he would have got would have been honest and objective.

However, Henry may have needed to seek a career that would have allowed him to make a worthwhile contribution. He may well have been happiest in a career that required him to solve difficult problems. R & D in psychology, medicine or industry would have allowed him to benefit society and so have come to know the joy of making a meaningful contribution.

<u>Middle:</u> Henry showed brilliance in management, in science and in unusual ways. His softened, aggressive nature could have proved an asset to him in his profession if it had been balanced by compromise and commonsense (which it was). But if he had not been able to control his temper, then he might only have generated a lot of bad publicity. Henry adapted his allegiances to lines along which he could have made his efforts count for the most. Yet he considered himself less important than his colleagues and fearing ridicule asserted himself defensively even when he knew he was right. His sense of humour may have saved the day when otherwise he would have been crushed emotionally. However, his superiors were aware of his competence. Probably, overall, he had become better prepared to take action than the average person.

The work that lay ahead of Henry may not have been clearly defined but with persistent effort and study, he would have come to understand the process. He had had to be alert to professional envy and to have had to be discriminating about the people with whom he shared information. Also, he had to have had a plan that was geared to success, even if he didn't feel ready for the position he wanted. He had to learn to resist any pressure to take liberties with the law otherwise his dedication to humanity would have become distorted. He had strong opinions about social conditions that needed to be changed but if he had wanted to derive any benefit from his ideas, then he must have had to accept the burden of developing and implementing them at the social level. Although he tried, both suddenly and creatively (and he should have done!), to support, help and fund foreign and more profound mental activities, he met with difficulty. There was frustration of plans when travel had been arranged, difficulties abroad with foreigners, or with journeys for carrying out duty. However, long-term results could have been good if duty had been realised and efforts had been made. Seriousness and concentration would have resulted in good, final results. Also, contacts with foreigners would have been better, if they had been elderly. Very hard work may have been done for idealistic ends. Results may have been disappointing and elusive because all was too imaginary. Irregular, over-glamorous and escapist ways could have contributed to any frustration, disappointment and failure.

There would have been a future for Henry in service to others but he expected these others to make concessions to his needs in return. It was rewarding for him to know that he had shown people how to become self-reliant and secure through their own efforts. He had a feeling of satisfaction when people realised that he had achieved his goals on his own, despite early, environmental frustrations.

Late: By developing his many good ideas, Henry could have achieved financial independence for his later years. With persistence, dedication and planning, he could have capitalised on these mental assets and thereby achieved this objective.

Appearance and Health

Appearance: Henry was somewhat taller than the average, well-formed with a strong, bony body and possibly short limbs. He had an oval face, fresh complexion, full, hazel or blue eyes, a tendency to a double chin and brown, plentiful hair inclining to baldness near the temples. He was unlikely to have looked distinguished.

Health: In general, Henry had good health, physical strength and good vitality but he tended to lose energy through fits of overwork by undertaking more than he could accomplish. His nervous system would have been important as any weakness would have caused worry that, perhaps, would have led to lung or intestinal trouble. A lack of correct working between his liver and his nervous system may have been at the root of his occasional poor judgement, woolly thinking and indiscretion. In addition, his health probably was undermined by strange fears and varying moods preying on his nerves. Possibly, he was susceptible to fish poisoning, harm from impure water and to accidents. He just may have suffered from unusual (wasting) diseases and paralysis. Probably, his death would have been unfortunate, would have occurred in a public place, either in sleep or under anaesthetic, but also as an easy release with a feeling of expansion into a new life.

Reference: "The Life and Times of Henry VII", Neville Williams, G. Weidenfeld and Nicholson, Ltd. and Book Club Associates, London, U.K., 1994 Edition.

Henry VIII

Speaking about Cardinal Wolsey's recent time as Chancellor:-

"Those who had the reins of government in their hands deceived me;
many things were done without my knowledge,
but such proceedings will be stopped in future."

Henry VIII (aged 18 in the picture) was the sixth child of King Henry VII and Elizabeth of York. As the throne was expected to pass to Prince Arthur, his elder brother, Henry was, at first, prepared for a life in the Church. Henry was a Renaissance Man and his court was a centre of scholarly, artistic and glamorous excess, epitomised by the 'Field of the Cloth of Gold'. He was an accomplished musician, author and poet. He was also an avid gambler and dice player, as well as excelling at jousting, hunting and real tennis. Although, initially, he suppressed the Protestant Reformation in England brutally, he is more popularly known for his role in the separation of the Church of England from the Roman Catholic Church leading to the Dissolution of the Monasteries. Henry also oversaw the legal union of England with Wales between 1535 and 1542. Henry's cruelty and tyrannical egotism became more apparent as he advanced in years, as he became obese and his health failed, partly due to Type II diabetes, but also due to a serious jousting accident in 1536, in which he suffered a leg wound that became ulcerated. As a result, he became covered with painful, suppurating boils. Possibly, he also suffered from gout. He is notorious for having had six wives, two of whom were beheaded.

Henry was born on the 7th July, 1491 NS, at 06:41 (see Appendix 1, Figure 4) at Greenwich, England. His Epoch occurred on the 1st October, 1490 NS at 18:00 (see Appendix 1, Figure 3).

Character Portrait

<u>General:</u> Henry was concerned mainly with practical and visible things. He expressed himself energetically. He attempted to surmount, adjust to or by-pass difficulties but nervously. His restless personality may have been tempered by an easy-going and comfort-loving disposition but too irresponsibly and lazily. Independent, proud and passionate, intellectual and a good mimic, Henry was also determined, ambitious and organising. A love of travel and change would have been characteristic of him from youth to old age. There was a love of power, fame, notoriety and leadership or for all four. He had a liking for popular, political measures as well as a love for shibboleths. Artistically, Henry had musical ability; he enjoyed dancing and embraced marine matters.

Henry was always "on the go". Activity, hospitality and optimism were evident. Pleasingly agreeable, Henry was fond of company, particularly that of females and delighted in any kind of sport. In fact, there was gay enjoyment of all pleasures, possibly involving harm, but also with teasingly caustic humour. Thus, generally, he was a free, jovial and good-humoured sort of person that did not easily take offence. He had an open, outspoken and free-handed disposition with courage, enterprise and the ability to work hard. Cheerful, happy with a love of peace and beauty, Henry was contented with his own surroundings. Additionally, caution, much prudence, worldly wisdom, sympathy and self-control were evident. <u>Importantly, his emotions and impulses were disciplined and well-regulated</u> (see following paragraph, the last sentence).

Henry went to extremes. He had a dominating insistence on being over-forceful with accompanying quarrels and hot temper. He tended to expend energy on cantankerous insistence on non-essentials. Not knowing when to be silent was his greatest liability. And so there was much impulse in his personal character, which would have brought sorrows into his life. Consequently, his inherent tendency to rash action had to be resisted strongly.

<u>Mentality:</u> Henry had a good, commonsense mentality and nervous force. His conservative inclination, within which he selected the

circumstances of his self-expression, showed that he 'moved' mentally as well as physically. Henry was inclined to neatness, orderliness and method that would have shown out in the habits of his mind, if not his outdoor life. Though constructive in a narrow, one-pointed way, his orderliness would have become rigid discipline involving dreary planning. Overmuch limitation of what he conceived to be his natural way of expression, or gratification, depressed him. Careless optimism when caution was calling produced unhappiness and guilty conscience. Mental loneliness could have resulted possibly through fear and apprehension. His resulting lack of poise forced brusque speech and writing. He had the capability of saying much in a few words yet met frustration trying to express his understandings when challenged. Although he could grasp the essence of things in a moment, he had difficulty stabilising himself in everyday, practical matters. Yet Henry had a gift for conversation and the necessary flair for effective delivery so that it would have been a loss if he had failed to take advantage of his acting ability. He became a master of debate and no-one who had provoked him would ever have forgotten the verbal attack that he had unleashed. While he may not have been physically violent, he lacked tact and self-discipline when challenged.

Although sensitive, receptive and conscientious, Henry's hyper—sensitivity caused trouble. His work would have been unsatisfactory through muddles made and through two-faced work people. There was a lack of clarity in his ideas on the philosophy of life possibly caused by troublesome, annoying dreams, visions and mental states. However, his dreams were more of a vision for mankind, rather than for any personal desires. Most of them were dedicated to how well he could serve creatively the society that had given him so much. He could see distant possibilities as very real probabilities in the here and now.

Henry was bound only by the deepest truth he saw within himself. Thus he avoided mass-movements, organisations, clubs, the institution of marriage and any other man-made structure that prevented him from experiencing all that he felt inside.

Lifestyle: Henry focused strongly on achieving a comfortable and abundant lifestyle enriched by a rewarding career and good friends.

He enjoyed being involved in the world around him, within which he would have had a rich variety of interests. His life became a flowing adventure that allowed him to taste the most rewarding experiences in human relationships. In order to fit into the social environment he aspired to, he may have had to overspend to acquire the right social image. Being accepted was very important to him. However, he fitted quite naturally into the mainstream of society and because of his easy-going manner and flair for communication, he qualified for the groups he may have wanted to join. Yet he was sensitive to responsibility, in which he was executor of his own opportunity. One difficulty was developing his ability to live in a world filled with dualities and hypocrisy. However, no-one criticised his own honesty (they wouldn't have dared!) but his methods left much to be desired. For example, he had to be careful not to develop an attitude of judging others. Thus Henry tended to act at all times under a consideration of opposing views, or through sensitiveness to contrasting and antagonistic possibilities. He existed in a world of conflicts. He appeared to be indecisive but his final choices and decisions would have been well-considered. Still, there was a particular and rather uncompromising direction to his life-effort. He dipped deeply into life and poured forth the gathered results of his experiences with unremitting zeal.

Henry was a free spirit with very few attachments that were meaningful to him on the physical plane. Bursting with life, he became an expression of "one's soul finally set free". In a way, he was the true 'Angel of Mercy'. He sought opportunities and situations where he would have been needed. He experienced a heightened consciousness of the world and of his place in it. He brought this worldly understanding down to a personal level, which, in fact, was difficult for him to do, where it could have become of practical use to others.

Henry had learned to live without anchoring himself to roots. Instead, he lived a more natural existence, flowing with the currents of his fortune. As a servant, without being a slave, he tried his best to live the life of a very dedicated humanitarian. In short, Henry felt that he was living a life of service, and the more he served, the freer he became.

Relationships

<u>Others:</u> Initially, Henry may have had some misgivings about being able to handle people because parental conditioning had made him doubt that he could have been influential. Yet he became especially skilled in dealing with people in his personal and professional affairs. He would have been good at achieving smooth working of any club, society or group to which he had become attached. He knew how to make people feel comfortable, which endeared him to them. Thus, people generally liked him and were eager to see him succeed in what he did. Because he didn't threaten them, people opened up to him confident that he wouldn't have violated their trust. This made them feel better about what they could do because of his influence. Generally, he had a fundamental power of organisation, i.e. a capacity for enlisting the fullest co-operation of others. As an endless giver of information and knowledge to others, he became their inspirer and instructor. Mostly, however, he had to learn not to force other people to think as he did because his biggest problem was to believe that his attitude worked best for those he thought he had to teach. Yet Henry was a useful worker for the good of others. It may have been difficult for him but he mustn't have lost his own identity through helping others. At the same time, he had to realise that others' needs had a high priority so that, occasionally, his personal desires would have had to come second.

Henry's ideas about the world to which he had become accustomed affected his everyday relationships. He was caught between trying to live out his present ideals and sacrificing those that prevented him interacting better with those around him. He was more a giver of advice than a listener to others and while many people filtered through his life, he did not become attached to any one of them. Often he was not always conscious of the people he was speaking to. Overly blunt (tact was foreign to his nature!) he tended to be abrupt with people because he liked to cover a great deal of ground in a short time, yet he himself was overly talkative. He was so unusually restless that he scattered his own mental energies, while silently judging others for doing the same thing.

Henry appeared to be arrogantly self-confident but, in fact, he couldn't bear to be upstaged by anyone. His lack of self-assurance made him put others on the defensive to distract them from his weaknesses. His potential lack of self-control could have got him into a lot of hot water, especially with people close to him in his immediate environment. But, eventually, even they may have thanked him for rousing them to action, when, otherwise, they would have missed an opportunity.

Henry was accustomed to basing his philosophies of life on the ideas of other people. He had learned, unconsciously, to become separated from his own truth while his own philosophical values became strongly influenced by those who surrounded him and who didn't actually understand fully what was really true for him. He became anxious to redistribute every piece of information he had received to those he was about to meet. Unfortunately, he tended to give out misinformation as well because he had not taken the time to sort the information out properly for himself. As a result, he needed to focus his ideas and likes and observe how other people used them. Eventually, he learned to settle into a practical outlook on life, thereby being able to distinguish between which of others' views he should adopt, or disregard, accordingly.

<u>Friends:</u> Henry was happy among like-minded friends but there were possible disappointments here. Yet his friends usually supported him in his endeavours, for which he should have been grateful.

<u>Family:</u> There was misfortune, or disharmony, with his parents. They would have affected his life very considerably. Henry tried too hard to live up to his parents' expectations. As a result, he may not have got on with them, or he may have lost them early. Perhaps parental conditioning had led him to believe that he was not qualified to make his own way in life. Once he understood that, then he needn't have felt that he had to prove himself to their satisfaction but only to his own. Later, he wanted to be sure that he had satisfied his family's needs, so that he was no longer obliged to them. Yet probably, he would always have had good relations with his brothers and sisters, even though their affairs would have called for his attention.

On the other hand, his own family was important to him. He worked diligently for those he loved; especially he enjoyed his children, and wanted to give them every advantage that he hadn't had. He hoped that they would have responded to these advantages and as they succeeded in their own way, he would have felt grateful for having had the opportunity to support them.

Lover: Henry's affections and partnerships were subject to disclosures, upheavals and new starts, accompanied by trouble and unpleasantness. Sexual relations would have been intense but not without quarrels. Partnerships would not have been easy. Feelings were strong but caused and received hurt. A cutting harshness entered into his relationships of affection. Possibly he was inconstant and all talk rather than having any real feeling for another. Alternatively, his strong physical desires may have been chilled by people who seemed coarse or vulgar. Yet Henry had fairly good judgement in handling his relationships but he hated to make decisions hastily. He didn't make commitments casually no matter how much in love he was. Basically, he sought a mate who shared his desire for growth and development.

Henry had to be sensitive to any residual resentment he held from his early years that could have disturbed the harmony of his personal relationship. He needed to have deliberated long and hard before he committed himself to a permanent marital relationship. It would have been better for him to marry because he felt he had met his ideal mate. He should have enjoyed an harmonious marriage because he didn't make unfair demands of his partner, and also because he was secure in his own identity. He would have enhanced his partner's social position and she would have shared his dreams for the future. He would always have looked ahead to see how well his current partner would have fitted into his future plans. In times of stress, his partner may have lent heavily on him for understanding and compassion, which, generally, he would have been willing to offer.

Career

Early: Although Henry's destiny lay in his own hands, it also lay more in the hands of others and depended on prevailing circumstances. Good luck and good fortune were to have been expected along with plenty of opportunities. He had been fortunate materially perhaps because opportunities had arisen for the use of his enthusiasm and energy. There would have been many new beginnings in his life with prominence at certain times.

Some change in his life related to parents or to early childhood. Henry's basic survival instincts and the foundation of his experiences early in his development had been at odds with his desire to achieve in life. The resulting disharmony in his nature would have urged him to accomplishment. Thus his rise to success may have followed severe limitation during which he developed his ability to cope with frustration. Because of this, he derived many benefits for later on. In addition, any success he achieved then became more precious to him.

Henry had the ability to work hard with a willing acceptance of duty. However, he hated the confinement of a daily routine because it limited his freedom. Yet he wouldn't have been really free until he had applied himself and earned it. Although he underestimated his ability to make an important contribution to society, he had a moral and spiritual responsibility to serve the best interests of the public and should have capitalised on his ability to communicate with people. Henry's doubts about himself were the only impediment to his success but he was more qualified and resourceful than he knew. His anxieties about the future would have been lessened by improving his earning abilities, which may have entailed him in making sacrifices. Additionally, any career would have had to provide him with self-determination and so freedom to perform his duties in his own way. This facet of his personality could have been a response to his early parental intimidation that had threatened his self-image. He had to find a career that made demands that would have forced him to use his natural ability. With his creativity, he could have built his future without having had to rely on others too much. Acquiring the appropriate skills to establish his authority in his chosen field was an absolute must for his own sense of worth. He needed to think about the goals he needed to reach and to remember that achieving them should have been his most important priority. High on his list of these must have been to establish realistic values and to have been willing to make some contribution to others. He could not have afforded to go forth with empty hands and then expected to succeed. When he worked on his priorities he might have realised that he was not investing sufficient mental energy for the greatest returns later. He knew that he would have reached his goals by putting his ideas to work. He may also have wanted to prove to those closest to him that he could achieve without their assistance, if necessary. He should have made long-range plans for using his natural assets efficiently and yet reserved some of his energy to preserve his physical well-being.

Realising that his future was bright, Henry capitalised on his talents and worked diligently at putting his ideas to work. He knew that others would do the job instead, if he didn't, so he strove constantly to improve his skills and proficiency. However, his lack of control caused problems in shaping his ideas and his lack of concentration made it difficult for him to focus on an objective. Additionally, he tended to spend money carelessly and get himself into situations that he was not adequately prepared for. As a result, it took him longer to achieve his aims effectively.

Henry's career demands may have seemed oppressive at first and he might not have been ready to accept the responsibility for exploiting his ideas for the future but he did have the enormous advantage of being able to withstand competition to reach and retain the position he wanted.

Henry was capable of unique achievement through a development of unsuspected relations in life but likely to waste some of his energy through his improper alignment with various situations. There was an inner frustration that resulted from his inclination to follow the line of least resistance against his conscious awareness that he had to assert himself to exploit his creativity. This resulted in difficulty in dealing with persons in authority and so he could well have assumed that they were somehow determined to obstruct him. Yet when given the opportunity, he himself proved that he could promote his ideas to achieve the goals that he had established.

Vocation: Although Henry could have succeeded in a communications field, his prospects, despite his own potential losses, were even better as an investment counsellor. However, as a disobedient servant, he would have had to change his situation more than once.

Henry had ability for drama as well as for writing romances about love and adventure.

<u>Middle:</u> Henry's most persistent adversary remained himself. His success had come through public affairs and his own fame would have been sought constantly. If he had been gainfully employed and had been making some contribution to society, he wouldn't have had to apologise to anyone, least of all to himself. Henry's competitors were impressed by his exciting display of aggression and fascinated by how successful his suggestions were in stimulating an active response from others. His driving ambition to gain recognition may have caused some problems with colleagues or superiors by reminding them that they weren't doing all they could. He may even have been envied because he was able to accomplish so much work.

Henry would have been interested in a cause but would have had less concern about end results, about the conservation of his resources and even about himself. He would have adapted his allegiances to lines along which he could have made his efforts count for the most. Any support, help and charity would have been directed conservatively towards his own interests.

Henry worked with potentialities immediately at hand. He was always successful in what he did because his measure of success was to do what was right for the moment, staying flexible about what tomorrow may have offered. Yet he was subject to upsets and to forced new phases. Although his ambitions and prominence had been achieved, there was also a real danger of his downfall.

Mostly, Henry may have been preoccupied with obtaining mundane objectives but he would have sensed a subtle, inner urge eventually to have become involved in attempts that would have increased the public's awareness of its pressing needs. In this way he would have been able to make a permanent impression on society. Probably, his greatest opportunities would have come through appreciating and learning from other people's opinions. Although his efforts had had to be focused on opportunities provided by others, he did have the talent for promoting them to his own advantage. Practical planning and determined self-will could well have united to produce brilliant results. Henry worked hard at his job and accepted long hours as part of his struggle to achieve and maintain the position and status he wanted. Success may have been achieved but at much cost of hard work, or of personal hardship, and may well have been long-delayed. In fact, very hard work may have been done for idealistic ends. Results here may have been disappointing and elusive because all was too imaginary. Irregular, over-glamorous and escapist ways tended to result in failure.

<u>Late:</u> No indicators and their interpretations were found under this category.

Appearance and Health

<u>Appearance:</u> Henry was a mixture of small, middle-or-rather-above—it, and large stature, spare body and unhealthy appearance. He had a somewhat defective, round and long face, of dark to ruddy complexion, broad at the temples and narrow at the chin, with sharp sight in grey to greyish-brown eyes. His hair was rough or wiry varying in colour from sandy to dark with bushy eyebrows but possibly balding at the temples.

<u>Health:</u> Although physically robust with good health, Henry's head and stomach were likely to have been vulnerable. His health may well have suffered through hidden, toxic causes. Food poisoning and drugs should have been avoided. His self-will and control were apt to alternate producing nervous tension since freedom and limitation do not go easily together. Danger was likely through accidents of the falling, crashing and limb-breaking kind. When attempting to overcome, adjust to or to by-pass difficulties, he would have been rarely without nervous stress. Overmuch limitation of what he considered to be his natural way of expression or gratification could have brought about exaggerated depression possibly with tragic results. Strange fears could have played upon his nerves thereby undermining his health. Even though his sleep may have been over heavy, he needed to have saved some of his energy to preserve his physical well-being and should have rested now and then to avoid physical exhaustion.

Reference: 'Henry VIII', J. J. Scarisbrick, 2nd Edition, 1997, English Monarch Series, Yale University Press, New Haven, U.S.A.

Edward VI

"I, with sixteen of my chamber, challenged any seventeen of my servants, gentlemen in the court, to run at base, shoot and run at ring."
Personal Diary, March, 1551.

Edward became King of England at the age of nine in 1547. He was the third monarch of the Tudor dynasty and England's first monarch raised as a Protestant. During his reign the realm was governed by a Regency Council, because he never reached his majority. The Council's first leader was his uncle, Edward Seymour, Duke of Somerset, and then John Dudley, later Duke of Northumberland. Edward's reign was marked by economic problems and social unrest that, in 1549, erupted into riot and rebellion. An initially successful war with Scotland ended expensively by military withdrawal. Additionally, Boulogne was lost in exchange for peace. The transformation of the Anglican Church into a recognisably Protestant body occurred under Edward, who took great interest in religious matters. The architect of this change was Thomas Cranmer, Archbishop of Canterbury, who's 'Book of Common Prayer' is still used.

In 1553, at age fifteen, Edward fell ill. When his sickness would prove fatal, he and his council drew up a 'Device for the Succession' designed to prevent the country returning to Catholicism, by naming his 2nd cousin, Lady Jane Grey, as his successor. However, following his death, his elder half-sister, Mary, deposed Jane to become Queen.

Edward, the only child of King Henry VIII by his third wife, Jane Seymour, was born on the 22nd October, 1537 NS at 01:33 at Hampden Court, London, England (see Appendix 1, Figure 6). His Epoch occurred on the 9th January, 1537 NS at 18:33 (see Appendix 1, Figure 5).

Probably the following Character Portrait is not as relevant as those presented in the rest of the book but, at least, it does give us an idea of the kind of talented individual he would have been if he hadn't so tragically lost his life to illness (see Health) at the age of fifteen.

Character Portrait

<u>General:</u> Edward was a mixture of objectivity and subjectivity. At his best, he would have had a dignified, self-reliant nature, ambitious for power and distinction, strong-willed, forceful, honourable and kindly. His hospitable, sympathetic and self-assured personality would also have shown zeal, ardour and quiet determination, which would have burned for success. There would have been a love of ostentation and display with some dramatic power. His ideals would have been very high regarding his surroundings, whether artistic, social or political. His energetic, self-expression was revealed in a robust, courageous and bold manner. Hard work and energy would have been expressed quickly in personal affairs and in starting new enterprises.

Although stirring in action, the downside here would have consisted of a dominating insistence on being over forceful combined with hot temper and antagonism. Whenever his ideas were threatened, he would have lost control of himself, becoming overly aggressive and overly quick in response. Yet all this assertiveness would have been softened. Generally, his emotions and impulses would have been disciplined and well-regulated. Caution, prudence, practical vision, self-control and perhaps even conceit would have been evident. Orderliness, neatness and method would have shown out in the habits of his mind, if not in his outdoor life. There would also have been some hurtful limitation to his self-expression in that life would have seemed hard at times, leading to self-pity. In addition, he had an anxious and hypersensitive side. Further, he would have had a tendency to let matters remain as they were and put-up with them. And so, he would have become patiently conditioned to trying circumstances but not without nervous stress. Although Edward's restless personality sought excitement, fulfilment and craved for adventure, it may have been tempered by an easy-going and comfort-loving disposition. A love of travel and change may well have been characteristic of him from youth to old age.

His sensitivity and deep feelings would have helped him to enjoy his music.

<u>Mentality:</u> Edward would have had a good, commonsense mentality and nervous force with keen, strong ideals but it was also too material in outlook and so led him out into the world around him.

Edward was trying to reach his past ideals. He would have delved continually within himself to assess how much of his life was living up to what he believed it should be. Although he might have seemed to have been overly concerned with details that shaped the structure of his life, ultimately it would have been through these details that he would have been able to create the neatly ordered world that would have made sense to him. Initially, he tried to crystallise all that was of value to him and then he tried to apply these values to his current situation. He kept collecting all that had offered him past security. Edward saw his world through all of its separate parts. Then he tried to fit these parts into all that had formed within him from his past. In this way, he internalised what he believed to be the correct segments from his outer world. Then, from these segments, he built his structured life. He thought that, in order to know himself, he had to understand the workings of everything that touched his life but inadvertently he pre-programmed his perception of things so that they could fit into his ready-made concepts. This made him unusually rigid and highly resistant to change. He tended to watch the world from somewhere in his past, where he once felt comfortable. As such, he stubbornly kept precipitating all that had held him back. The truth would have been that he wouldn't really have understood how his values fitted into the world he then saw around him. Thus he experienced a barrier between what he felt and what he was able to live, and this, perhaps, could have alienated him from all that he wanted. He would have felt forced to live the idealised world that he would have liked to have seen around him. Once he became sensitive to how unrealistic some of his expectations were, he would have become more comfortable with the world as it was. After he had carried out an enormous amount of observations of other people's lives, the perfection that already existed in his world would then have become apparent to him.

Edward's mind and mental outlook were helped by charm of speech and pleasantness of manner in which balance rather than worry was evident. Ease of writing would have been gained but rather at the expense of strength. Conversation would have revolved around affairs to do with the home, domesticity and any business to do with collecting. Mental occupations were carried out at home. He had a precipitate mentality that was powerful with revolutionary intent, independent, inventive, unconventional, dissimulating and even brilliant. Edward would have preferred to study the unusual, for example: astrology. Quick intuitions could have been used advantageously in serious study and in work to be published. His mind and nervous system would have been energised and so tended towards irritability, temper and carping incisiveness. Although his mind threw off worries and began thought anew, it took place over violently, explosively and with nervous stress. Edward could have been intense mentally, penetrative and emotional, yet his inclination to hurtful ways tended to be softened. In general, though, his communication was too brusque and independent so that it lost good contact with others. His revolutionary, strong mental action with his addiction to the unusual could have become so awkwardly expressed that he would have seemed eccentric, odd and even tiresome.

Edward's imagination was also expressed strongly but, again, any assertiveness would have been softened. His sensitivity would have been used to bring impressions to his mind so that it became a channel for inspirations, fantasies and ideas, as well as for prophesies and dreams. Highly introspective, he would have spent much of his time alone with his thoughts. He could well have been born with mediumistic talents that if properly developed would have led to a rich life of continuing, worldly realisation. Yet even when he searched for spiritual answers, he would have become overly zealous, too possessive and much too prideful of whatever awareness he had reached.

Lifestyle: Achieving significance in Edward's life endeavours would have required him to focus on the affairs of others, either personally or professionally. However, there were highly individual, or purposeful, emphases in his life, in which his temperament jutted out into reality by means of his unusual experiences as a result of his own very special tastes. Edward would have been both particular, and yet impersonal, in his tastes. He had a high nervous energy and would have wanted to do everything right away, because he never would have known what was going to happen tomorrow. Truly, he was the original commander of his life. He made his own anchorage in existence by a rugged resistance to pigeon-holing, either in the neat, conventional components of nature, or in the idea pockets of his associates. Edward would have striven to establish his own sense of uniqueness so that he could have distinguished his own personal identity from the myriad of identities that he saw around him. He had little interest in the rules or traditions of the society he lived in and would have identified with all that was new and unique. As a result, he would have gone out of his way to rebel against anything that caged him or made him appear to be anything like others. Thus he experienced a great fear of waiting for others to pull him into their realities.

Edward would have had a 'splay'-foot certainty to every approach he made to life's problems. Yet he would have experienced constant turmoil between the unique and the conventional, after which he would have identified with whatever gave him the strongest feeling of individual power. His biggest area of disharmony would have been that his rebellious, freedom-loving nature had had to be lived out within traditional confines. No-one could have solved this dilemma for him because if he was truly to reach the power that he could have had, then he would have had to have found its source within himself. Accordingly, he would have become power-hungry and also constantly discontented with whatever he had. In fact, he could have lived his entire life totally off the track, missing the point, hearing everyone of his friends, neighbours and relations telling him the same thing yet never listening. Thus there would have been continuous change until he had understood that his true purpose would not have been to dedicate his life to any particular principle or course of action because that might have smothered his spirit of adventure. Instead, he would have had to have followed his insatiable curiosity. As a seeker of the first order, he would have sacrificed much of the comforts of traditional society in order to be free to discover that which existed just beyond the limits of his contemporaries even at the risk of much personal sadness.

Relationships

<u>Others</u>: Edward would have developed his keen insight into the values of others because he would have tried very hard to understand them. By being a good listener, he had learned a lot about people. He would have enjoyed those who wouldn't have been afraid to speak their mind, provided that they had something worthwhile to say. People would have told him their secrets because they sensed that they could have trusted him with privileged information so he had to make promises only if he truly intended to keep them.

Edward would have extended himself freely, perhaps even making personal sacrifices, if someone had needed help (this was also true for those to whom he was emotionally drawn, but he would have rarely made a commitment until he was sure that the feeling was mutual). Yet he also felt that others could have helped themselves as he had, and he resented it when others wanted him always to be available to them. On the other hand, he would have gained a feeling of satisfaction when people realised that he had achieved his goals on his own despite early environmental frustrations.

Edward would have been responsible and trustworthy but he could have become suspicious when people made demands. He would have become curious about their motives and would have tried to pin-down what his efforts would have cost him. Although he may have been suspicious of people's motives when forming alliances with him, the chances were that he wouldn't have resisted them very much. He let others get an edge on him in competition by giving them the impression that he didn't mind doing favours for them, but that only enhanced their position. He needn't have had to indulge them simply because they asked him to. It would have been devastating for him to have found out that he'd been taken by somebody whom he shouldn't have trusted.

Edward would have refused to conform to norms established by those he saw unconsciously as being of lesser value than himself. He would have been rarely led by others and would hardly have ever asked for advice. Unconsciously also, he would have poured out the residue of his unhappiness onto everyone around him. Basically, he wouldn't have liked his ideas to be questioned by others. People tiptoed around him in fear of triggering him off while he continued his mental game of shattering everyone's ego but his own. Yet despite all this, on balance, Edward would have been a useful worker for the good of others.

Friends: Edward mustn't have had to shrink from asking favours of friends when an opportunity arose because he would have been able to reciprocate later.

Family: There was likely to have been some misfortune or disharmony connected with Edward's parents. At first, it wouldn't have been easy for him to express himself except in ways that would have offended his parents. Later, he would have realised that unless he resisted his family, he would never have had an opportunity to make a life for himself.

<u>Lover:</u> Sensuous, Edward would have experienced a great deal of semi-conscious visualisation based on what he felt he needed from life. Yet others must have shown an interest in him before he would have been willing to make an emotional commitment to them. However, he would have extended himself and made substantial sacrifices for the person who showed definite signs of affection for him.

Edward was a poor prospect for marriage because his nature was highly unpredictable as he tried to break with conventional society. In addition, he would have been a very difficult person to live with because he constantly would have tested the loyalty, sincerity and honour of those around him. Furthermore, his nature was inharmonious in that his personal tendencies towards affection conflicted with his internally ambitious instincts, yet conjugality could have been well-expressed. Moreover, he would have found it difficult to understand his partner's feelings of emotional frustration that he was not completely devoted.

Accordingly, Edward may have felt that his expression of love was blocked. Every time that he tried to give his affection to another, he was brought to question whether or not he was fulfilling his values. He would have always sensed that something was wrong but he would have had difficulty putting his finger on it. Usually, this would have been due to an underlying feeling of guilt in terms of how he had treated people in relation to things. However, he would have reached happiness the moment he clearly realised how untrue he had been to himself in the past. His eventual partner may well have been older than he was. She was likely to have had an ego drive that matched his own but his marriage, for one reason or another may well have been long delayed.

Career

<u>Early:</u> Edward's destiny would have been in his own hands but also in the hands of others and would have depended on prevailing

circumstances. There would have been gain for him either by legacy or through marriage. A cleavage in his life relating to his parents (death of mother) at his birth, or in early childhood (death of father) would have caused disharmony in his nature, which could have urged him to accomplishment later. To help here, there were indicators for his success in the affairs of the world and so there would have been ease of accomplishment through frequent, good opportunities. Success would have been in material ways, in which extremes would have been kept in bounds, since commonsense control would have been combined well with optimism and the desire to expand both his viewpoint and his circumstances. This desire for expansion, again, would have been in material ways although with a love of the beautiful.

Probably Edward had applied himself diligently to get an education. He would have known that his earnings would have increased if he had been well-informed and had been willing to work, if necessary, to pay for his education. However, he was a realist and probably would have selected a course of study that could have been translated easily into increased security and have provided stability in his career. The best way for him to have handled any of his resentment of authority would have been to become an expert himself in some area. As an intensive personality, he could not have been limited to any steady point of application. He may not have been the most adaptable person but he could have adjusted to learning new skills when required. He mustn't have assumed that he could have asserted himself in any way he wanted. He had to build substantial character values that would have helped him to gain the security he wanted otherwise his efforts would barely have been remembered. As a result, he would have been able to have met people on mutually agreeable terms and then should have taken advantage of every opportunity to earn a reasonable income.

Probably Edward would have earned his living working with people. This being so, he would have had to concern himself with the public's requirements. Quite apparently, he would have had every resource he needed to satisfy this kind of responsibility but he may have been apprehensive about the value of applying his efforts in this way. He could have been filled with plans for the future but he would have had difficulty converting them into practical efforts that would have yielded tangible results. Seemingly, there would have been nothing that he couldn't have accomplished with self-discipline, but first he would have had to get over his feeling of inadequacy.

<u>Middle:</u> Edward would have valued the training and education he had gone through, appreciating how much hard work it had required. Hence he would have taken every opportunity to improve his skills when special training became available. He would have adapted to job assignments fairly well and have learned new skills easily. His social and spiritual obligations had been largely the product of early conditioning when he had felt that his teachers knew more than he did about life. Unfortunately, he would have become very disappointed when he had learned that much of what he believed was illusory.

Popularity, public recognition, ambitions achieved and prominence in some sphere would have been obtained but there would also have been some danger of downfall. Probably he would have changed direction often during his life, which would have been fine, as long as he had kept to a plan that, eventually, would have brought him the security he needed.

Edward would have been engaged in an inner struggle to carry out his ideas in the real world in an orderly way. His need to be both free and secure would have inspired him to try and capitalise on his ideas. In fact, he would have been a whirlwind of ideas and with only a little help he would have been able to use these ideas to obtain his basic necessities. However, his wealth of ideas would not have been enough to guarantee success; he must also have been willing to promote them. He would have been able to make it on his own but he would have needed to have been convinced of that fact. His greatest problem would have been that he tended to reject responsibility for his actions. People would have resented him for this but they would have admired him if he had helped them to convert their liabilities into assets, so that they could then have succeeded by means of their own efforts. Edward would have understood the value of money and he would have had as much as he needed if he had put his resources to work. He would have been clever at devising money-making schemes because he would have understood how money talks and he would have used that knowledge to further his ambitions. As a rule, Edward wouldn't have discussed his financial affairs openly. Instead, he would have talked about them privately only with those he trusted. However, care would have been needed when taking on increased financial obligations. In the world of business and finance he may well have needed direction to avoid any confusion. But he would have been wise enough to get advice about investing in the future.

In Edward's work he could have become unusually efficient, particularly when he knew that others were depending on him for order and efficiency. Probably he would have been well-trained and would have done his job well so that it would have been unlikely for him to have lost it to a more capable person. Although he may have been inclined to do the right thing and stay within the bounds of acceptable practices, he would have had to have been alert to deception by those who would have used him to satisfy their own ends. Additionally, he would also have had to be alert to the possibility of professional envy from fellow workers and to have been discriminating about the people with whom he shared information.

<u>Late:</u> Only determination and persistence would have brought Edward his required security during his later years.

<u>Comment:</u> Overall, we could well conclude that Edward VI was clearly not only his father (Henry VIII)'s son but also his paternal grandfather (Henry VII)'s grandson.

Appearance and Health

<u>Appearance:</u> Edward would have been above average height with large bones and muscles, broad shoulders and with a tendency to stoutness that would have resulted in a square build. He would have had a round, full-sized head and a round face with full cheeks and a somewhat ruddy complexion. His eyes would have been grey to light blue, his nose would have been a short one with a prominent tip, and possibly accompanied by a double chin. His hair would have been light in colour with a tendency to baldness at the temples. His upright walk may have looked somewhat awkward and possibly heavy.

<u>Health:</u> Generally Edward would have had good health, physical robustness and a vitality of spirit that could have been almost too intense. He may have expected to live long even though there was a small possibility of an accidental, or sudden death. He should have avoided acting hastily or on impulse because accidents, falls, physical exhaustion and collapses were risked. Even less likely problems would have included mental disability, nervous trouble and disorder, chronic complaints, stomach problems, infection, deep-seated diseases and degenerating tendencies.

More specifically, Edward suffered intermittently from Quartan fever as a small boy. Poor aspects to Mars (his sub-ruler, see Figure 6)) rising in Leo may well have made him more prone to this fever than others.

A brief, astrological diagnosis of the root cause of Edward's early death concerns the poor position of the Moon in Capricorn (its detriment) in the 6th House (of health, work and service) and poorly aspected (again, see Figure 6). We note that the strong square of the Moon to the Sun would have made him liable to indigestion (dyspepsia). The sesquiquadrate of Saturn (the Moon's ruler in this case) to the Moon would have tended to make this indigestion chronic. In addition, his anxious disposition would not have been helped by the strong opposition from Uranus in the 12th House to Pluto also in the 6th House, weakly conjoint the Moon. Two external factors would have continuously aggravated this situation further. Firstly, Edward's diet would have been far too rich in fatty foods supplied by well-intentioned servants. Secondly, the woeful state of Tudor medicine probably caused more harm than good.[2]

References: 1) 'Edward VI', Loach, Jennifer; Bernard, George and Williams, Penry, eds., English Monarch Series, Yale University Press, New Haven, CT: U.S.A., 1999.
2) 'Edward VI: The Lost King of England', Chris Skidmore, Weidenfeld & Nicholson, London, England, 2007.

Mary I

"When I am dead, and opened, you shall find 'Calais' lying in my heart."

Mary was the only child, who survived to adulthood, of the marriage of Henry VIII to his first wife, Catherine of Aragon. Mary's younger half-brother, Edward VI, succeeded Henry in 1547. When Edward became mortally ill in 1553, he tried to remove Mary from the line of succession because of religious differences— he was a protestant and she, a catholic. On his death, Lady Jane Grey was, at first, proclaimed queen. However, Mary assembled a force in East Anglia and successfully opposed Jane, who was beheaded later. In 1554 Mary married the future Philip II of Spain, becoming queen consort of Habsburg Spain on his accession in 1556. Unfortunately, she twice suffered from a false pregnancy.

As the fourth crowned monarch of the Tudor dynasty, Mary is remembered for her restoration of Roman Catholicism after the short, Protestant reign of Edward VI. Her motto was: 'Truth is the daughter of time.' During her five year reign, she had over 280 religious dissenters burned at the stake in the 'Marian' persecutions, thereby gaining the sobriquet "Bloody Mary". Her younger half-sister and successor, Elizabeth I, reversed the Roman Catholic re-establishment, after Mary's death in late 1558. In the January of that year, French forces had taken Calais, England's sole remaining possession on the European mainland. It was an ideological loss that damaged Mary's prestige. Mary was born on the 28th February, 1516 NS, at 04:03, at Greenwich, England (see Appendix 1, Figure 8). Her Epoch (see Appendix 1, Figure 7) occurred on the 10th June, 1515 NS, at 23:12.

Character Portrait

General: Mary was rather more subjective than objective. Her strongly artistic personality showed widespread (instead of personal) interest in psychic, mystical and marine affairs. However, her personal and gifted artistic expression showed through in music and dancing, which became necessities of life bringing happiness and benefit. She had strong, imaginative faculties but needed her strength to activate her visions, ideas and aims. Although she displayed a receptive, self-distrustful disposition showing reserve, diffidence and coldness, a positive, quietly affectionate nature could easily have been coaxed out. As well as prudence, steadiness (more so than mercurial types in general) and commonsense, her disposition basically was good, kind, loving, generous and so much respected. Optimism, cheerfulness, contentedness with her surroundings and ways, as well as sweetness of character and behaviour, would all have been displayed. More negatively, she would have tended to squander gains, to be extravagant and to trust to luck too easily.

Alternatively, when the occasion demanded, Mary could have proved excessively wilful and independent in unconventional, expansive ways. All her strengthened will, determination, authority, invention, spiritual energy and her ability to read character well, would have come to the fore. All of this would have been particularly helpful to Mary as her own conditions were big enough and free enough for it to have found vent (but otherwise it would have appeared as resentful rebellion).

<u>Mentality:</u> Mary showed much mental and physical activity, in which critical, inspirational intuition and intellect blended well. She would have had interests of a scientific kind and of those deemed to be for the good of humanity (sociology) but also towards a linking with other minds similarly inclined/motivated. Balance rather than worry would have been evident. Independence, originality and even eccentricity could have been outstanding characteristics and she could well have been attracted by new and unusual theories. She became broadminded, metaphysical and would have gained a deep insight into human nature. Occasionally, self-will, the desire to make breaks and to start anew would have found vehement and assertive expression. She was a born student and whereas it may have taken her longer than many to learn something, ultimately she would have

understood it on a deeper level. Herein, probably, lay the source of her humane, scientific and sociological inclinations.

Although sometimes erratic, Mary always remained inventive and original. She would have been an unusually agile and eloquent communicator even though her thoughts, at times, may have seemed disjointed. Although talkative, times of quiet and withdrawal would have been needed. Because she was inexperienced at expressing herself outwardly, she experienced confusion between domination and submission and so tended to take any conflict inside herself. It was only through experiencing new and higher emotional levels that afforded her security to express herself adequately on the mental plane. All this was difficult for her because her past emotional thoughts, which, dependent on their nature, would have either allowed, but more likely, would have inhibited, the remainder of her nature to express itself. Although this could have been constructive in a narrow, one-track way, any order was more likely to have become rigid discipline and to have required dreary planning.

On the other hand, Mary's strong, fertile imagination gave her a mind that could take varied patterns as wax takes an imprint, coupled with a nervous system exposed to all that touched it. She would have been good at poetry and music, but sometimes would have got herself into mazes by trying to test herself mentally. However, any limitation through these maze-like worries would have cleared up in the long run through patient endurance and quiet keeping out of the limelight.

Mary would have had some inclination to the psychic, to the occult and to the artistic but her psychic sensitivity would have needed rapport for expression. She may have been misled about the realities of life through too much living in the clouds, lovely though these may have been. Even so, glamour and clouds of glory would have been expected rather than any real delusion. She may well have had moods of dreaminess and inattention and could have become lost in a world of imagination. Thus, she could have had a tendency to be impractical and to have concentrated on visions of the future rather than on those of the present. Yet, despite all this, her mind would not have wandered but would have ordered and controlled in practical, cautious and methodical ways. As a result, her visions would have been detached and impersonal because she could easily have dissolved previous difficulties by not holding onto opinions about them. Instinctively, she knew that the past had no basis in present reality. Similarly, she would have been capable of mediumship without becoming personally involved.

In time, she would have developed great insight into worldly reality, seeing the whole of things without having to dissect them. Subsequent ideas and hunches, which would have come easily to her, should have been acted upon.

<u>Lifestyle:</u> Mary always had something to bear. She knew that she was set off against a definite part of the world, i.e. there was a complete half of experience from which she was excluded in some subtle fashion. Accordingly, she tended to capture things, or would have tried to consummate various life phases. During the first part of her life she would have experienced an inner sorrow that would have made her a kind of collective rubbish bin for everyone with whom she came into contact. But once she had begun to see the true essence of things, much of her own self-pity would have become replaced by a greater tolerance of the world in which she lived. She reviewed all that she had been through so that whatever she didn't need to carry with her into the future would have become loosened. She would have absorbed all her past memories of security. Thus, she spent much of her time in this backward, introspective, absorbing place, where she felt safest.

There was a particular and rather uncompromising direction to Mary's life-effort. She dipped deeply into life and poured forth the gathered results of her experiences with unremitting zeal. As an idealist, she would have been the advocate of some cause, the furtherer of some mission or would have had an introspective concern over the purpose of experience. Unfortunately, she tended to fantasise about victories before she had shown that, actually, she had won. The uncomfortable contrast between her active desire nature and her passive emotional nature was often projected as confusion about who and what she was. She wanted to find the answer reflected in those around her, especially with people to whom she was close. As a result, there might have been disappointment and grudge against life because of setbacks and failures. But, generally, she knew how to use her experiences to benefit her continuing development so that her self-expression became more inspired and imaginative. Fortunately, she would have had the ability to attune herself to her true worldly identity. Her inner harmony became reflected in her serene disposition under the most disturbing of conditions. This composure had resulted from the satisfactory integration of her will with her emotions. She had become capable of dealing with hypocrisy well. Her gravity and her determination would have increased with age.

Relationships

Others: Mary had a love of freedom and a hatred of interference that may have extended to a headstrong disregard for the feelings of others. She should have focused on serving others in the best way that she could (and what she was inclined to do!) for that would have given her great returns. If her energies had remained self-seeking, then the stability of her affairs would have been undermined.

Mary showed a kindly, humane disposition of gentle, inspirational desire to help others. She made acquaintances easily, got on well with strangers, yet managed to stay somewhat reserved and independent. She had a calming effect on people, which could have proved useful when she had learned to apply it. She always had something to give to her fellows, literally or psychologically, whether constructively or vindictively, probably out of frustration and uncertainty.

She did more for others than she did for herself. She had a deep, spiritual devotion to people who were somehow disadvantaged. In fact, she wanted so much for people to need her that she sometimes pursued them in the hope of making them dependent on her. However, it would have been painful for her to know so much about people because it suggested that she would have had an obligation to use her creative ideas to help them to solve their problems. She would have become an instructor and inspirer of others. Eventually, she would have learned just how resourceful she had become from the people who had benefitted from her efforts.

Mary's ideal state lay in relationships with others and all that she went through in her life was a part of her learning to understand the nature of the duality within herself. Through others she wanted to learn more about how she functioned, so that, eventually, she hoped to gain a truer perspective of herself coupled with an even more serene outlook on life. She attracted those to her who could have given her a glimpse of herself as she was reflected in them. As a rather harsh example, she might have attracted cantankerous or argumentative people because she hadn't dealt with that inclination in herself and so she needed to see it dramatised in others.

When Mary compared her accomplishments with those of other people, she felt stimulated to match or to exceed them. She envied people who were successful and she found it profitable to form alliances with others in money-making schemes. As a result, success came through co-operation with others. However, her lack of ambition may have annoyed those who were constantly struggling to succeed, but that reaction wouldn't have disturbed her.

Friends: Elderly friends would have been the most satisfying ones for Mary. However, there would have been a lack of real friendship and, instead, she would have concentrated on well-defined objectives. Yet she could have depended on friends when she needed them. Generally, her many friends were very important to her but she had to be wary of those friends who gave her advice, because they might not have understood her at all.

Family: Mary's parents' love for her may not have been as warm as she would have liked. There would have been frequent changes in her home, or separation from it, and her family. She would have had an unusual but attractive family background. However, the unconventionality may not have been pleasant for her.

Her career often had had to come second because of pressing family responsibility. For example, she had reservedly dealt with detail in her mother's affairs. Accordingly, she may have thought that the needs of her family were holding her back, but, in fact, it was her need, most of all, to be able to express herself in an environment in which she would have been positively surer of herself that was required, because her outer world did not present such an opportunity. Hence, she didn't always express the uniqueness and purpose of her identity through the right channels but instead had a strong tendency to linger in child-like stages of complaining about why her life was not blooming in the way that she thought it should. As a result, it may have seemed impossible for her to have attained a prominent position because of her dependence on her family, but she would have liked to prove that she could have done it anyway.

Any children she may have had, would have felt that she was unable, or unwilling, to understand them, because she would have seemed pre-occupied with her partner and with deriving contentment for herself. Yet, at the same time, she mustn't have sacrificed all of her own needs to satisfy her children's expectations.

Lover: Mary's affection was most difficult for her to express so that her life tended to be solitary. There would have been sorrow and loss through her affections. Any partnership would have brought responsibility. Her partnerships may not have been what they seemed partly because the conditions were hidden and possibly because of her possessiveness. Her partner may have tried to tell her that doing more for him was her obligation. He might have expected so much from her that it would have been difficult for her to cope with the tension. However, if she had persisted, she would have been able to deal with this problem.

Career

Early: Mary's destiny lay in her own hands. There was gain through her mother, through application and through honest endeavour. She would have had plenty of opportunities in life and a feeling that good luck was to have been expected. There would have been success through both science and art together with a tendency towards a fortunate journey through life.

Mary's early upbringing would have taught her to become self-reliant. Her childhood was important because much of her adult thought revolved around the feelings she had experienced during those early years. Although spoilt early on, probably she had grown up in austere circumstances. This increased her determination to acquire as many comforts as possible, even to the extent of having to take a second job. Possibly, there would have been a cleavage in her life relating to parents or to early childhood. The disharmony created in her nature could have urged her to accomplishment. Fortunately, she would have been capable of receiving a good education. Clearly, she must have made her own way and risen to excellence by using her own skills as the basis for her accomplishments.

Mary should have appreciated her imaginative talent because it allowed her to reach many goals. Her intuition helped her accomplishment as well. Orderliness and caution stopped her ideas from becoming too vague. She had good, all-round ability, was a good worker and was fond of useful work. She had to decide on an area that gave her the most satisfaction and then develop the relevant skills as her major priority. She needed to try to get the training she required so that she could serve people better, which was her social obligation. Living for the moment, as she did, meant that it was important for her to concentrate more on her goals and objectives. She had had to have evaluated them carefully and to have made plans for achieving them. It would have been a good idea for her to have meditated on her objectives, which may have been buried in her subconscious. She had the potential to succeed in most of her endeavours though she may not have chosen to do so. With a little self-discipline and careful planning, she could have achieved most of her objectives.

Vocation: Mary's imagination could have been used for works of art, for psychism or with her intuition for both everyday and professional life. As a writer or speaker she would normally have had ease rather than strength. When she had resolved her fear of competition, she could have done well in a career in which she worked from her home, for example as an estate agent or in insurance or in accountancy. Her good education made her suitable for literary, legal, business or medical pursuits. She could have succeeded in business because she would have been well-informed about all the details, which she would have handled with complete control. She may have had to travel during a business career, which she would have been willing to do, provided that success and future growth of the business depended on it. Alternatively, it might have been advantageous for her to select a career in which she helped people (perhaps impulsively) with their problems, such as in medicine, in research or in counselling. If she had cringed at brutality, or at human suffering, and had been distressed by injustice, she should have worked to help to change the conditions that allowed them to persist. Social service, medicine, institutional work, the ministry or geriatric work would have provided areas within which she could have found satisfactory expression.

<u>Middle:</u> Mary would have been interested in a cause but would have shown less concern over end-results and over her resources or herself. She would have adapted her allegiances to lines along which she could have made her efforts count for the most. Her greatest fear should have been failing to live up to her potential. Additionally, her fear of being dependent on others made her eager to take advantage of her gifted imagination. Accordingly, she applied herself seriously to the business of getting on in life and so she developed many ideas for gaining a good position with all its benefits. She had had to plan her financial moves so that she didn't have to be preoccupied with money because she couldn't have afforded to have been distracted from her most urgent goals. Freedom of thought and action would have been achieved but only through long study, application and determination. Her desire to control and limit would have become freed to a certain extent so that her scope would have become widened. She dreamt of a more abundant way of life, and she wanted to make the most of her basic resources so that she could have satisfied her anxieties about the future. She mustn't have been content with only moderate gains because apathy and indolence were signs of failure. She worked hard to develop her skills because she knew that she could make a good living by applying them in her chosen field. As she developed them, her reputation would have grown and she would have received the recognition she deserved. She was determined to promote all her ideas to her own advantage. In addition, she would have been willing to do without some of life's pleasures temporarily in order to guarantee her future security. With her imagination and sensitive intellect, she could have made a worthwhile contribution to the world. Although much may have been done in a quiet way, she would have been rarely fortunate in a worldly sense despite being greatly esteemed. There would have been no easy path but eventual success would have been achieved through plodding care and wise-looking ahead.

<u>Late:</u> Mary wanted to enjoy a more leisurely time in her later years. If she had wanted to, probably she could have retired early. She would have had to have worked to gain a place in society, if she had wanted security in her later years. She knew that her financial security then

depended on using her resources as productively as possible. During these later years, she would have looked back with contentment at the contributions she had made to improve the quality of life for others.

Appearance and Health

Appearance: Mary would have had a rather fleshy, middle stature, strong and well-formed, with stoutness and a square build later, and possibly small or short limbs. She would have had a full, fleshy and long face with a good, pale and delicate complexion. Possibly good-looking, but with a tendency to a double chin, she would have had full, blue eyes of a somewhat sapphire tint. She would have had abundant hair, the colour of which could have been anything between dark and flaxen.

Health: Mary should have avoided too much excitement. She would have had general good health, strength and endurance but may have been susceptible to gout, liver, stomach and blood disorders. She would have had a resigned attitude towards her own death that would have occurred in a public place.

References: 1) 'Mary Tudor—The First Queen', Linda Porter, Little and Brown, London, U.K., 2007.
2) 'Mary I—England's Catholic Queen', John Edwards, Yale English Monarch Series, 'The University Press', New Haven, CT., U.S.A., 2011.

Elizabeth I

"Though God hath raised me high, yet this I count the glory of my crown:
that I have reigned with your loves."
'The Golden Speech', 1601.

Elizabeth was the fifth and last monarch of the Tudor dynasty. The daughter of King Henry VIII and his second wife, Anne Boleyn, she was born into the royal succession, but her mother was executed two and a half years after her birth and Elizabeth was declared illegitimate. On his death in 1553, her half-brother, Edward VI, bequeathed the crown to Lady Jane Grey, cutting his two half-sisters, the Roman Catholic Mary and Elizabeth, out of the succession, despite a statute law to the contrary. His will was set aside, Mary became Queen and Lady Jane Grey was executed. In 1558, Elizabeth succeeded her half-sister, during whose reign she had been imprisoned for nearly a year on suspicion of supporting Protestant rebels.

Elizabeth set out to rule by good counsel, depending on trusted advisers led by William Cecil. She established an English Protestant church, of which she became the Supreme Governor. Elizabeth had been expected to marry and to produce an heir, but she never did, despite numerous courtships. As she grew older, she became famous for her virginity. One of her mottoes was *"video et taceo"* (I see and say nothing) [another was *"semper eadem"* (always the same)].

Elizabeth was more moderate than her father and half-siblings. She was relatively tolerant in religious matters, avoiding systematic persecution. In 1570, the pope declared that she was illegitimate and released her subjects from obedience to her. Several conspiracies then threatened her life but all were defeated with the help of her ministers' secret service. Elizabeth was cautious in foreign affairs, moving between France and Spain, and only half-heartedly supported military campaigns in the Netherlands, France and Ireland. When

Spain finally decided to conquer England in 1588, the failure of the Spanish Armada associated her with one of the greatest military victories in English history.

Elizabeth's reign saw the flourishing of English drama (Shakespeare) and of the seafaring powers of English adventurers (e.g. Sir Francis Drake). At times, especially later, Elizabeth became short-tempered and indecisive. Such was the case with her rival, Mary, Queen of Scots, whom she imprisoned in 1568 and eventually had executed in 1587. Near the end of her reign, a series of economic and military problems weakened her popularity. However, her forty four years as queen had provided welcome stability for her kingdom and had helped to forge a sense of national identity.

Elizabeth was born on the 17th September, 1533 NS, at 14:44 at Greenwich, England (see Appendix 1, Figure 10). Her Epoch occurred on the 7th January, 1533 NS, at 13:33 (see Appendix 1, Figure 9).

Character Portrait

General: Elizabeth was both subjective and objective. Argumentative, daring, courageous, robust, quick, and hard-working, her self-expression was shown energetically. Her energy was vast, her sympathy over-ruled her reason and she was unstable emotionally. On the other hand, she was reserved, secretive and overly cautious. These limitations, possibly deriving from her father, enabled her to accept lessons of duty and self-control willingly. She became conditioned to what was lacking. Subconsciously, she didn't really like herself enough, so that when she suffered a reversal it was "just what I expected." However, her scientific, practical, methodical and persevering capabilities made her suitable for the business world.

Elizabeth's personality was friendly and cheerful. Her desire for enjoyment and for widespread activity of mind, were very keen. There was a love of pleasure and social life that helped to bring popularity. Spiritual as well as physical pleasures would have brought joy and happiness. However, a tendency to be too easy-going could have led to difficulties, unless firmly controlled. She had power of synthesis, awareness of truth, self-sufficiency and easy elimination of the unwanted. More negatively, she was self-willed, self-insistent, conceited, sarcastic, disruptive, brusque and precipitate.

Elizabeth's refined and humane disposition helped her to read character and to study human nature but she did not always act on her own intuitions. She made up for any lack of aggressiveness through quiet determination and persistence.

Mentality: Elizabeth's mind was powerful and enterprising. She was enthusiastic and "all-out" for far-flung ideas and for cheerful ways of enjoyment, but somewhat exaggerative and off at a tangent. There was charm of speech, friendly discussion and contemplation of all beautiful objects. Communication was accomplished in affairs to do with profound studies and in foreign interests. Possibly she had a wavering manner coupled with an inability to make decisions.

Elizabeth's interests were mainly intellectual and her skills largely in the development of ideas. Thought, speech and writing were vivid, unusual, scintillating and inventive, and inclined towards unusual subjects for study, but with difficulties through these. Her mind devised ingenious ways to avoid being obliged to others, and any attempt to restrict her, or alter her opinions, was futile. Her obsession was detachment with a compelling need to achieve free self-expression. She wasn't afraid to speak her mind but she should have listened too. Her ideas and intuitions tended to be strong through heightened receptivity but may have been expressed nervously in a perverse or cantankerous manner. Altogether, she had to avoid displaying her intellect in an arrogant and pompous way.

It irritated Elizabeth when she didn't know the answer to a question. This indicated how important it was to ask herself if she should have been better informed in any area. Her insatiable curiosity provoked her to learn as much as possible about everything so that her knowledge amazed listeners. However, nervous tension was likely since freedom and limitation did not blend easily together. Limitation was displayed as wise control, caution, commonsense and willing acceptance of responsibility in all matters of correspondence, communication and in all educational or literary work. She was overly repressed, sceptical and prone to holding to herself alone that which was cherished, whether it was family, or knowledge, or valued collections of any kind. When withdrawn and contemplative, she became a good student of human nature. In this mood, she wasn't a fast learner but what she did learn left a deep impression.

In addition, Elizabeth's mind could take varied patterns as wax takes an imprint together with a nervous system that was exposed to all that touched it. There would have been gentle kindness, a fertile imagination, intense sensitivity and ideas that could have been communicated awkwardly. She could well have been mystical, fantasy loving, metaphysical, penetrative, prophetic, inspirational, dissimulating and quickly perceptive. She may even have been interested enough to work for research into psychic matters. Although talkative, times of quiet and withdrawal would have been needed.

Elizabeth went through conflict between the input and output of information. She had had to spend much time early on learning how to learn. She became a victim of habits that had led her to fill herself with more information than she really needed. As a result, she had to learn how to develop a clear priority of thoughts, throwing away all that was unimportant, while, at the same time, learning to express better that which was meaningful. Actually, she weighed herself down with one question after another, but, interestingly, she had already pre-programmed the answers. This hampered her learning process, for what she often sought was only that which would have substantiated what she had already formed solidly in her belief system. Often she blocked her conscious mind from being sensitive to the signals that came from her deeper mental levels. Thus, she was not fully integrated within herself. Those parts that she was able to comprehend consciously were in great measure a façade of thoughts, rationalisations and the constructed ideas that she found socially acceptable. Accordingly, she crystallised all her current, life-thought forms very strongly. As a result, she had great difficulty communicating. She could not put her thoughts easily into words she knew that others would have understood. Partly, too many of her ideas were formulated in black and white and she wasn't aware of the many shades of grey that existed between them.

However, there was a touch of genius/madness added to Elizabeth's mentality. She would have been a highly ingenious, yet very rebellious person. Now, as a rapid learner, there was a tendency to slip over things; now, her approach to understanding was helter-skelter rather than thorough.

Undoubtedly, in later years, she would have gone back over much she had raced through earlier. She desired instant responses to questions about all her feelings, but in her search she tended to move right past her answers. She could have become highly intense, trying over and over again, to solve problems that, actually, she had lived through many years before. Her disharmonious, emotional make-up was caused by constantly questioning and analysing everything, to the extent that she never truly allowed a settled, emotional life to develop fully. Her biggest difficulty became synchronising herself in the time dimension where she kept re-evaluating her past in the hope that it would have created a better future. And yet, because she did all this, her future actually became the mirror image of her past.

<u>Lifestyle:</u> Elizabeth needed to understand her fears and anxieties so that she could have put them into perspective. This would have allowed her to understand others better and to have realised that she was not alone in her fantasies. She was born with a craving for adventure and a rebellious attitude, which continually sought fulfilment, perhaps without cause. She would have enjoyed travel with its unexpected situations and developments. However, there had been a tendency towards disappointments in travel abroad as well as in study and in intelligent interests. Hence, she had developed a feeling of inadequacy concerning foreign travel and profound mental study. However, there was enjoyment of games and pleasures, but here also there were possible disappointments. Force was frittered away in constant changes of direction. Nevertheless there was a particular and rather uncompromising direction to her life-effort. She dipped deeply into life and poured forth the gathered results of her experiences with unremitting zeal.

At her best, Elizabeth would have reached a high standard of refinement and purity in her affairs, in which she tried to maintain the highest ethical standards. She was highly responsive to the new order of civilisation and she was never content with her knowledge or accomplishments. She sought continuously to learn more about the world so that she would have been ready to assume a more responsible position. Her wisdom, patience and constructiveness would have grown and brought success in later life. On the other hand, at her worst, her addiction to the unusual and the unconventional would have been so strong and awkwardly expressed that she would have become eccentric, odd and tiresome.

Elizabeth was on a life-long quest to purify herself. She experienced transformations as her constant urge to seek brought her many intense experiences. In all she did there was a powerful inner drive that motivated her. She was rarely content and extremely difficult to please because what she was seeking was usually beyond the grasp of those who tried to help her. She would have spent much time transforming her personal concepts and learning to transcend her ideal state as she uncovered worldly reality. She would have been anxious to achieve this but, in fact, her true evolution always came from after-the-fact realisations. During youth she had been highly impulsive. After mid-life, she became more introspective. Then, instead of trying to impress herself upon the world, she sought to understand how much she was a product of the world she lived in.

Elizabeth kept dwelling on emotions that had burdened her past. Unfortunately, the more she tried to free herself from these emotional blocks, the more she created other blocks that would have blocked her in further. The trick was, if possible, to try and flow through the blocks without using force. Because of the blocks, she tended to be slow making progress in life as she felt she had to be sure of herself constantly. Her need for security was high. Her strong, earlier attachment to a figure representing protection and safety was transferred to an older, authority figure as she didn't understand how she could live without a protective womb. When she did try to come out of herself, she was not sure that she would have been fully accepted by others. As a result, she tended to wall her emotions in, as if to save them for the one individual she may have hoped to meet in the future, who would have been symbolic of the past security she had given up.

Elizabeth tried to keep the concept of familiarity in her mind. Even when she travelled she kept identifying each new phase with a past that she was already comfortable in. In this way, she could have moved through life with the feeling that she was securely rooted, no matter where she was, or whom she was with. Because she was living in a world that seemed to be changing around her, it would have been better if, instead of trying to make her present fit in with her past, she realised and accepted within, the past securities she had known, so that she would not have had to seek them continually in her outer world. In this way, she could have fulfilled her ideal state of ever present birth.

Elizabeth spent her entire life learning how to learn and although her sources may have consisted of bits and pieces from many different individuals, phrases from many books (the complete texts of which she did not have the patience to read) and spots of different experiences, her life had a tremendous richness to it in terms of the scope of knowledge that she had touched.

Elizabeth absolutely insisted on being different from the society in which she lived. As such, her ideals and principles kept changing along with her erratic behaviour patterns. There was constant emotional upheaval stemming from experiences that she was unprepared for. For example, should the question of abortion arisen, she would have been confronted with her need for motherhood conflicting with her need for personal freedom. Somehow or other, she would have had to learn emotional contentment. The totality of all that she was, came to represent so much of what her traditional environment was not. She changed so often that it became difficult to see any real pattern to her lifestyle. Because of this, however, she became one of the most original thinkers. Her inventiveness was without cause, or definite purpose, yet she was unhampered by the boundaries that tied others down.

Relationships

<u>Others:</u> Elizabeth became an inspirer and instructor of others. Yet eccentricity was displayed in taking care of anyone (or anything). However, she wanted to help others and not offend them, which was admirable. People needed someone who was genuinely interested in their problems, and no-one was better qualified than she, to give them her assistance.

It annoyed Elizabeth to have to concede to people when they were wrong, but she feared that she would have alienated them if she didn't. Once she had become established, however, she would have gone back to being honest with others and with herself. Then she would have appeared to be more obstinate than she really was at heart. Still, only limited help, support and charity would have been given aggressively, and with difficulty, to others.

Her communication with others tended to be too brusque and independent so that it lost good contact with them. In conversation, she would have shocked people in order to drive home a point, and so she would have been confident that she had made an indelible impression on them. Because she tried overly hard to get her thoughts across to people (while inwardly believing that they were not as receptive as she would have liked them to be), she experienced great difficulties in all her relationships. Additionally, because there was so much insistence on expressing individuality no matter what the cost, there was difficulty getting along with others in work or in personal relationships. Although she was not that easily influenced by others, she often had doubts in her own mind, which she may not have admitted to. However, her willingness to make both concessions and compromises, coupled with her success in reading people, did result in forming good relationships.

<u>Friends:</u> Elizabeth had many friends and acquaintances, who were never able to get too close to her. However, her fate depended upon the friends and acquaintances she gathered around her, as she was relatively easily influenced by her associates. In addition, there was a tendency to break with friends.

<u>Family:</u> Elizabeth experienced changes in her family structure, including separation from siblings. Her emotional identification with her parents was a powerful force in her life. Coping with her feelings of divided loyalty to each of her parents may have been difficult. Probably she leaned towards the dominant parent (her father?), which could have caused some guilt feelings. From her past, she had not yet developed within herself a true sense of gratitude to her family while still benefitting from all that it had given her. Thus, there was always emotional frustration as she tried to rebel against her family. She had to let this situation be, because, one day, she would have looked back and realised just how inconsequential all of it was in terms of the destiny she had to fulfil.

Elizabeth would have been a good parent because she realised how vitally important it was to offer children every chance to mature in their own way so that they would have become self-sufficient adults. She would have wanted to share her experiences with her children and she would have been deeply pleased when they indicated that they wanted to follow in her footsteps.

<u>Lover:</u> Elizabeth's sexual life was of importance. Her sexual relationships would have been harmonious. She had a strong desire nature, which she often expressed in extreme ways. For example, there was a somewhat impulsive exaggeration of licentious behaviour coupled with a desire for freedom at any price. Alternatively, when the object of her desire nature was not immediately available, she patiently bided her time until s/he was, and then she wouldn't have accepted rejection easily. There was gay enjoyment of love making (and of children). Her affection was demonstrative but she didn't

want to be enchained. Sex wasn't the most important concern in her life: if it was available, then that would have been fine, but if not, then she wouldn't have got too uptight about it. The tendencies were that: (1) partnerships were disappointing and undependable, (2) there was confusion and deception in love affairs, and (3) there were secret partnerships.

Elizabeth was always seeking "the other half" and never being satisfied. Duty, or some form of limitation, stopped the full expression of love and harmony, but the duty was acceptable, or less heavy, because of some happiness, which it brought. There was a tendency to free herself from bounds or ties. Her social and domestic nature, and her inclination to marriage, would have depended upon a fair amount of geniality and popularity. To sum up: freedom was preferred to marriage.

In any case, marriage (and other relationships) would have been difficult because her inner turmoil made her continually attempt to uproot and transform her needs and basic desires. Consequently, marriage would have been delayed. Probably, any partner would often have been older than she was.

Career

Early: Elizabeth's destiny was mainly in the hands of others and depended on circumstances. Probably, she had been born into a prosperous environment; she would have inherited money or risen in life to earn a good income. However, there was likely to have been a cleavage in her life relating to her parents, or to early childhood. The disharmony produced in her nature could have urged her to accomplishment.

The restrictions of Elizabeth's early conditioning may have prevented her from being even mildly optimistic about her future. She may not have cared about others' needs, or have wanted to know how they thought, which only indicated that she was determined to get as much as she could from them to satisfy her own desires. Identification with her parents may have caused her some delay in becoming established independently. It was to her credit that she could look forward eagerly to achieving her goals because, probably, she had had little help from her parents. In fact, burdensome obligations, strong parental conditioning and family ties at home, caused her to alter her plans until she could have felt comfortable fulfilling her objectives, taking on her own responsibilities and establishing her own identity. Gradually, she should have relinquished her grip on the security provided by her family and made her own way whatever the outcome. She didn't have to win her parents' support for her career or lifestyle.

Elizabeth needed to have put into perspective the obligations she had to others and those that she owed to herself. Despite her past, she may have become motivated by a strong, spiritual commitment to serve others, in which case her results would have been much greater than the sacrifices she had made to get them. She had to examine her motives carefully to determine why she felt compelled to take the career direction she'd chosen. She had to have been directed by only the noblest reasons, including the desire to help to satisfy pressing human needs. She had to be wary of the temptation to relax her ethics while pursuing her objectives; giving in could have resulted in massive losses in earnings and prestige. Her task was to have made the transition from feeling inadequate to knowing that she could have exploited her creativity to derive whatever she wanted out of life. She wanted to be free to use her creativity in activities that were far removed from the usual boring routines. She wanted to be self-employed, or if employed, then to have self-determination. She may have had to give a lot before she realised any rewards for her efforts but then she would have enjoyed very substantial earnings because she handled responsibility so well.

A formal education would have revealed the realities of life to her and prepared her for occasional setbacks, so that she didn't have to rely on feelings and hunches. She had to try not to contaminate her ideas with irrelevant emotions. She had high aspirations and a vision of herself in a position of trust and authority. This vision would have convinced her to get the formal training she needed; she knew that, otherwise, her aspirations were little more than fantasies. If she had spent some time developing her mental assets, she could have been rewarded abundantly. She then had to learn to convert her ideas into tangible assets and to have used them to build a life of her own without being dependent on others. With her education, she would have realised that she had plenty of talent and creativity to have succeeded on her own; her progress would have accelerated until she had gained complete command of her destiny.

Elizabeth over-reacted to her superiors' expectations and did more than was required. However, complaining about the way things were run may have been risky, if her superiors had been offended easily.

<u>Vocation:</u> To avoid having to do physical labour, Elizabeth looked for a field in which she could have exercised her mental faculties. The chances were that she would have grown into a staff, or management position, on the job. She was not particularly fond of menial tasks either, so she would have preferred a career that allowed her to grow and develop according to her own particular abilities. She could have been a successful employee, or executive, in her own field, getting on well with people in her charge. Some career fields that may have interested her include: medicine, consumer services, family planning or creative writing. Surgery and psychology would have attracted her mind. Any of these would have provided her with opportunities to extend herself creatively. Ideally, she would have become qualified for management enterprises, at which she would have excelled. She had splendid organising ability, with success in large undertakings, for public companies, for example. Government service, social programs, political interests, land development and estate agency management comprise some of the outlets through which she could have found meaningful expression. Temperamentally, she would have been qualified for a professional field such as economics, education and law. However, in the end, she may have preferred a career that allowed her some privacy and still provided a useful product, or service, for the public.

<u>Middle:</u> Elizabeth tended to put so much nervous energy into her career that she would have become rather irritable. Although she may have been restricted by the demanding obligations of her daily routine, she managed to use her innovative ability to make her work interesting. She was clever at devising new and better ways to make the job more exciting. Much progress was made in life through careful forethought and steady persistence. She was an effective salesperson especially when promoting herself and she was willing to work hard to gain the approval of her fellow professionals. However, she was unusually vulnerable to the danger of fellow workers conspiring against her on the job. She had to have been constantly alert to this problem, and completely informed, to prevent it from happening.

Elizabeth was interested in a cause but less concerned about end-results, about conserving her resources and even about herself. She adapted her allegiances to lines along which she could have made her efforts count for the most. She tended to act at all times under a consideration of opposing views, or to sensitivity to contrasting possibilities. She existed in a world of antagonistic conflicts. Yet she was capable of unique achievement through a development of unsuspected relations in life, although she would have wasted energy through her improper alignment with various situations.

Usually, Elizabeth would have been fortunate in money matters. She had good business ability with success in financial operations and investments. Financial independence was very important to her. She was even willing to do without some of life's pleasures temporarily in order to guarantee her future security. Thus, she was determined to promote her own ideas to her own advantage. She also felt the necessity for dealing with financial matters for others.

Elizabeth realised that unless she was willing to devote some part of her life to helping people become more self-reliant, her growth would have been limited. She felt a responsibility to communicate her knowledge skilfully to anyone who needed and wanted it. Her knowledge sustained those who needed intellectual nourishment. She was deeply sensitive to the problems of society and to people who were victims of political, social and economic injustice. Because she understood people's individual difficulties and problems, she was better able to cope with larger social issues. She used any tool she needed to help those who could not help themselves. Privately, she felt that she was destined to serve society by helping others and so, in the future, she would have become dedicated to public service.

In her own personal and business dealings, she insisted on fair play and justice. She spoke out against offensive, socio-political conditions. She had an affinity for solving problems that required sophisticated solutions. Practical planning and determined self-will would have united in an unusual way to produce brilliant results. Additionally, her good education would have given her enormous leverage to promote better government and a better society. But her rise to public prominence would have been easier, if she had understood how much she needed to know to win people's respect.

Late: If Elizabeth had been successful in her career then she would have enjoyed her later years knowing that she had made an important contribution to others. Undoubtedly, she would have been long remembered by those she'd helped or influenced. She wanted to have security so she could have enjoyed retirement in relaxed comfort. She hated the idea that she might have had to live out her final years in an institution.

Appearance and Health

Appearance: Elizabeth was of middle stature, strong and well-formed, with a square build that inclined to stoutness/plumpness later. Her hands would also have been plump, short and broad. Her face would have been long and fleshy with a short, strong neck and forehead, nose, lips, cheeks and mouth, all full. Her speech could have been drawling yet soft and attractive. Her jaw may have been heavy but both her complexion and appearance looked well. Her eyes would have been round, prominent and dark, and her hair any colour from light to dark and possibly curling. Later on, she may have stooped.

Health: Her health should have been very good but her eyes may have suffered. On the other hand, she had a strong nervous system implying good eyesight, hearing and sense of touch. Changes, new ideas and "differentness" were applied to food and precautions about health. Possibly, there would have been sudden upsets in health relating to her breasts, stomach and upper alimentary system. Possibly, there would have been kidney or liver trouble (deriving from over-indulgence?), and also possibly colds, chills and rheumatism, all coupled with poor recuperation. There may have been danger through accidents of the falling, crashing, limb-breaking kind. She may well have had an easy, peaceful death.

References: 1) 'Elizabeth I' (2nd Edition, Illustrated), Christopher Haigh, Longman Pearson, Harlow, U.K., 2001.
2) 'Elizabeth I—A Biography', Simon Adams, Yale English Monarch Series, 'The University Press', New Haven, CT., U.S.A., 2013.

James I

*"Hath God not made us all in one island, compassed with
one sea, and of itself, by nature, indivisible?"*
Addressing the English Parliament, 1604.

James was King of Scotland as James VI from July 1567 and King of England and Ireland as James I from the union of the English and Scottish crowns in March 1603 until his death. The two kingdoms were individual sovereign states, with their own parliaments, judiciary, and laws, though both were ruled by James in personal union. He succeeded to the Scottish throne at the age of thirteen months, after his mother, Mary, Queen of Scots, was compelled to abdicate in his favour. Four different regents  governed during his minority, which ended officially in 1578, although he did not gain full control of his government until 1583. In 1603, he succeeded the last Tudor monarch of England and Ireland, Elizabeth I, who had died without issue. He continued to reign in all three kingdoms for 22 years, a period known as the 'Jacobean Era' after him, until he died in 1625, aged 58. After the Union of the Crowns in 1603, he based himself in England, only returning to Scotland once in 1617, and styled himself "King of Great Britain and Ireland". In his reign, the plantation of Ulster and the British colonisation of the Americas began.

His reign in Scotland for 57 years was longer than any of his predecessors. He achieved most of his aims in Scotland but faced great difficulties in England, including the Gunpowder Plot in 1605 and repeated conflicts with the English Parliament. Under James, the 'Golden Age' of literature and drama continued following Elizabeth I. James himself was a talented scholar, producing three main works. He also sponsored the translation of the Bible that was named after him: the Authorised King James Version. James had been termed "the wisest fool in Christendom", an epithet associated with his character.

However, since the late twentieth century, historians have revised James's reputation and have treated him as a serious and thoughtful monarch.

James was the only son of Mary, Queen of Scots and her second husband, Henry Stuart, Lord Darnley. Both Mary and Darnley were great grandchildren of Henry VII of England through Margaret Tudor, the elder sister of Henry VIII. James was born on the 29th June, 1566 NS, at 09:23 in Edinburgh, Scotland (see Appendix 1, Figure 12). His Epoch occurred on the 1st October, 1565 NS, at 01:27 (see Appendix 1, Figure 11).

Character Portrait

General: James had an ambitious and power-seeking personality that would have burned for success. He showed strong will-power, controlled persistence and intuition but also impulsiveness. He had a hot and hasty temper, yet was free and generous by disposition. Generally this disposition was moderately good but rather passionate. There was a great power of concentration that combined with will to give quiet, yet unequalled, determination. Happiness with a love of peace and beauty were indicated mildly. Hopeful and optimistic, he had good personality feelings that enhanced his spiritual and refining tendencies. In short, he had a balanced and harmonious nature. He tended to be very happy with life in the world and was greedy for its good things. He longed for a comfortable life surrounded by beautiful objects and for that he would have resisted those who opposed him. Sensitivity and protection were emphasised with a dislike of conflict. He tried to adjust to difficulties, or attempted to by-pass them but with strain. His manner appeared to be cool, cautious and more limited than he was really. Duty, conscience and orderliness were of importance. Although charming in speech and manner, there was a tendency to be timid through a feeling of personal inadequacy. He tried to compensate for this emotional insecurity by accumulating material possessions. Unfortunately, his energy and his limitation did not combine well. Force and initiative was canalised and ordered, while caution and patience were enlivened. These effects would have been depressing for him when feeling lively, and hurtful when wanting to be slow and solid.

James was more subjective than objective. He had a great love of drama and showed particular enthusiasm in pursuit of an ideal. He had poetic and musical ability and either his artistic, or moral nature, would have had many opportunities for development.

<u>Mentality:</u> James was independent and original with a tendency to success in inventive, flashing thought. He knew the importance of thinking for himself. He was restless and eager and when stimulated his aggressive nature sprang into action. It was the thrill of competition that made him accept challenges. He was energetically talkative with a tendency to wild extravagance, mainly of thought. Although his mind was powerful, courageous and enterprising, it would not have wandered but would have ordered and controlled in practical, cautious and methodical ways. His mind was good for narrow-pointed applications but order may have become dreary planning and rigid discipline. Accordingly, there would have been a tendency to mental loneliness and a lack of poise that forced brusque speech and writing. However, in general, balance, harmony and a sensitive will contributed to a good mind and mental outlook.

Communication was expressed in affairs to do with the home, domesticity and collecting. Mental occupations would have been carried out at home. He used his mind to express beauty and in hand and arm work, such as in painting, designing and craftsmanship. Often, his mind schemed in an involved way yet action tended to occur through intuition rather than from reason.

James was emotionally sensitive and needed independence of thought along with emotional security at the same time. Seeking both emotional and mental fulfilment simultaneously he was incomplete when receiving one without the other. Because of this he did not fully understand the concept of growth and so kept thinking himself incapable of letting go of earlier phases of his life. He also found it difficult to establish a sense of meaning, yet he still found it necessary to keep moving. Striking a balance was difficult to achieve because if he had leaned on others for security, he would have lost his independence of thought, and <u>vice-versa</u>, i.e. he would have lost the emotional security he had gained at the cost of his independence of thought. His easiest bargain would have been to grow emotionally possessive of his thoughts but unfortunately, this could have led him into many neurotic complexes that he would have found himself unable to let go of. Thus, it became difficult for him to bury the past and to move ahead freely and clearly into the future. Because he analysed his emotions rather than let them flow, he could actually have given power to negative emotional states thereby making them larger than they really were, without even realising it.

James experienced more mental freedom than he did the practical application of his thought. It was more important for him to have freedom of mind than the ultimate result of how he applied it. He needed space to think and became uncomfortable in crowds. He could have become a complete day-dreamer, pondering all that he could have done but hadn't. As a result, he would have experienced a great deal of impracticality in his thinking.

James was able to absorb the consciousness of all those individuals who brought him back to re-enacting the thoughts, stored in his memory, of all he had experienced. His mind and emotions were so linked that all thought created feelings and vice-versa. Both were so deeply rooted in past experience that he kept trying to recreate his childhood. Because of this, his upbringing had been most important, for many childhood experiences would have been carried as a residue all through his life. He had many dependency thoughts from his past. Through these he kept re-enacting child-parent roles with everyone he related to. Later on, he would have developed a very beautiful rapport with children, that, eventually, would have turned out to be one of his greatest strengths.

Ideally, James was engaged in studying levels of consciousness without necessarily committing himself to any particular one:—He compared past ideas with present realities and future dreams so that, he may, one day, have understood what it was he thought he was looking for. Without knowing the questions, he could hardly have understood the answers, but he was still a seeker of the highest order. He may have done well to study the modern ways of Taoism, or of Zen, where some of his unconventional ideas could have actually found a haven of truth on a worldly level. He was in search of the unreachable, intangible rainbow that he believed actually existed. Accordingly, he could well have been the person who would have thrown away the bird in his hand to go after two in the bush.

A strong inclination towards spiritual things sometimes made James too idealistic. His tendency towards the intangible, resulting in good imaginative faculties, involved visions, ideas and boundless aims. These would have been of the ethereal and inspirational kind but would have required strength to actualise them. More negatively, emotional intensity together with a stimulated, morbid imagination and a sentimental susceptibility possibly would have led to delusion, unrestrained self-expression, self-criticism, restlessness, hallucination, recklessness, perversion and cruelty. Touchiness induced may well have resulted in escapism.

Lifestyle: A home of James's own would have given him a sense of 'belonging' and the comfort of having roots. He knew that he needed to establish these roots before embarking on a gainful life endeavour. However, he had a great deal of difficulty pointing his life in sensible directions through balanced means. Here, the memory of his childhood environment should have guided him. James was interested in a cause, but showed less concern over end-results, his resources or even himself. He dipped deeply into life and poured forth the results of his experiences with unremitting zeal. He undertook a vital search for the meaning of life both anarchically and obsessively. He was very much a worldly seeker, focusing a great deal of his mental energies upon understanding the progress of the human race. He became intrigued by the progress of evolution and of mankind as a theory rather than as a fact. Actually, he didn't like to confront the central core of life. Instead, he was almost happy to view it as an outside observer. Eventually, James would have become the special spokesman in literary and religious realms for the vast, deep and hidden knowledge assembled by the end of the middle ages.

James's unusually high awareness level was due to society neither traditionally nor restrictedly binding his imagination. As a dreamer and a seeker of awareness in life, he had to learn how to balance all he intuitively felt with all he had to deal with on more mundane and practical levels. It was not enough for him to imagine something idealistically wonderful. He had to find the ways to impress his dreams into his reality. He became deeply appreciative of life itself so that creating things for himself became far less important to him than just experiencing the essence of that he could absorb. He became idealistic to the point that he didn't easily discipline himself to the standards of society. He always felt that there was a higher music, a more subtle meaning to life and a deeper understanding of what the world called love. As a result, he tended to withdraw from creativity, retreating into a dream world that became his reality. Hence, he tended to be impractical as the scope of his imagination far surpassed the reality of the world around him.

However, little in life went by him without him studying it clinically. His drive was not merely physical but mental and world oriented as well. Whether he expressed it physically or transformed it to mental regions, this drive was powering all he sought to understand in the world. He sought to understand the deepest mysteries. To him sexuality represented the most unfathomable question of all. The more he grew discontented with the world around him, the more he began to fathom the mysteries within himself. He aggressively created constant destruction of old, traditional habit patterns so that ultimately he could undergo a rebirth within himself on the deepest of levels.

Relationships

<u>Others:</u> James was not fully aware of all his talents because he had allowed others to tell him what to do. He didn't argue when others disagreed. But he mustn't have let others dominate him, or have interfered with him, while he developed them. Despite this, he knew that he had to make a dramatic break and exploit his imagination in his own way.

Sociable, James easily attracted others in the public by his innate charm. At his best, he would have been an instructor and inspirer of ideas for others, i.e. his main strength would have been as a disseminator of ideas to them. He was lucky because he met helpful people. People respected his determination and self-discipline and knew that they could depend on him to help them solve their problems. James was constantly questioning the values of others. He was so linked with the values of others, that whether he liked it or not, he was strongly influenced by mass consciousness.

James was attracted to those who were as polished and as charming as he was. He admired people who were free, and he aspired to emulate them in seeking his own goals and gaining financial freedom. He didn't expect others to give him anything because he had the talent to gain his goals on his own. He preferred not to be limited by obligations to others. Yet because he was apprehensive about the stability of his material resources, he never refused gifts from others, and he didn't necessarily reciprocate. Support, help and charity was given to, and received from, others cautiously. He was suspicious of people who made demands, so he questioned their motives and tried to pin-down what his own contribution would cost. On the other hand, he was highly compassionate and often would have sacrificed much for the needs of others. He was keen to act for their good and often in unrecognised ways. He could have given generously, not only without expecting something in return, but also not even wanting the other person to know that he had been the giver. At other times, however, he found it difficult to get free from obligations to the people around him in his personal and professional life. For example, he was fond of the people who had loved him and had helped him as a child. He appreciated any kindnesses and tried to reciprocate.

James was a hard person for others to reach, because he could have rebelled against anything that bound him. He was a loner, yet he needed people, if only to add colour to his ideas. At the same time, he had a way of remaining detached mentally. Normally, he didn't like the ways of thinking on the part of others. He himself found it easier to personalise problems in society rather than deal with those things that were closer at hand in his own life. Becoming indignant at social reforms long overdue, he could have ignored the need for personal reform within himself. As a result, he experienced distortions in the priorities of his relationships to his society, to his family and even to himself.

Friends: Although popular with many friends, James was selective about making them. He was drawn to persons who were mature enough to stand on their own. Basically, however, he was a friend to all and rarely too busy to listen when someone needed him, especially when it concerned their future goals and aspirations. James liked to feel needed by his friends. However, he had to help them when they needed it, because, probably, they had helped him previously. He had to get help from his associates, and to learn from his competitors, because they could have proved a catalyst for his success. Generally, his friends helped him to achieve his objectives. Even when the going got rough, he could have relied on them for support, because they weren't likely to have been fair-weather friends. Fortunately, for James, he was able to detach himself from old friends, because he knew that he could have made new ones easily.

Family: James was grateful for his parents' (guardians') influence in helping him to shape his own life and he wanted to win their respect and admiration for his accomplishments. He may have felt that he owed his guardians so much that he had had to put a low priority on his own personal interests. Unless he had changed that attitude, he would have let precious time pass without focusing on what he owed himself. Doubtless his guardians wanted the best for him but they may have denied him the opportunity to learn from experience. He may have felt such a strong obligation to them so that he may have put aside working towards his own goals in order to help them. Indeed, he may have come to resent them for imposing this burden on him. Yet he shouldn't have blamed his guardians for his problems on getting started on a career that was satisfying to him and rewarding to others, for his early environment had allowed him to express his imagination. Perhaps his family had urged him to make a life of his own anyway. Whatever the situation, he would have had to exploit his talent when he realised that that was the only way to achieve the freedom he wanted from family obligations and responsibilities.

James had found that a tranquil home had been soothing for him and he hoped that his own home would have had that quality. He needed a family, or close friends, who would have shared his good fortune, and would have made his efforts seem both satisfying and worthwhile. His home would have been harmonious and delightful containing beautiful objects coupled with smooth and loving family relationships. Warmth and enthusiasm entered into relationships of affection both in sexual life and as expressed to young people in a family. James was reasonably fond of children, but they might have interfered with his personal objectives. Giving his (wayward?) children the advantages he hadn't had, was an important component of his goals. However, he had to remember that they had to fulfil their own potentials, according to their own interests, and so he inspired them to assert their own identities.

Lover: Early on, James's love affairs would have been numerous and happy so that partnerships would have been beneficial and successful. However, the animal side of his nature would have been awakened, with the liability to go to extremes, especially where love was concerned. He had a powerful, very intense sexual drive coupled with the desire to be the dominant partner in all relationships, whatever their nature. He craved ardent feelings and sensation. Thus, he was an ardent lover but too prone to mistake passion for love and intensity for depth. He was not accustomed to having his desires frustrated, and he became very impatient when his lover became non-committal about their relationship. A cutting harshness could have entered into relationships of affection. These were likely to have been intense but not without quarrels. Feelings would have been strong but would have caused and received hurt. Additionally, unusualness was apt to be fascinating, but edged with unpleasantness. Partnerships would have been unconventional and apt to be broken because of insistence on freedom. Scandal and disfavour would have been possible. Moreover, James found affection most difficult to express. He avoided close communication in intimate relationships. In some instances he could have become sexually unresponsive because he did not feel comfortable. Overall, his partnerships were not easy. Later on, life would have tended to become solitary. Although keen, sensitive, sincere and in love with love, he was often unrealistic in his romantic affairs and so often became disillusioned. As a secret romantic, he could have enjoyed many imaginary love affairs.

James could have paid lip service to marriage, children and tradition. However, he was a good candidate for marriage, and would have worked to make it stable. He would have been a warm, loving person, who clearly would have enjoyed doing things that pleased his partner. He wanted to share as much as he could with his mate so that boredom wouldn't have arisen. Thus, it would have been difficult for him to remain single, so that he was apt to marry in haste, and repent afterwards. His partner must also have been a friend, have shared his dreams and have given him the freedom to serve others in his own way. In fact, he was happiest with a congenial 'other', either in work or play. He wanted his partner to hold him in high esteem so that he became a credit to his partner as he pursued his career. He would have had to listen to his wife's suggestions in this regard, because, probably, he had chosen her for her versatile mind.

For James, the limitation of his affection, or of a happy social life, had a serious, one-pointed direction. Love may have meant sacrifice, or of a life lonely, except for the chosen one. His partnership was serious but successful practically. On the downside, however, he could have become overly possessive of loved ones; there would have been sorrow and loss through his affections, and any partnership would have brought responsibility.

Career

<u>Early:</u> James's destiny lay mainly in his own hands. He had a tendency to a lucky journey through life from meeting good opportunities. Transformation would have come through learning rigorous lessons of duty and self-control. His early conditioning would have allowed some misgivings to develop about his ability to gain the security he wanted. Consequently, he grew up not knowing if he could have succeeded on his own. He underestimated his own worth and so was apprehensive about meeting competition. But his fear of challenge was groundless. Generally, he maintained a low profile because he assumed that his creativity was not very special, yet, at the same time, he hadn't to neglect to exploit his talents. All his potential would have meant little unless he had willingly invested the time and energy to develop a skill that the public would have paid for. However, it would have been easy for him to neglect this task in favour of more self-satisfying pursuits. He had felt that he would always have had the privilege of indulging himself as he chose, and yet he expected to be well-paid for his professional skills. How independent he became depended on how far he was able to accept another person's authority over him. Resisting authority only impeded his progress and showed his own incompetence. Rather than assume that he couldn't have done something, he needed to have got the training that would have qualified him to succeed in it. His future success in his career depended completely upon fully exploiting his skills before the public. The benefits he derived here were exactly proportional to his ability to face up to and deal with his responsibilities. Once he had gained the credentials he needed, he probably would have become a specialist in some area of endeavour.

One of his goals should have been obtaining substantial monetary rewards for his efforts, to provide financial security coupled with a reasonably independent lifestyle. He looked forward to achieving his goals in the future. Simultaneously he also looked forward to the time when he could have pursued his hobbies more freely. Achieving this goal would have given him the freedom to come and go as he chose without having to endure the frustration of limited ambitions. He should have become self-sufficient as soon as possible and have had a place of his own.

James was serious, cautious and responsible in his undertakings. He was better informed than he realised and so was more qualified to achieve his goals. There was a patient working out of what was begun but not with ease. Reaching the goals he had set depended largely on improving his self-image so that he could have felt that he deserved them. James knew that his future financial security must have come from using his resources effectively. He hoped to derive all possible benefits from his career so that his future needs would have been met. Probably, he would have had to guard against seeming too indecisive, weak and wanting peace-at-any-price during his career. Yet worldly success would have been achieved eventually.

Vocation: James should have selected a career that made sufficient demands on him and had allowed him to use his creativity. He would have inclined towards the arty-crafty. These pursuits would have seemed to be consistent with his temperament and would have given him some flexibility in using his talents. Security would also have been an important consideration when he came to choose a career. Potentially, he had good business sense and would have been capable of managing and controlling large enterprises. Banking and investment would have allowed him to grow steadily with some assurance of security later on.

James's intellectual awareness of social injustice provoked a compassionate response, suggesting that he might have worked in an enterprise that offered solutions to social problems. Once he had become involved, and realised how effective his contribution would have been, he could have laid the foundations on which he could have built a career that would have enriched him as well as those he served. He may have met some painful situations, which he could have learned to handle by becoming more objective.

James delighted in fire-arms, shooting, wars, surgical operations and in maritime affairs. Work in hospitals, correctional facilities, in medicine, physical therapy, in pastoral care or in programs for the deaf, blind and mute would have comprised suitable careers in which understanding and compassion were critical.

<u>Middle:</u> James was subject to upsets and to forced new phases. He felt that he had a job to do, even though he may not have been sure of what specific role he could have played. He was willing to work for life's necessities, and because he was basically honest in his dealings, he would not have met any uncomfortable moments when he reflected on his achievements later on. He tried to maintain high ethical standards because he knew that otherwise he would have sustained severe losses. He didn't like to work with people who took liberties with the law. He had had to learn to make appropriate plans to ensure security later in life. He became clever at devising money-making schemes, for he came to understand how money talks and he used this knowledge to further his ambitions. He came to know how to use his talents and resources to plan for the future. Usually, he was greatly concerned over resources. However, in general, he didn't discuss his financial affairs openly, and he talked about them privately, only with those that he trusted.

James planned carefully so that he always had something to do. Whenever he reached a goal, he established a new one to replace it. He adapted his allegiances to lines along which he could have made his efforts count for the most. He had excellent prospects for getting everything he wanted out of life, partly because he didn't live in the past. However, he considered himself to be less important than his colleagues, and fearing ridicule, he asserted himself defensively even when he knew he was right. Yet he knew that he had to adjust to the fact that if he had been reticent in his job, then someone else would have got the promotion. So, when a promotion came up, he would have let his superiors know that he was qualified to take on greater responsibility. Hence, he came to know how to put his best foot forward with finesse. Even though he may have been preoccupied with obtaining mundane objectives, he would have sensed a subtle, inner urge to become involved eventually in enterprises that would have increased the public's awareness of its pressing needs. He was physically sensitive to the social chaos that resulted from public indifference. Yet he remained concerned about social problems at all levels of society—local, national and international. His sensitivity to unacceptable social conditions may have forced him to make sacrifices to ensure their limitation. Many legal resources would have been available to help him to force the public to re-examine the social values involved. Also, he himself could have aroused enthusiasm for a positive effort to stimulate better social conditions. With his many ideas, he could have pursued a rewarding career and made a truly important and permanent contribution to society.

<u>Late:</u> Probably, James would have been very active in retirement. Being useful was so important to him that he would always have found ways to keep busy and gain fulfilment. Knowing that he had done a good job would have given him much contentment when he came to reflect on it during his later years.

Appearance and Health

<u>Appearance:</u> There was little that was personally attractive about James. A large, bony and muscular individual, James was tall, of full stature with broad shoulders and firmly set with a square build in middle age that all the high-living in the world could not have made fat. He had a full-sized, round head and face (possibly scarred), round, full, grey eyes and a florid, or ruddy, complexion. His flaxen hair was light brown and tended to baldness. His walk would have been upright and possibly his speech would have been drawling, but soft and attractive.

<u>Health:</u> Generally, James had good health and a vitality of spirit that could have been almost too intense. He had an ability to withstand arduous, rough and pioneering conditions as well as to bear personal hardships. Even so, extremism in work and play could have led to overstrain. He had an harmoniously working, strong nervous system, hence good eyesight, hearing and sense of touch. He would have been a good sleeper. Nevertheless, there would have been a tendency to tenseness that would have been hard to relax, and which could have led to nervous storms. Additionally, adjusting to difficulties usually produced nervous stress. Yet there was a controlling tendency operating here, that prevented his nervous system from becoming energised to the point of overstrain. In a general way, he may have been susceptible to malnutrition, bruises, colds, fevers and accidents.

Despite many contacts, he may well have become sad at the end of his life, culminating in an unfortunate death in a public place.

Reference: 'James VI and I', Roger Lockyer, Longmans, London, U.K., 1998.

Charles I

"The season is so sharp as probably may make me shake, which some observers may imagine proceeds from fear. I would have no such imputation."
30th January, 1649.

Charles was monarch of the three kingdoms of England, Scotland and Ireland from 1625 to his execution at the end of January, 1649. Charles engaged in a struggle for power with the English Parliament, attempting to obtain royal revenue whilst Parliament sought to curb his royal prerogative, which Charles believed was divinely ordained. Many of his subjects opposed his attempts to overrule and negate parliamentary authority, in particular his interference in the English and Scottish churches and the levying of taxes without parliamentary consent, because they saw them as those of a tyrannical absolute monarch.

Charles's reign was also characterised by religious conflicts. His failure to aid Protestant forces successfully during the Thirty Years' War, coupled with his marriage to a Roman Catholic, Henrietta Maria of France, generated deep mistrust among Calvinists. Further, Charles allied himself with controversial ecclesiastics, such as Richard Montagu and William Laud, whom Charles appointed Archbishop of Canterbury. Many of Charles's subjects felt that this brought the Church of England too close to Roman Catholicism. His religious policies generated the antipathy of reformed groups such as the Puritans. His attempts to force religious reforms upon Scotland led to the Bishops' Wars, which were lost, thereby strengthening the position of the English and Scottish Parliaments, which, in turn, helped to precipitate his downfall.

Charles's last years were marked by the Civil War, in which he fought the forces of the English and Scottish Parliaments. He was defeated in the First Civil War (1642-1645), after which the English Parliament expected him to accept its demands for a constitutional monarchy. Instead, he remained defiant by attempting to forge an alliance with Scotland and escaping to the Isle of Wight. This provoked the Second Civil War (1648-1649) and a second defeat for Charles, who was subsequently captured, tried, convicted and executed for high treason. The monarchy was abolished and a republic called the Commonwealth of England was declared.

Charles was the second son and third surviving child of King James I of England and Queen Anne of Denmark. He became the heir to the throne upon the death of his elder brother, Henry Frederick, in 1612. Charles was born on the 29th November, 1600 NS, at 23:06, in Dunfermline, Scotland (see Appendix 1, Figure 14). His Epoch occurred on the 26th March, 1600 NS, at 06:08 (see Appendix 1, Figure 13).

Character Portrait

General: Charles had an ambitious, power-seeking personality that burned for success, displaying firmness, zeal, ardour, energy, enterprise and self-reliance. Courage, daring and the ability to work hard were the main attributes of his personality. He was well-informed and fond of acquiring knowledge, of intellectual pursuits, of debate, of argument and of always being at the front. He actively enjoyed games, sports and all pleasures but perhaps not altogether harmlessly. He was good-humoured, cheerful, honest, candid and with a fondness for show, ceremony, fine clothes, decorated rooms and large houses. This inclination to beauty and ease was too irresponsible and lazy but being subjective and somewhat artistic, he tried to surround himself with the finer things of life. Music, dancing, poetry, drama and painting would have become necessities of life bringing happiness and benefit. He had an appreciation of good food and thoroughly enjoyed it. Also, he liked journeys, the law, religion, philosophy and exercise and so felt free to explore both physically and mentally. Life, on or by the sea, would have been liked and he may even have been fond of looking into ancient customs and strange religious rites.

Charles had developed a very good opinion of himself but had he been really sure of himself, he wouldn't have needed to defend himself by stating that he was, or by complaining that everyone else was unqualified or untrained. He had to prove himself by becoming satisfied.

However, Charles did have an inherent tendency to rash action that had to be resisted strongly. His initiatory, resourceful individuality sought excitement and unusual experiences. His obsession was might with a compelling need to achieve emancipation. He often said more than he meant in unrealistic, impulsive outbursts, being enthusiastic and aspiring. Although his moods were suddenly changeable, they resulted in an ability to throw off the static and then start new, receptive ways. At times, egotistical, avaricious, harsh, foolhardy and brutal, he was precipitate in action, but full of power and revolutionary intent; hence his refusal to tread the beaten path.

Charles's energy was expressed with a dominating insistence on being over-forceful with accompanying, possible hot temper. Proud, commanding and combative, yet loyal, defensive and with noble ideals, his behaviour seemed to be based on a belief in the survival of the fittest. He insisted on his right to assert himself when he felt the impulse. He didn't feel that he had to explain his actions to anyone, and he didn't. He had a strong desire nature and when his mind was made up, he wouldn't have taken 'no' for an answer. On the other hand, he took enormous chances that he wouldn't encounter someone, who would have resisted him more strongly than he would have bargained for.

However, certain other personal characteristics, such as sincerity, hope, refinement; reasoned, intuitional will-power and quick, accurate perception coupled with a power of comparison, tended to equalise and modify his impulsiveness. Also, and still on the other hand, his self-expression tended to be hurtfully limited because life had been hard thereby causing self-pity. Accordingly, he had a tendency towards retirement, to philosophise and to day-dream. However, "clouds of glory" were more to have been expected rather than any real delusion.

Mentality: Charles received correct mental impressions, which he coupled with his power for clear thinking. There was some originality of thought and action that tended to be both precipitate and changeful. His mind was sympathetic and worked by swift intuition, rather than by ordered reasoning. Although he tended to be confused by practical issues, he was highly receptive to artistic and benevolent ideas. Mentally, he was occupied with pleasures, love-making, with children and with artistic creations. Also, his speech and letters would have been concerned with these. However, his communicativeness would have been hidden unless otherwise brought out but similarly would have been concerned with creativity, maritime matters or with work in seclusion. Being well-informed was so important for Charles that he learned as much as he could about many subjects. The unusual (such as astrology) may have been preferred as a study. Because of this, he always made a worthwhile contribution to a discussion often amazing people with his wealth of information. Indeed, there was possible conceit deriving from his width of mind, rather than from any good grasp of detail. His mind worked enthusiastically in a "far-flung" manner, somewhat with exaggeration and off at a tangent. He was restless because he was far-seeking, which he satisfied by gaining knowledge. Additionally, he would have been interested in travel and in acquiring languages. There would have been a tendency for scientific thought and rebelliousness.

In general, his mind was jovial, optimistic and contented. This acted on his feelings, making his spiritual and religious aspirations keen. He had an innate sensitiveness to his surrounding thought sphere. Charles would have been extremely sensitive, mysterious and reserved, full of schemes and yet never thoroughly to have been known. He had inspirational yet practical vision and as such his ideas and "hunches" should have been acted on. His own spiritual ideas were chaste and calm but he was liable to be critical in psychic matters. He would have tended to have moods of dreaminess and inattention and could have lost himself in a world of imagination. However, the fruits of this could have proved useful for works of art, for literature and in everyday/professional life.

Previously Charles had developed crystallised conflicts in his value systems, which would have had to have been broken up if he was to make progress within himself. While these crystallised parts kept tempting him to hang onto the safety and security of his past, events kept lifting him from his lower self, making him aware that much of his safety to sense of well-being had been built on false foundations. Constantly, he shifted from calm serenity and the exciting exploration of new boundaries that may have had little or no promise of practical outcome.

Charles would have tried to break up his earlier sets of thought patterns but he was not yet ready to detach himself from the primary importance that they had put on the physical side of his life. On the one hand, he anxiously assimilated new philosophies and spiritual awareness, along with the desire to ingest all that he could. There was a reaching of all that had value for his higher being. Charles sought to explore all that he perceived in the world. Wisdom came as soon as he learned that he was allowed to walk with his head in the clouds as long as his feet were on the ground. Ideally, he was learning how to cope with the full essence of thought streams that were unbounded by individual possessiveness. He was one of the few people, who really knew that a person was not just what he thinks. Whether he was aware of it or not, he tended towards astral projection from one place to another, and from one realm of consciousness to another, on an almost continuous basis. His individual consciousness was the one least connected to his physical body. He was constantly attracted to world thought, and much of his personal thought had less to do with his own life than with the world that he was unconsciously exploring at any given moment. Sometimes he could have lost his conscious train of thought because he was so interested in everything that he had difficulty narrowing his field of focus. Ideally, he was learning how to be spiritually, philosophically, religiously and emotionally independent. Naturally, his reading would have included philosophy, religion, (psychology and metaphysics).

Charles was a rebel against restrictions; seeing the world as a playground in which he could exercise and grow. Having fought against rules, he would have known the inner rules that would have done him the most good.

Charles had the ability to understand so much that he had to have learned how to focus himself on one thought, or one project, at a time. He felt compelled to develop his understanding of life regardless of what was socially acceptable to the rest of the world and have been able to stand on what he knew worked for him. Because he saw so much, he eventually became very sure of his opinions and attitudes that could have caused him much difficulty in relating to others, who did not fully understand his sources of information. Often this would have led him to experience much criticism from his friends and peers. It may even have caused breaks in his marital ties. But still, his ultimate truth must have come from his own uniqueness of identity rather than from any need to compromise what he knew for the sake of personal acceptability. When used correctly, and with proper training, his vocation could have become an extremely spiritual one.

On the other hand, on a deeper level, he was bringing up a spiritual consciousness, developed previously, into his current life. Thus, he may well have experienced an abundance of holy knowledge from Biblical days in his past, which had created in him a powerful desire to bring such understandings into his present life. Charles's great awareness of life seemed to be coming from a different source than from the average norm, because the ways in which he expressed himself were always rather unique. He had a great love for the ideas of "God" but not for the official format of any specific religious tradition.

<u>Lifestyle:</u> Charles had an easy flow of life because he was at ease with himself, hence a pleasant person, whom others liked to help and favour. He maintained an orderly, harmonious lifestyle that gave him a good perspective about his relationships, career goals and personal interests. But he had to be careful not to become too 'wishy-washy'. He had to stand firm when he was right, because although it was fine to be all 'heart', he mustn't have lacked 'backbone'. "Make love, not war" may have been his motto but he was too vulnerable to those who would have taken advantage of his passivity to win his submission. His desire for the finer things of life made him careless about his financial resources. He found it difficult to hold onto his money when he was tempted to splurge on buying things he wanted rather than on those he really needed. Thus, financial and emotional security became shaky, but this only made Charles more determined to establish himself.

Charles kept re-evaluating all that he had already lived through. He wanted to have his cake and to eat it too. He liked to be married but, at the same time, wanted to believe that he was free. He liked to work at a steady job while convincing himself that he was not bound to it. He liked to follow one religion while thinking to himself that truly, he had no obligations to it. Hence, he was untraditional in a very traditional sense. When faced with the opportunities actually to be free from marriage, job, religion and all other parts of the form nature of his lifestyle, he quickly jumped back into the safety that he had always sought.

Charles's temperament leaned towards the impulsive side encouraging him to give full rein to his creativity. His environment exercised compulsion on him, marking his response to the social trends of his day. He could see the deeper and more unsuspected compulsions, under which everyone lived. His deep satirical skill would have been shown together with the incisive pointing and psychological soundness of his actions.

Charles had a capacity for self-discipline. Limitations occurred through maze-like worries but these tended to clear up in the long run through patient endurance and quiet keeping out of the limelight. Inner maturity was added to otherwise indecision. In the long term, his judgement was quite sound and he would have been able to steady himself. As a peacemaker, he was often thrown into the middle of opposing people or ideas. He tried to bring harmony by establishing a balanced third point that expressed the positive aspects of both sides.

Charles had the opportunity to take an objective look at his purposes in life so that their validity could have been re-assessed. For him, life was a series of turns and twists, until he understood that his mission in life was not for himself. In this regard, he was able to recall past idealism so as to develop new insight into old ways of thinking. He was able to be re-born as he could release old value systems forever, which were never really his, but which he had tried to conform to in the past. Eventually, he reviewed and transformed all that mankind, previously, had crystallised as past tradition.

Relationships

<u>Others:</u> Young people were drawn to Charles mainly because he was conciliatory and didn't make impossible demands on them. He enjoyed stimulating them to take part in activities.

Charles was an instructor and inspirer of others. As a result of meeting him, people began to re-evaluate and weigh proportionately their own past beliefs and the direction in which they had been moving. He helped others to a more balanced purpose. This was done by setting an example of balance through harmonising apparent opposites of thought. In turn, he brought this about by finding the essential unity of human ideals. His flexibility allowed him to change depending upon the need of the moment. Thus, he truly became the most versatile and valuable of helpers.

Charles felt a strong responsibility towards others. Yet he was emotionally at odds with those who seemed unable to accomplish anything without his help. He was grateful for any opportunity to show how much he cared about people but despite this he often complained that he didn't have enough time to take care of his own needs and he resented the fact that others expected him to do everything. He offered to help people who needed it but resented having anyone impose their demands on him. Additionally, he hoped that he wasn't being naïve when he offered to help others, assuming that later he would have been repaid for his efforts, perhaps when he least expected it. While he may have resented all this apparent intrusion on his time and energy, the truth was that he was psychologically dependent on the people he had met in his professional affairs, who had given him the opportunity to show them how competent he really was.

Moreover, there was much idealistic interchange with others. Charles tended to live other people's values in order to transform himself through what others had found to be worthwhile. As he had not yet learned a sense of purpose for himself, he wavered under the influence of his marriage partner and of close people in his life. Not everyone would have let him have his own way!

Charles was upset by people in important positions who had distorted social values. His compassion went out to those who were sociologically and economically locked into unfortunate situations. As an idealist, with a deep appreciation of philosophical and spiritual matters, he was pained to see how little was done to improve the quality of life for many people in society. He was disturbed by the failure of those who were largely responsible for dealing with this and felt that government officials needed a much more comprehensive understanding of current social problems.

Charles was very sensitive and easily influenced to submit to people and situations. Fearing the loss of his resources, Charles asserted himself cautiously towards others. His uncertainty made others apprehensive about dealing with him. This uncertainty was aggravated by Charles's tendency to advance himself by ruthless behaviour towards others and by being prone to intrigues.

Potentially, Charles was good at achieving smooth working of any group or society to which he was attached but there were disappointments here. He preferred not to be involved in other people's affairs, so he avoided any group functions that required donations of time, energy and money.

Yet Charles's warm and kindly disposition did attract others. He responded warmly to people who exhibited substantial human values, and he loved them for the stability that they gave him. He preferred the company of people who shared his refined interests. He enjoyed their good opinion of him and he even enjoyed their flattery!

Friends: Charles mustn't have let his preoccupation with security interfere with his social life. If he had cut the lines of communication with the people who could have enriched his life, he would have become very lonely. He was often unhappy because he got from others the repercussion of his own awkwardness as a companion. He tried to be a friend to others and hoped to reap their loyalty in return. Knowing that people would have sought his friendship if he had been willing to compromise, he made every effort to be on his best behaviour. And so he came to know how to win friends and influence people effectively with his charming manner and warm, winning ways. As a result, he could have relied on their support when he needed it. When he had gained some popularity, he became happy among, and attracted to, like-minded friends and acquaintances, who would have been congenial to him, may have benefitted him, and amongst whom he may have married.

<u>Family:</u> Charles mustn't have forgotten the people who had helped him in his past, especially his parents. It's not likely that he would have done this because he felt a close tie with them. Their contentment gave him much happiness but he had to be careful not to short-change himself by helping them. His parents had given him the confidence to gain financial and emotional security and he appreciated their efforts on his behalf. In addition, his parents should have instilled in him a respect for education so that he could have achieved many objectives that would have been beyond them. But he may have had to devise a way to get his education while still satisfying family obligations.

There was little that Charles wouldn't have done for those he loved. He was willing to make sacrifices for them provided he knew that they would have reciprocated. There was a tendency for harmony at home in which warmth and affection entered into relationships as expressed to young people in a family. He expended energy in gay enjoyment of his children. He wanted them to enjoy the best, and to be self-reliant too, in pursuing their own identities. He would have disciplined his lovely children so that they would have become a credit to him thereby leading to happiness and success. He demanded opportunities for them and he offered himself as an example of what someone could accomplish through individual fulfilment. Unfortunately, the time he would have had to spend away from home would have caused problems with his children but these would have become resolved eventually.

<u>Lover:</u> There was happiness through Charles's love affairs. Warmth, affection and enthusiasm would have entered into his sexual relations. His naturally romantic nature inclined him to make concessions to those he loved. Energy was expressed in gay enjoyment of love-making. Although his affection was demonstrative and gay, he did not want to be enchained. Freedom was often preferred to marriage. Yet he had this strong desire nature that wouldn't have wanted to take 'no' for an answer. As a result, there was trouble through the opposite sex because he was sensual, prodigal and too passionate. Also, there was a tendency to confusion in love affairs and even deception. Affections, liaisons and partnerships were subject to disclosures, upheavals and new starts but with good results in the end. Sometimes his happiness was secret.

Charles's sexual nature was rooted in the past. Depending upon the current sexual evolution, much time was spent retesting old traditions against society's present standards. Although he experienced a strong sexual interest in anyone who seemed exciting or different, there was a restriction bordering on impotence owing to the many fears that he had collected. Thus, he could have seemed to be too cool in affection at times, also. This caused him much worry and he repeated tests of sexuality almost to see if it was still there.

Feelings of obligation to his family may have kept Charles from forming lasting ties in a personally satisfying love relationship. Great anxiety would have resulted if he had felt torn between loyalty to his parents and the desire to gratify his own emotional needs. He wanted a partner who would have needed him and also supported his goals; someone to whom he could have turned when he had faced reversals, yet who would have allowed him to have stood on his own when conditions improved. At the same time, his partner would have expected a lot from him, which wouldn't have been difficult to provide, assuming that he would have known that it would have been appreciated. His innovative talent would have made him a creative lover and his partner would probably have been quite content with his skill in love-making. His mate probably would have urged him to succeed in his career, believing in his potential for taking on more and more responsibility.

Career

<u>Early:</u> Charles's destiny lay in his own hands, in the hands of others as well as being determined by circumstances. Sudden reversals and many changes were indicated. Similarly, losses were possible through investment and speculation, while there was risk in enterprise. His early conditioning may not have given him either the financial resources or the opportunities he would have wanted. He would have had to pursue them on his own with determination to succeed. Although he identified with his family, especially his parents, he came to know how to use his resources to sustain himself. His parents may have chosen a career for him but he should have thought for himself and found a profession based on his own beliefs and needs. His upbringing had given him an understanding of human frailty and serving others could only have enhanced him in his career.

Freedom was so important to Charles that nothing would have stood in the way of his getting the education he needed to achieve his goals. In his view anyone who was uninformed was likely to have become trapped in a life situation or career that limited their personal privileges or their ability to assert their individuality. Charles needed an education to help him to grow and to reveal his talents. Self-doubt and procrastination were his greatest liabilities. When he had discovered what he could have done, he would have been motivated to reach his goals successfully. He developed enormous faith that he could have succeeded in anything that he attempted and his devotion to his responsibilities would have made it possible for him "to move mountains." Additionally, he would have gained an even greater advantage over his adversaries if he had developed his mental assets.

Charles wanted the opportunity to develop his own creativity and prove what he could have done with it. Gaining financial and emotional security would have been high priorities in his life. He had a mind of his own that should have allowed him to gain plenty of security. In fact, he had an obligation to himself to take advantage of his creativity. He mustn't have underestimated it and hadn't to let any of his family convince him that he couldn't do something. By using his creativity, he could have established a secure place for himself in his career and in society.

Charles wanted to be the best in whatever he did. He knew exactly how to reach his goals but he had to stay within his limits so that he wouldn't have been disappointed unnecessarily. Although he didn't enjoy routine physical work, he would have endured it if it had helped him to grow. He wouldn't even have minded working without recognition while developing his creativity so that he could have shown it to the world when he was ready. He had a notable capacity for administration and so there was a strong possibility that he would have achieved success early in life. Also, his intuition helped in accomplishment as orderliness and caution would have stopped his ideas from becoming too vague.

Vocation: Finding a suitable career should have come first on Charles's list of priorities. He believed in himself and when he had decided what he wanted to be, he would have dedicated himself to becoming the very best. A career that allowed him to serve the public would have appealed to him. His sensitivity and concern would have been ideally suited to helping others with their problems. Probably, he would have done this in direct contact with the public. By developing his own skills he could have made a substantial contribution through political or social activity. Obviously, he cared enough to make this effort but needed training to accomplish his objectives. Serving the public's needs would have exerted a positive influence where it was most needed and would have given him a feeling of spiritual enrichment as well.

Middle: Charles translated his need for personal security into a desire for financial independence and all possible material comforts. He may have had to adjust his plans if they had depended on huge expenditures of money. Lack of money would have taken the wind out of his sails until he had learned to conserve his resources. He would have had to learn to build slowly and consistently and to have expanded his plans as he went along.

Charles's attachment to whatever was of mature value in others gave him a great deal of confidence and commonsense in the world of business, where his caution worked to his practical advantage. He was easily intimidated when others showed their excellence, but it also stimulated him to excel. His greatest challenge came from comparing what he got for his services with what others got for theirs. Knowing how capable he had become, he put a high premium on his services, and he didn't mind letting people know that they would have had to pay dearly for them. Probably, he would have earned their respect although he might not have won their friendship.

Although Charles did everything enthusiastically, he sometimes lacked the self-discipline required to get the most from his efforts. His impatience made him less efficient but his aggressiveness became useful when the time came for action. His uncontrolled outbursts could have put him temporarily out of commission, so he had to conserve his energy. Also, it was important that he learned to postpone taking any action until he was sure that his plans were valid. He needed to be as well-informed as possible to avoid being deceived or misled. He planned carefully because he knew that this was the best way to achieve his goals. When his plans did go awry, he would have made excuses since it was painful to realise that he had made a foolish mistake.

Charles adapted his allegiances to lines along which he could have made his efforts count for the most. He avoided activities that would have taken him away from the mainstream, where everybody was. There was a willing acceptance of duty and success was gained through orderly and practical ways even though these may have caused personal limitations and a lack of gaiety. There was a patient working out of what was begun but not with ease. His results had to have been battled for. The narrowness engendered would have produced selfishness and egocentricity. Hardship would have been endured and sternness given. Much may have been achieved but with nerve storms, many breaks and new starts. Gaining public attention would have turned Charles on but unless he had had a genuine contribution to make, the public might easily have been turned off by his actions.

Appearance and Health

<u>Appearance:</u> Charles would have been of middle stature tending to shortness with a square build of body in middle age. Earlier, he would have had a spare body, a long face and neck, and a head full-sized, (broad at the temples and narrow at the chin) with brown to grey,

very luminous, wistful and mobile eyes. He would have had a ruddy complexion, sharp sight and delicate ears with abundant hair that was wavy, varying in colour from dark to sandy and a tendency to baldness at the temples. He may well have had bushy eyebrows and sandy whiskers but a neat appearance and an upright walk. Also, he would have been shy, demure and somewhat mysterious, with curious tastes.

Health: Generally, Charles would have had good health, a good nervous system and a vitality of spirit that could have been almost too intense. Because he burned up energy so rapidly, he had to take time to recuperate after any arduous task but he did have the ability to revivify. Nevertheless, physical overstrain was risked. For example, his health could have been seriously impaired through disappointments in his love-life. In addition, his health varied according to his moods and circumstances; when good, lots of accomplishment; when low, he suffered discomfort because of nervous tension, which tended to upset his digestive system. Thus, his nervous system, although good, was sensitive, so that elation and depression alternated quickly. As a result, his mind and nervous system could have been energised to the point of overstrain. Breakdown would have followed with irritability and temper.

There was potential danger from burns, falls and scalds. Chills and orthopaedic troubles were also possible as well as unusual diseases.

References: 'Charles I: A Political Life', R. Cust, Pearson, London, U.K., (2005).
'Charles I: The Personal Monarch', 2nd Edition, C. Carlton, Routledge, London, U.K., (1995).

Oliver Cromwell

"Lord, though I am a miserable and wretched creature, I am in Covenant with thee through grace. And I may, I will, come to Thee, for Thy People. Thou hast made me, though very unworthy, a mean instrument to do them some good, and Thee service."
Reputedly taken from Cromwell's last prayer, September 1658.

Oliver Cromwell was an English military and political leader best known for his involvement in making England into a republican Commonwealth and for his later role as Lord Protector of England, Scotland and Ireland. He was one of the commanders of the New Model Army, which defeated the royalists in the English Civil War. After the execution of King Charles I in 1649, Cromwell dominated the short-lived Commonwealth of England, conquered Ireland and Scotland, and ruled as Lord Protector from 1653 until his death in 1658.

Cromwell was born into the ranks of the middle gentry, and remained relatively obscure for the first 40 years of his life. At times, his lifestyle resembled that of a yeoman farmer until his finances were boosted thanks to an inheritance from his uncle. After undergoing a religious conversion during his fourth decade, he made an Independent style of Puritanism a core tenet of his life. Cromwell was elected Member of Parliament (MP) for Cambridge in the Short (1640) and Long (1640-49) Parliaments, and later entered the English Civil War on the side of the 'Roundheads' or 'Parliamentarians'.

An effective soldier (nicknamed 'Old Ironsides'), he rose from leading a single cavalry troop to command of the entire army. Having been chosen by the Rump Parliament (1649-53) to take command of the English campaign in Ireland during 1649-50, he then led a campaign against the Scottish army between 1650 and 1651. In 1653 he dismissed the Rump Parliament by force and set up a short-lived nominated assembly known as the Barebones Parliament before being made Lord Protector at the end of 1653 for life.

Controversially, Cromwell has been a regicidal dictator to some historians and a hero of liberty to others. His measures against Irish Catholics were described by some historians as genocidal. To this day, he is still widely hated in Ireland.

Oliver was the only surviving son of Robert Cromwell and Elizabeth Steward along with his seven surviving sisters. He was born on the 5th May, 1599 NS, at 04:13, in Huntingdon, England (see Appendix 1, Figure 16). His Epoch occurred on the 23rd July, 1598 NS, at 20:55 (see Appendix 1, Figure 15).

Character Portrait

General: Oliver was interested practically in what things meant and in what they were. He "scooped up" impressions and information in a kind, protective and sympathetic way, to initiate new experience. Determination and leadership were marked characteristics. Courage, enterprise and the ability to work hard were the main attributes of his personality, which would have been out of the ordinary. Yet his nature was at one with itself, being cheerful, conservative, hospitable, reliable and resistant to change. Although contented with his surroundings and ways, he longed for a comfortable life surrounded by beautiful objects and to obtain that end he would have resisted those who opposed him. He had an inherent tendency to rash action that had to be resisted strongly. He could have become extremely assertive, pugnaciously aggressive and even hurtful to others. He was good at starting new enterprises but antagonistically so, with a cantankerous insistence on non-essentials. His intention to surmount difficulties led to nervous stress.

Being subjective, Oliver had a strongly artistic personality with a love of beauty and possibly an interest (suppressed?) in the psychic, the mystical and the occult. There was a tendency for him to be impractical in that he was inclined to concentrate on visions of the future rather than on those of the present. In this way, his methodical tendency would have been lessened but only to the extent that economy, persistence and usefulness would have become increased. In addition, his ambition would have been reinforced by his internal power that was necessary for him to have risen through merit and adaptability without passing through vices. Although he was inclined to music, art and good living, his perhaps lazy and irresponsible indulgence in personal pleasures may well have been limited by a lack of funds. As alternatives, he would have travelled for pleasure, circumstances permitting, and going here and there for social occasions and visits would have been much enjoyed.

On the positive side, he would have been optimistic, enthusiastic, exuberant, vigorous and resourceful with a desire to reform. At a neutral level, he would have been a self-sufficient, authoritative and independent individual, who sought excitement. More negatively, he would have been dominant, revolutionary, disruptive, awkward, combative, self-(willed, seeking, and insistent) with a craving for adventure.

Mentality: Oliver was emotionally sensitive, needing both independence of thought and emotional security at the same time. This was a difficult balance for him to achieve for if he had leaned on others for security then he would have lost his independence of thought. If he had developed his independence of thought then he would have lost the emotional security he would have gained by leaning on others. His easiest bargain would have been to grow emotionally possessive of his thoughts, which, unfortunately, could have led him into many neurotic complexes that he would have found himself unable to let go of. It would have been very difficult for him to bury his past and move ahead into the future freely and cleanly. Because he analysed his emotions rather than letting them flow, he could actually have given power to negative emotional states, making them larger than they really were, without even realising it.

Oliver would have been able to absorb the consciousness of all other individuals who brought him back to re-enacting, through his memory, the thoughts of all he had experienced. His mind and emotions were so linked that all thought created feeling and all feeling created thought. Both were so deeply rooted in past experience that he kept trying to recreate his childhood. Because of this, his upbringing would have been important, for many childhood experiences would have been carried as a residue all through his life.

Oliver retained many dependency thoughts from his past. Through these, he kept re-enacting child-parent roles with everyone he related to. Seeking both emotional and mental fulfilment at he same time, he was incomplete when receiving one without the other. He did not fully understand the concept of growth and kept thinking himself incapable of letting go of earlier phases in his life. In his later years, he would have developed a very beautiful rapport with children, which, eventually, would have turned out to be one of his greatest strengths.

Oliver had good, clever and original commonsense combined with a well-balanced outlook and good practical vision. Communication was expressed in money-making ways, in which his mind, mainly, would have been used commercially, clerically, rationally and educationally. He would have learned a subject if he had liked it but he would have been inclined to be lazy otherwise. He would have had a love of philosophy and a tendency towards religious thought that would have led to a keen, internal aspiration to become a channel through which good forces could have flowed. He had a good power of concentration with drive but without mental width. Through apprehension, his prudence would have become increased. In a scientific way, he sought new and interesting ways of doing things, even of letting go of the old. For this, he would have needed spiritual energy, a stimulated desire to reform, a good flow of thoughts and an ability to read character.

Oliver was magnetic, inventive and inspiring yet also prophetic, pious and penetrative. Although there was strong mental action through revolutionary thought, his communication became too brusque, precipitate and independent so that it lost good contact with others. A tendency to wild extravagance of thought (and deed!) coupled with a desire to make breaks and start anew, would have found vehement expression. Fortunately, his mind threw off worries and began new thought but over-violently, explosively and with nervous stress. Unfortunately, his addiction to the unusual and unconventional would have become so strong that he would have become eccentric, odd and tiresome. Additionally, vague but well-intentioned ideas would have led to an inflation of self-approbation and idealistic notions about his organising powers and about the governance of countries. His vivid imagination would have become gullible and confused so that his mind would not have been well-directed. Although sensitive, mystical and fantasy-loving, he would also have been dissimulating, inscrutable and sceptical. Touchiness could have induced escapism and his mind would have schemed in an involved way. Action would have come from intuition rather than from reason. Foolishness and craziness about "-isms" would have become possible.

Experiencing difficulties in focusing his mental energies, Oliver worked on an ideal way of learning how to make his mental plane productive creatively. Curiosity had led him to leap ahead into the multitude of ideas that he would have liked to create. Yet it was much easier for him to think about creating, or to tell others what he would have liked to create, than actually to have carried out his projects himself completely. His ideal situation would have been getting to understand how to organise and to create his present from that he had been conscious of, in his past.

Oliver was attracted to reading romantic novels as well as to reading stories of how people reached greatness but he had difficulty putting his knowledge into practice. He often thought that he should have been doing more than he was, and this kept his mind racing further and further into the future, while his natural instinct to look back, kept him receiving glimpses of how little he had accomplished in his past. He must have had to learn how to overcome these frustrating mental pictures, which kept impeding him in all he thought he could have been or done.

Attracted to younger people, Oliver found it easier to express to them his radiating qualities. With people of his own age or older, he became more inhibited. He would have been confronted with the conflict between being the actor at the centre of his life, or of being a spectator of it, through observing the actions of others.

Lifestyle: For Oliver life was a series of turns and twists until he had understood that his mission in life was not for himself but rather to help to direct others to a more balanced purpose. As a peacemaker, he was often thrown into the middle of opposing people, or ideas. He tried to bring harmony by establishing a balanced third point that expressed the positive aspects of both sides.

Oliver had the opportunity to take an objective look at his purposes in life so that their validity could have been reassessed. His prime concern was getting down a real foundation for life, and in re-ordering the basis of the society in which he found himself. He was completely centred in a cause, or in a sense of mission, or in an introspective concern over the purpose of experience, to which he had responded. Courage, energy and assertiveness showed how he sought to carry out his mission that gave him his everyday justification for existence. His obsession would have been might with a compelling need to achieve emancipation. He would have formed his own opinions and would not have been led by others. There would have been the tendency that his ideals would have been carried into actuality by an unusual power of leadership in spiritual, scientific and advanced ways. As a complete idealist, he could well have sacrificed everything for his mission. On the other hand, loving kindness would have been shown in a general way while organising. However, overmuch careless optimism, when caution was calling, would have produced unhappiness and guilty conscience. Yet in the long run, his judgement would have been quite sound and he would have been able to steady himself. Inner maturity would have been added to otherwise indecision.

Relationships

Others: Oliver was attracted to those who were as polished and charming as he was. He responded warmly to people, but was interested only in those who showed substantial human values. He felt a strong responsibility towards others and was happy as a host. He also felt that he could have learned something from everyone he contacted. As a result of meeting him, people began to re-evaluate, and weigh proportionately, their own beliefs and the direction in which they had been moving. Thus, he was fulfilling his role to help to direct others to a more balanced purpose. He achieved this by setting an example of balance through harmonising apparent opposites of thought. In turn, he brought this about by first finding the essential unity of human ideals. Additionally, his adaptability allowed him to change depending on the need of the moment. Hence, he became one of the most versatile of helpers.

On the other hand, Oliver's direct and sometimes blunt approach alienated people, and he incurred their displeasure because he was unable to compromise, or to meet them halfway. Also, his irresponsibility may have irritated people who accepted their responsibilities, and his disregard for rules made him seem somewhat unstable. In these cases, he judged people by their physical assets, paying little attention to their human qualities. At the same time, he was immediately aware when anyone tried to undermine him or resorted to unfair practices. This lack of reciprocity from others could have brought on depression and loneliness for him, along with an inability to realise that these were springing from within himself.

Overall, Oliver always had something to give to his fellows, whether literally or psychologically, whether constructively or vindictively, because his orientation to the world was one of division, i.e. from frustration and uncertainty. Talking about what he could have done may have fascinated people but it was action that counted in the final analysis. He gained a feeling of satisfaction when people realised that he had achieved his goals on his own, despite early environmental frustrations. If he had been motivated by the desire to do whatever he wanted with his power, people would have been likely to resent him. In addition, he mustn't have forgotten the people who had helped him in his past.

Friends: Oliver's tactlessness antagonised his friends.

Family: Oliver had good relationships with his parents. His home conditions and childhood circumstances were comfortable in that his parents provided him with warmth, affection and material security. Strong family ties would have made it painful for him to detach himself from obligations to his parents. His relations with his siblings would have been happy and they were likely to have been good-looking and attractive. They felt that they could have turned to him for help with their problems. Possibly, his parents may have tried to intimidate him by insisting that they should have come first in anything he did. However, he hadn't to forget his parents. It's not likely that he would, because he felt a close tie with them. Although he wanted to show his appreciation for his parents' assistance throughout his formative years, perhaps he would have simply been paying off a debt that he had incurred from them earlier. But because of his fond memories of those years, he would have liked to have helped them during their twilight years. Their contentment gave him much happiness, but he had to be careful not to short-change himself in helping them.

Oliver's own home was harmonious, delightful and happy with smooth and loving family relationships. Pleasure was taken in all matters of furnishing, decorating and arranging both flowers and pictures. Thus, there was benefit to him through the affairs of home and family. He would have extended himself for his partner and his children because they would have given him so much joy. They may even have provided the stimulus needed for him to capitalise on his creativity. If he had truly cared about the people he loved, he would have tried to live up to his potential. In fact, providing for his children's needs did stimulate him to extend himself. If furthering his goals had required him to be absent increasingly from his domestic scene, then he would have justified his dedication to the demands of his career by saying that he was only satisfying his children's needs, which would have been difficult to challenge.

Unfortunately, Oliver's home and home conditions were likely to have dominated his mind to an unhealthy degree. There were peculiar happenings regarding his children. Also there was a tendency for him to project his own childhood inadequacies onto his children. His children would have disappointed him. For their part, his children may have resented his permissiveness. Although they may have admired his exciting lifestyle, they may not have wanted it for themselves.

Lover: Oliver may have been inclined to shy away from the opposite sex as childhood problems were re-projected onto members of the opposite sex both in their present time and in their future. Oliver experienced great sexual tensions whose energies were constantly spilling over into his mental centres. Danger seemed possible from the opposite sex and from passion. Easy expression of affection was intensely charming, fluent and overdone but could have been all talk rather than with any real feeling for another. Nevertheless charm of personality was often a strong element in attracting women to him. Oliver was forceful in intimate relationships. Sexual relations were likely to have been intense but not without quarrels. Although his sexual drive was strong, it was not all powerful. Yet there was a necessity for restraint where his deep and possessive feelings were concerned. Additionally, his affection was changeable and often for more than one at a time. Trouble was caused by too many love affairs. Thus partnerships were not easy and breaks occurred in personal relationships. Moreover, deceit was likely through love affairs. Muddles arose through idealisation of the loved one without enough commonsense evaluation. Disappointment occurred when realisation came.

Still, love remained an important consideration in Oliver's life and may well have been the catalyst for his success. He wanted a partner who would have been a loyal friend. Also, he wanted his partner to hold him in high esteem, so that he could have become a credit to her as he pursued his career. He was willing to make 'sacrifices' for the 'right' person, whom he hoped would have shared his life and no gift would have been too costly when he had wanted to impress that person. Although he was slow in making a partnership, he was reliable, steadfast and still possessive, when once settled. However, if his parents hadn't approved of his chosen partner, he might have had to make a painful choice. He could have experienced anxiety about this, but making a life of his own depended on it.

Oliver was given the opportunity not only to work out childhood problems with his dominant parent, but also by selecting a similar type of mate for marriage. He would share his life unfoldment with another, who, although she appeared to be the backward student, in reality turned out to become the teacher. Oliver learned much from this experience, through which he would have become receptive to ideas that would have seemed to have been beyond his present maturity level.

However, frustration and disappointment would have been expected from others in close connection, such as in marriage. A combative partner would have led to irritation and quarrels. Also, his own explosive temper and wilful impatience would not have made things easy in marriage. And so a cutting harshness may well have entered into relationships of affection. His partner might have brought much responsibility or caused losses. All this may have strengthened him by building up an ability to stand on his own feet without a partner, or alternatively may have caused depression and loneliness because of the loss of his partner, coupled with his own inadequacy in forming other happy relationships.

For Oliver, the ideal state of marriage was to be learned at its fullest. He often felt that his spouse was holding him back. Even when unmarried, he would have felt the weight of others trying to get him to retrace his steps in order to gain a more balanced and mature view of himself. Possibly marriage would have occurred with an older partner, whom he may have known from earlier. His biggest lesson centred around his establishment of harmony with others. He knew this but his ego tended to rebel when the going got heavy. Nevertheless, he had learned previously that his real security came more from others than it did from himself. He needed to feel protected. Even though he may often have complained that marriage was boring, he knew that it was a stabilising anchor that had kept him from what might otherwise have proved a lifestyle that either would have been too hectic for him to experience, or for him to have learned from.

Career

Early: Oliver had a thirst for experience and great potentiality. His destiny lay mainly in his own hands but also lay in the hands of others as well as being determined by circumstances. He would have been subject to upsets and to forced new phases, yet his fate would have been marked and his life most eventful, but the rise and fall, or honour and degradation, would have depended considerably on his (good) individuality. There would have been plenty of opportunities, the meeting of helpful people and the feeling that 'good luck' was to have been expected. Thus, he would have had a lucky journey through life. He knew that he could have controlled the general direction of his destiny. There would have been success in life because he was independent and could have made his own way, being self-reliant, firm, positive and generous. Also success would have come through exercising his humorous and witty mentality. Additionally, there was gain through literature, travel, the law, the church and the young. Overall, he felt secure and was well-organised for achieving his goals. Moreover, he knew that he had the necessary resources with which to succeed, and that he had a talent for making the most of them. Furthermore, he had well-developed values. Hence he was well-qualified to reach his objectives. However, he did have some feelings of uncertainty, but his need to express his creativity in a worthwhile endeavour assured his eventual success.

Oliver appreciated his early upbringing and the benefits he had gained from close ties with his parents. His experience with them had given him a firm base on which to build his future. His parents had allowed him to develop freely according to his own abilities and had encouraged him to cultivate his own ideas, talents and dreams. His early conditioning had led him to believe that his role in life was to serve others. He had to use the advantages of his upbringing to become self-sufficient on his own merits. He hadn't to avoid the responsibility for making his own life. He could have achieved any goal he had set his sights on, if he had spurned apathy and indolence. However, he might have encountered problems if his parents had disapproved of his goals. His early training had stimulated him to make the most of any opportunity. Whether or not he could have reached his objectives depended on getting the right training and good education. He needed polished skills and total awareness of his abilities in order to reach the limits of his potential. However, his fear of risks made it difficult for him to exploit his creativity fully. Additionally, he underestimated both his abilities and the value of his creativity, and so failed to capitalise on them properly. At the same time, he tended to overestimate his power based on his accumulated assets. Moreover, an innate lack of concreteness did not help in his work but he was able to mitigate most of it by using his self-control. His tendency to dawdle and to day-dream was too much of a luxury. He must have put his ideas to work if he had wanted any rewards. Also, he had to remember that others were free with their advice when their own security was not at stake. Knowing that his future security depended on his willingness to work, he was able to mobilise all his assets and resources to achieve the greatest yield and get it. Even though he knew quite a lot, he needed constant reminders that he was doing the right thing with his knowledge. He had the creativity to meet crises and to adapt whatever resources he had to succeed despite obstacles. He could have reached any goal he had set for himself if he had continually added to the vast amount of information that he already had. He mustn't have been afraid to extend himself in unfamiliar situations that showed same promise of greater security, for it would have been unlikely that he would have over-reached himself to the point of diminishing returns. He should have cultivated a more optimistic attitude in order to enhance the likelihood of succeeding more often than not.

Working with young people would have given him the satisfaction of knowing that he had helped them to prepare for the future so that they could have achieved greater fulfilment. Working with the public would have been easier if he had developed greater self-discipline and had learned to make concessions at the right time. With a moderate amount of effort he could have adequately satisfied his needs and have even accumulated a financial reserve. Similarly, with a little more imagination and a willingness to work at developing his talents, he could have earned a comfortable income. This would have improved his self-image. Eventually, he would have had to stand on his own but first he had to grow up, use his creativity and accept the fact that he had to earn his independence. However, it was difficult for him to stand on his own because he lacked the necessary self-confidence. Thus, there might have been some delay in achieving his level of greatest efficiency if he had wasted valuable time in his early years trying to decide what to do and, most of all, learning to apply himself to that commitment. A rebel at heart, he insisted on being allowed to develop in his own way. Though he may have gone to extremes, he had the sense of purpose to change conditions in his environment, which would have improved his chances for success. He may have encountered much competition in trying to get a job but with his aggressive nature, he would not have been deterred from his objectives. Probably, he would have left home early in life, so that he could have made his own way independently. His action may have been restricted if he had felt guilty about this decision. It would not have been easy but he had to have been more independent so that he could have taken advantage of any opportunities that had arisen from social contacts.

Oliver came to know his abilities as well as his limits. On the plus side, he had magnetic leadership and unusual ability so that good results were possible. There was extremism in work and play but control was available within himself. Facing rejection, he may have procrastinated unduly in taking advantage of his creativity. Constructively, he could have forced to a patient working out of what had been begun, but not with ease. Results would have had to have been battled for, producing selfishness and egocentricity. Hardship would have been endured and sternness given. Success may have been achieved but at he cost of much hard work, personal hardship and long delay. Overmuch limitation of what he conceived to be his way of self-expression and self-gratification would have brought about exaggerated depression, possibly with tragic results.

Oliver came to realise that without patronage his future was in doubt. He required lots of money in order to satisfy his desires. He had to have become financially secure before he could have really achieved independence from those who fulfilled his needs. He must have had to work to develop patronage for the services he offered. In this way, he could have earned a comfortable income and improved his ability to aim for even greater goals and ambitions. But he mustn't have done more than he'd agreed to do, and have set aside some time for rest and recuperation. As soon as he had got the feedback that would have convinced him of his abilities, he would have made his most significant contribution to society and to himself. He would have enjoyed financial rewards while at the same time helping those who had required his services.

<u>Vocation:</u> Hard physical work was not really consistent with Oliver's temperament. He would have made a good servant, or subordinate, and would have done well with someone either to lead him, or to have worked with him.

Oliver should have chosen a career that allowed him to use his creativity in helping people to manage their material resources. His critical faculties were accentuated by his practical nature making him one of the best commercial types of men. In business, he would have been precise, persistent and very pronounced in his judgements. Also, he would have been firm, conscientious and pliable but with a fixed determination that would have enabled success. Furthermore, he could have succeeded in business because he would have been well-informed about all the details and would have handled them with complete control. His greatest asset was his skill in solving problems, which could have been applied in many different situations. He was a 'can-do' individual, who was sometimes impatient with theory, when practical sense was required. In addition, he may have had to travel in his business, which he was willing to do if the success and future growth of his business had depended on it. While sometimes lacking in enterprise (but remember his assertiveness!) he could quickly have applied and developed the suggestions of others. Probably, he would have done best if he had been self-employed, so that he could have paced his own growth. He could have felt restricted in organisations that limited his progress, or had failed to recognise his capabilities. Yet he had ability in several different directions and so would have been eminently adaptable in order to have managed more than one type of business.

Careers in masonry; carpentry; heating and refrigeration; or in general construction, would have been rewarding for him. In any case, he would have risen to a level of responsibility in managing operations.

<u>Middle:</u> Oliver had become acceptably conditioned to his limitations. Wisdom, patience and constructiveness had grown and brought him success later on. At first, he may have avoided competition for fear of failing, but as he matured, he would have learned that competition was the key to his greatest accomplishments. He hadn't needed anyone's approval to rise to prominence, if he had been willing to use his talents for the benefit of the public. However, he had to be careful not to distort his objectives by a lust for personal gain, for that power could have become destructive. When he was trying to convince people of his talents, he drove a hard bargain. However, instead of trying to match others' performances (which he'd probably overestimated), he should have developed his own talents to the utmost, so that he could have accepted any challenge and known that he could have succeeded.

Oliver wanted to be the best at whatever he did and he strove to improve by learning new skills. Knowing that the public wanted the best service it could buy, he worked to provide that service. His achievement had to have been public in nature, and it had to have been rooted in his sympathy with the affairs of men and women generally. Once he had been trained to use his talents wisely, the lives of everyone he contacted would have been immeasurably improved. When he had helped others with his creativity, his accomplishments became unlimited. When someone had appreciated a service he had done, his vitality was regenerated.

Security remained Oliver's most important consideration and he put a lot of energy into acquiring the necessities of life, to gain an advantage over those who lacked them. His mind became able to calculate the true value of any item before he bought it. He had come to understand money and how to manipulate his affairs to get the most financial benefits. Investments should have been in maritime affairs, in oil, or in businesses connected with art. To summarise, he translated his need for personal security into a desire for financial independence and all material comforts. Once he had become established in his career, he could have then begun to enjoy himself more freely.

<u>Late:</u> Oliver had a program for maintaining his security during his later years. He wanted to be remembered for the important part he had played in the lives of the people he had dealt with.

Appearance and Health

Appearance: Oliver was of middle stature or rather above it, strong and well-built, with somewhat short and small limbs, but inclined to become fleshy. His head, broad at the temples and narrow at the chin, would have contained a long face and neck with a ruddy complexion. He would have had grey to greyish-brown, full eyes with sharp sight, bushy eyebrows and a tendency to a double chin. His hair would have been plentiful, rough and varying in colour from dark to sandy, but with possible baldness at the temples.

Health: Oliver had robust health, physical strength and endurance. However, his health varied according to his moods and circumstances. When he was positive and generally optimistic, much was accomplished. On the other hand, when his spirits were low, he suffered from many discomforts through overstrain and nervous tension, which would have played havoc with his digestive system. Yet after exhausting himself completely, he would have had the ability to revivify. In addition, vagueness would not have helped his attempts to keep healthy. Sleep could have become over-heavy and there may have been danger from drugs, poisons, (gas and anaesthetics). Additional danger could have come from paralysis, from accidents to limbs, from burns and scalds and from falling. Depression may have become frequent.

Reference: 'Oliver Cromwell', Peter Gaunt, The British Library, London, U.K., (1996).

Charles II

"Tis agreed on all sides that if Mr. Holles were not so Dogmaticall, he would be very useful and necessary to the Royal Society, for there are few people that can see further into things than he, or have applied themselves so long to the Study of Natural Philosophy."
1662.

Charles II was monarch of the three kingdoms of England, Scotland and Ireland from 1660 to 1685. Although the Scottish Parliament proclaimed him king from 1649 onwards, England entered the period known as the English Commonwealth, making the country a *de facto* republic, led by Oliver Cromwell. Cromwell defeated Charles at the battle of Worcester in 1651, and Charles fled to mainland Europe, where he spent the next nine years in exile in France, the United Provinces and the Spanish Netherlands.

The political crisis that followed the death of Cromwell late in 1658 resulted in the restoration of the monarchy and Charles returned to Britain. He was received in London to public acclaim.

Charles's English parliament enacted laws known as the Clarendon Code, designed to support the re-established Church of England, even though Charles favoured a policy of religious tolerance. Charles, a patron of the arts and sciences, actively supported the foundation of the Royal Observatory as well as the Royal Society, a scientific group whose early members included Robert Hooke, Robert Boyle and Sir Isaac Newton. He could well have been called the first, scientist King of England. He was also the personal patron of Sir Christopher Wren, the architect, who helped rebuild London after the Great Fire, constructing St. Paul's Cathedral and the Royal Hospital Chelsea, the latter for retired soldiers.

The main foreign policy issues of his early reign were the second and then the third Anglo-Dutch Wars. Help from France resulted in Charles secretly promising to convert to Catholicism at a future, unspecified date. Charles attempted to introduce religious freedom for Catholics and Protestant dissenters with his Royal Declaration of Indulgence (1672) but the English Parliament forced him to withdraw it. In 1679, Titus Oates's uncovering of a supposed 'Popish Plot' sparked the Exclusion Crisis when it was revealed that James, Duke of York, was a catholic. Charles dissolved the English Parliament, having sided with the anti-exclusion Tories, and following the discovery of the Rye House Plot to murder Charles and James (1683) ruled alone until his death in 1685. He was received into the Catholic Church on his deathbed.

Charles II was popularly known as the *Merry Monarch,* in reference to both the liveliness and hedonism of his court following the general relief at the return to normality after the English Commonwealth. Charles's wife, Catherine of Braganza, bore no live children. As Charles's illegitimate children were excluded from the succession, he was succeeded by his brother James.

Charles was the second, but first surviving son, of King Charles I of England and his Queen, Henrietta Maria of France. Charles was born on the 8th June, 1630 NS at 11:45, in London, England (see Appendix 1, Figure 18). His Epoch occurred on the 19th August, 1629 NS at 23:36 (see Appendix 1, Figure 17).

Character Portrait

General: Charles's personality was optimistic, friendly and cheerful. He was happy as a host. Generally, he had considerable energy, endurance, perseverance and determination. His self-expression was shown energetically in bold, brave, initiatory, forceful, hardworking and quick ways. There was firmness within a sensational nature. Actually, overdoing could have been disastrous unless control, sport or career, etc. had used up his excess energy.

Yet Charles was also practical, idealistic and chaste with good business instincts but, at the same time, he showed tendencies to be very critical, restless and anxious. Probably, keen appreciation, sterling qualities and musical talent would have been evident. His ideas on love, art and beauty would have been out-of-the-ordinary, hence more exciting and attractive but there was also an inclination to be "off with the old and on with the new". Too much force, applied for change, produced unhappy results.

Charles was both objective and subjective. He showed independent behaviour that could have become rebellious, disruptive and awkward. Force was used in financial ways (and also for agricultural work?) but it was also frittered away in constant changes of direction. He had a tendency to squander gains, to be extravagant and to trust to luck too easily. He could also have become moody and quarrelsome. In fact, he had to beware of becoming so self-indulgent that it would have interfered with his development.

On the other hand, Charles could also appear to be on the strict, cold side becoming overly stern, rigid, narrow, and grasping; while showing little tolerance for social disorder.

Overall, Charles possessed great potentiality, a robust personality containing courage and adventure, unusual and magnetic ability that generated good, general success, yet somehow, many of his larger scale projects tended to become ruined.

Mentality: Charles's mind worked in a detached, sensible and thoughtful manner in affairs to do with home, domesticity and in any business involving collecting. Charles felt most comfortable absorbing all that represented past memories of security. He spent much of his time doing this because then he felt the most safe. His childhood had been important because much of his thoughts centred on the feelings he had experienced during those early years.

Charles was critical, clever, intuitive and discriminative. His mind and mental outlook were good in so far as charm of speech, pleasantness of manner and the generally beneficial results of an harmoniously working nervous system, were concerned.

Often he blocked his conscious mind from being sensitive to the signals that came from deeper parts within him. Those parts, which he was able consciously to understand, were mostly a façade of thoughts, rationalisations and the constructed ideas that he had found to be socially acceptable. He crystallised all current life thought forms very strongly. There was so much importance attached to each thought that he actually weighed himself down with one question after another. However, interestingly, he had already pre-programmed the answers. This hampered his learning process because what was sought was only that which could have substantiated what he had already formed solidly in his belief system. He went through conflict between the input and output of information. He had spent so much time learning how to learn that he became a victim of habits that led him to fill himself with more information than he needed. He had to learn how to develop a clear priority of thoughts, throwing away all that was unimportant, while learning to express better that which was meaningful. Nevertheless, balance, rather than worry, was evident.

Charles's personality was a studious one, devoted to books and reading, within which quick-wittedness and adaptability were outstanding characteristics. There was a tendency towards, and success in, the more profound lines of study. Actually, he had an immense thirst for knowledge, was fond of study and of intelligent interests and because he was so well-informed, he felt that he would be successful.

Charles had an exceptional intellect so that, at times, he was struck by inspired ideas for ways to solve his own problems and for those relating to his immediate environment. However, he had to examine these ideas very carefully to determine their objective value. Fortunately, his mind would not have wandered but would have ordered and controlled in practical, cautious and methodical ways. He assimilated information easily and was knowledgeable about a wide variety of subjects, which enabled him to take advantage of opportunities to widen his ambitions. However, as indicated (see foregoing, small-print paragraph), there were occasions when he wasn't a fast learner, but what he did learn would have made a deep impression on him.

Charles was utilitarian in outlook. Although he was liable to wild extravagance of thought (and deed), his tendency to pensiveness, brooding, stubbornness, defiance, uncompromising dogmatism and possibly even artistic genius, were easily stimulated, rendering him magnetic, inscrutable, sceptical but also less extravagant.

Charles had strong, freedom-loving expansiveness but with difficulty of expression. He could have been brusque, precipitate, conceited, and imprudent. He hated asking questions but he would have valued a good suggestion if he could have benefitted from it.

Charles experienced confusion between dominance and submission because he was so immature emotionally at expressing himself outwardly. He took the entire conflict inside himself, thereby closing off his expression, except for more limited forms that did not entirely make him happy. His past emotional thoughts, which, depending upon their nature, would either have facilitated, or impeded, this self-expression.

Charles's greatest growth occurred when he came to understand that the world around him was very much like the Tower of Babel, i.e. people were unable to communicate with each other; in this case, because they had different conceptual understandings of the simplest words. Thus, the quality of communication with others was always less than he knew it could be. He sensed the interruption in the steady flow of thought that was caused by language barriers. Hence, overall, he experienced much difficulty putting what he knew into words. His ideal state would have been to know, to understand and to teach where he was asked, but never to impress himself on those who were unable to comprehend his wisdom. In a roundabout way, he could have been maturing his understanding of himself and of the world around him.

Although Charles would have been able to understand his higher mind, he didn't always believe that he would have been able to communicate its contents to others. He may have had strong religious insight. For example, he may have had a very strongly developed understanding of God, or he might have expressed this through an explanation of how the mechanisms of the world worked. Charles had undergone experiences that had taught him a particular method of thinking about how to rationalise all the intricacies within himself and with his surrounding world. He had come to see a major gap between how the world works in reality and how it could work in his ideals. He would have discovered that machinery of all kinds could have been closer to the ideal he saw, than the machinery of human relationships. In addition, he had the ability to weigh things, so that, ultimately, they were balanced from a centred perspective. Often, he could have paralysed himself by considering things to the point that he used more scope than actually he needed. In this way, he could have over-exaggerated the importance of certain things by seeing too much of life either as supporting, or as negating, the principles he believed he stood for.

Charles also had strong imaginative faculties, i.e. visions, ideals and boundless aims that could have been of the most ethereal and inspirational kind (but strength of character would have been needed to actualise them). His interest in maritime affairs, in mysticism and in hidden things, was pursued with energy and with the desire to experiment in new ways. Additionally, he showed enthusiasm for the arts, dancing and the psychic, or for any form of idealism. His strong response to external stimuli added to his substantial creativity and would have provided him with many outlets for self-expression. His good sensitiveness was due to his intellect being coupled with his sensational nature so that his mind became a channel for all inspirational ideas and dreams.

Charles could have been highly psychic, but until he had developed more confidence in himself, this gift could have proved more of a hindrance than a help. However, once he overcame his own negativity, he would have received a very clear and inspiring insight into the people he would have liked to relate with. Charles was living through an ideal state of learning an unusually subtle and well-evolved form of communication that ultimately would have brought him understandings that the current language of his time would have been unable to express.

Charles would have been at his greatest strength during mid-life as he fulfilled his ideal state of gently helping the world onward. This was done by replacing all that was dying with new spiritual consciousness that only he was capable of understanding at its true depth. He was one who, on an individual basis, dissolved the past. He was a forerunner of the future—reshaping the formless for the needs of meaningful growth.

Subtlety and scope would have been added to Charles's depth. His visionary qualities would have been increased along with his intuitive understanding of the unconscious. He would have been able to transform himself gently as well as the world around him. He could have been impersonally intense about his needs and about the directions he felt that the world was moving in, but, simultaneously, his detachment and dissolving influence prevented him from becoming weighed down by his sensory impressions. He would have been a part of starting to bring about a transformation in music, the arts and in medicine; bringing to the surface many overlooked qualities that only his keen awareness was capable of finding.

Although Charles had good sensitivity, at the same time his tendency to escapism, daydreaming, deceit and self-gullibility, may have prevailed. There may well have been frequent muddles and many poorly fulfilled ideas. Treachery, foolishness and craziness about "-isms", could have ensued. Hence, his vivid imagination could have led to chaos, in which limitation would have been felt through difficulties that would have been hard to grasp, to come to terms with, or which would have been better kept hidden.

Charles operated largely on a subconscious level and tried to avoid any of his unpleasant truths. With a little honesty, he would have become free from fears about his hang-ups (of which everyone has some). However, he had to learn to take advantage of his hidden talents and to have used his creativity better.

<u>Lifestyle:</u> During Charles's youth he often tried to act older than he was. Even though he may have been very wise, he wasn't heeded until considerably later. But inner maturity became added to otherwise indecision and in the long term, his judgement was quite sound and he would have been able to steady himself. However, in his active life, he experienced a very strong 'stop and go' vibration that didn't always allow him to do all the things he would have liked to have done. He had a great deal of difficulty living through mundane situations and circumstances. He liked to move about and conversely didn't like spending too much time in any one place. As such, he was very much a nomad, wandering through life to test the knowledge he had gained from former and recent experiences. His moods and ways were changeful in an acceptable way since he liked new phases in life. There was a love of pleasure and of social life that helped to bring popularity but a tendency to be too easy-going could have led to difficulties unless it had been kept firmly under control. He tended to respond to an immediate promise rather than to a future one. His obsession became wealth with a compelling need to achieve permanence. There was also an implied adjustment to difficulties and an attempt to by-pass them, though rarely without nervous stress. His force and limitation did not combine well but were canalised and ordered. On the other hand, inertia could have been energised. Thus, caution and prudence would have become enlivened somewhat thereby providing some help for the bearing of arduous, rough or pioneering conditions, or for personal hardships, even at the risk of being hurtful.

Charles's life was a series of turns and twists until he understood that his ideal mission was not for himself, but rather to help others to a more balanced purpose. This was done by setting an example of balance by harmonising apparent opposites of thought. In turn, he brought this about by finding the essential unity of human ideals. His adaptability allowed him to change depending completely on the need of the moment. Thus, he became truly one of the world's most versatile and valuable of helpers.

There was a particular and rather uncompromising direction to Charles's life effort. He would have been interested in a cause but with little concern over end-results, or over himself and his resources. There would have been highly individual or purposeful emphases in his life, in which his temperament jutted into experience with a robust resistance to pigeon-holing, either in the neat conventional compartments of nature, or in the idea pockets of his associates. There was a persistent insistence on individuality. He also had a splay-foot certainty in every approach he made to the problems of life, in which he could not have been limited to any single point of application. He was inclined to be particular yet impersonal in his interests. He dipped deeply into life and poured forth the results of his gathered experiences with unremitting zeal. Although, basically, he was not an optimist, he would have become more so, the more he succeeded.

Relationships

<u>Others</u>: Charles fraternised readily with others. As an excellent tactician, he let everyone believe that he had shared their views. He made a point of asking people about their needs and opinions and they appreciated that kind of attention. He endeared himself to others by indicating that he was attracted to people of quality. Conversely, he tended to appreciate any kindness and was inclined to try and reciprocate. He was fond of the people who had loved and helped him as a child.

Generally he felt a strong responsibility towards others. Often he experienced their ideal state more than they themselves did. Naturally, this could have thrown him off-balance. Actually, he had the ability to change the ideal directions of those people he came into contact with. As a result of meeting him, they began to re-evaluate and to weigh proportionately their own past beliefs and the direction they had been moving in. Thus, for many, there was the opportunity to take an objective look at their purposes in life so that their validity could have been re-assessed. He became a real instructor and inspirer of others. Probably he felt that the needs of others (particularly those of his own family) were holding him back, but actually it was his own need, most of all, to express himself in an environment where he was positively sure of himself. The outer world did not present such an environment. Thus, he didn't always express the uniqueness of his identity and purpose through the right channels, but instead, had a strong tendency to linger in child-like stages of complaining about why his life was not blossoming in the way he thought it should.

Charles's ability to promote himself was his best asset and he let others know that he was ambitious. In general, people admired and respected him for his professionalism, and they may have sought his help with their problems. In response, he was willing to help. His pleasure came from his confidence in solving problems that involved details that others were unable to handle. In all his dealings with people, he tried to make everything fit into computer-like ideals he'd established many years previously. Usually, he knew instantly the point that he was going to make. However, he would have avoided making it until he was sure that his language would have been accepted by the other person.

Charles had great difficulty in communication being unable, easily, to put his thoughts into words he knew that others would have understood. Partly, too many of his ideas were formulated in black and white, and he didn't realise fully that many shades of grey existed between the two. Because he tried overly hard to get his thoughts across to people, while inwardly believing that they were not as receptive as he would have liked them to be, he experienced great difficulties in all of his relationships.

Charles tried to be in tune with whoever he was communicating with, but often had difficulty coming to the point. He could have beaten around the bush, taking his listener in circles, before saying what he knew he had wanted to say right from the beginning. There could have been a great deal of earlier sorrow in relationships, which he was unconsciously trying to forget. This gave him difficulty in expressing confidence in his current relationships. He was easy to please but found it difficult to believe that he was really capable of pleasing others. Often he went far out of his way trying to gain acceptance.

Because Charles was unusually sensitive to others he had to teach himself to believe in the positive qualities of those surrounding him. The moment he could have done this, was the one when his life would have changed dramatically for the better.

Unfortunately, Charles's wilfulness and insistence on being "different" produced tactlessness and bluntness that offended others.

He had strong opinions for what was right and wrong in terms of how others should live their lives. He had a highly eccentric view so that he ideas and ways of all others were scorned, "Everyone was out of step but our Charles". His emotional responses would have become galvanic and intense. Additionally, there was some tendency for him to advance himself through ruthless behaviour towards others.

Charles's most difficult task was to admit that he may have been wrong and to have realised that he had to make compromises to win the support of those around him (which would have been favourable for dealings with foreigners). It annoyed him to have to concede to people when they were wrong, but he feared he would have alienated them if he hadn't. As soon as he was firmly established in his career or social position, he would have gone back to being honest with himself and with others.

Charles tended to be too susceptible to the attractions of others, with possible deception. He had to avoid people who expected him to do more than his fair share. Difficulties would have arisen through service given to others.

Friends: Charles's tactlessness antagonised his friends, causing breaks in personal relationships. His natural instinct for freedom made him a poor candidate for any kind of involved commitment of a lasting nature. He tended to pull away from people as he desired to experience more and more of his natural environment in place of the sophistication necessary in living up to the social expectations of others. Thus, his life tended to cause discomfort for those close to him.

Charles shied away from the tightness of entangling relationships, feeling much more comfortable when there was a slight distance between himself and those around him. He may well not have had many friends but those who were close to him would have been discriminately hand-picked.

Family: Charles's home had tended to be harmonious, a tranquil home would have been soothing to him and he hoped that his own home would have had that quality. Yet he mustn't have waited for parental approval before exploiting his talents. He knew the importance of thinking for himself, even though he had been conditioned to pattern his thinking after his parents' beliefs. Eventually, he may have been inclined to resent their intrusion.

Charles had a tendency to strong family ties but his desire was for the unusual and the unconventional, especially in his home, which resulted in a lack of peace. He was reasonably fond of children, but they might have interfered with his personal objectives. He would have been a good parent because his youthful joviality was immediately disarming. His children would have adored him and his partner would have known that he would have wanted a comfortable lifestyle with an abundance of happiness and contentment. He would have wanted the very best for his children (as well as for his lover) and he would have encouraged them to take advantage of the opportunities he had provided, so that they too, would have reached their goals.

Lover: Charles's affection was cool, undemonstrative and critical, but with a retiring, modest yet sensual charm. Although not being particularly warm in his personal relationships, he did have the abilities of a highly skilled, impartial thinker. He was very wary about forming close ties with associates, or with people who showed a romantic interest in him. He studied these contacts carefully to learn people's motivations for wanting to become aligned with him.

Charles's tendency to popularity, his ease of attracting others (or the public in general) was due to sheer, innate charm. Love affairs inclined to be numerous and very happy. (Similarly, partnerships would have been beneficial and successful.) Unusualness in expression of love, or in artistic accomplishment or in any kind of partnership, would have been delightful, intriguing and fascinating. He enjoyed giving presents to show how much he cared and sometimes he was extravagant in this regard. On the other hand, he was likely to have been inconstant in romantic relationships unless he felt secure with the loved one. There was an easy slipping away from one attraction and the quick forming of another. Thus partings were likely but for good reasons and with pleasant replacements or reunions. However, explosive temper, wilful impatience and nervous strain would not have made for easy partnership in marriage or business.

Charles should have been able to find a partner who shared his objectives and goals. It would have been ideal if their career interests had been on similar lines because if they had understood each others' problems they would have helped each other maintain harmony in their relationship. Although he was slow to make a partnership, but reliable when once settled, he would have been steadfast in love but possessive.

Charles wanted a partner who supported him fully in his goals, and who would have given him strength to persist in them. He may have married a foreigner, or lived abroad after marriage or may have gone into such partnership for business or profession. His partner would have admired his skill in handling people, which, in fact, would have helped them both.

Career

Early: In general, Charles's destiny would have lain in his own hands. He had a special capacity, or a gift, for some particularly effective kind of activity, or important direction of interest. His fate would have been influenced also by external and concrete, matter-of-fact experiences. His burden to bear, or responsibility to take, would have been through work, which would have been taken seriously. Long term results could have been good, if patience could have been used and his character strong enough to bear what had to be borne. As a result of the challenge of events, i.e. the stimulus, which circumstances had provided for the actualising of his inner potentialities; success would have led to character reinforcement, whereas failure would have led to rationalisation and defence. Subconsciously, he didn't really like himself enough, so that when he suffered a reversal it was, "just what I expected." However, his determination and persistence made up for his lack of aggressiveness. There would have been success in life abroad, foreign countries and through foreigners. Additionally, there was gain through relatives and through literary pursuits. Moreover, his fate was determined by the social and political world, in which distinction was generally sought and obtained.

His parents had given him many opportunities to promote his creativity and they had been willing to sustain him in developing them. However, he underestimated his own potential, and he may have hesitated to apply himself as he should have done. As a result, he would have maintained a low profile, yet he mustn't have neglected to exploit his talents. His parents may have chosen a career for him but he should have thought for himself and found a profession based on his own feelings and needs. The frustration he experienced with his parents should have given him the ambition to succeed on his own merits. He may have had to break with his past to improve on early circumstances but his future had depended on it. Probably, he would have been impatient to grow up because he would have been anxious to prove that he could have succeeded, if he had been given the opportunity. He may have been misled into assuming that his goals would have been limited to serving the needs of others. The fact is that he had the ability to gain a high position in his chosen field, once he had the self-confidence to think for himself and to have stood on his own. The restriction of his early training may have prevented him from being even mildly optimistic about his future. Withdrawn and contemplative, he became a good student of human nature. However, getting an education should have had a high priority in his plans. He knew that further education would have improved his competitive position and would have enabled him to convert his knowledge into tangible assets. Without it he would have been less effective. He had to get the training he needed so that he was better prepared to meet the challenge of rising to his highest level of accomplishment. He more than satisfied his superiors' demands, but he still became depressed when he didn't come up to the level of work they required. Perhaps he felt, subconsciously, that he had to live up to the goals chosen by his parents, which he resented.

Charles's romantic nature often distracted him from capitalising on his gifts. He often daydreamt, when a more decisive approach would have given him the yield he wanted from his efforts. He disliked working at ordinary jobs that didn't make sufficient demands on his talent. But all the talent in the world was a waste, if he hadn't applied it. He couldn't have afforded to take time away from training if he had really wanted to establish his worth as a truly talented person.

To achieve the many goals that Charles had in mind, probably he would have had to make some kind of investment. However, if financial return had been his only motive, he would have been denying himself the truly significant achievements he could have accomplished. Yet he shouldn't have been afraid to capitalise on his ideas by investing in them. In fulfilling his goals and objectives, he must have had to expect some loss of freedom and privacy. He would have had to use his financial resources wisely, if he had wanted to satisfy his material needs and still have had sufficient funds to develop his creativity. With a little imagination and willingness to work at developing his talents, he could have earned a considerable income. This would also have improved his self-image. He had a mind of his own, which would have allowed him to gain plenty of security. His own ideals and imaginative intuitions were kept in bounds and give shape and form so that they would have been useful in his material world. His ability to learn and to find ways to use his imagination would have been strong points in his favour, and his resourcefulness would have allowed him to achieve security in his endeavours. He came to realise that the sacrifices he had made, at any time, in developing his ideas, had been the best possible investment for his future.

Charles would have had to apply himself diligently to secure his rightful place in the world. Realising that his rise to prominence would have required a great deal of creative effort, he tried to use all his talents to achieve it. He would have needed to have sought the help of those who were already established because he would have benefitted from their inspiration.

Wealth was acquired through industry, thrift and through practical, commonsense business methods. Business ability and mental alertness would have led to early success in his career. By making a courageous effort to put his ideas to work, he could have achieved the position he wanted. That was the only way to get the recognition he felt that he deserved. With his many ideas, he could have pursued a rewarding career and made a truly important contribution to society.

Vocation: Charles was fitted for responsible, subordinate posts and as head servant, either in public or private life. His mind inclined to become that of a writer, artist, poet, mimic, mystic, visionary and spiritualist. As a writer or speaker, he would have benefitted by ease rather than strength. However, his ability to absorb diverse kinds of information may have qualified him for many different, professional positions. As such, his career should have involved considerable self-determination and have offered unlimited potential for growth. There was ability for either music or literature, or chemistry and hygiene, and indeed, for many subjects where the ideal and the practical are blended. He would have had good, practical business ability for organising, planning, acting as an agent, manager or lecturer. He might also have enjoyed the performing or graphic arts as media for expressing his creativity, although he would have realised that the latter required considerable training. Working with the public would have given Charles the best opportunity to achieve his goals and to feel comfortable with his achievements. Fulfilling the demands of a career here, would have earned him the public's respect and appreciation. His temperament would have been suitable for a career working with young people or children. Some fields that would have been suitable for him include: politics, government service, education, vocational guidance, business management, law, psychology and for the many services offered by government agencies. Charles could well have had a taste for science, antiquarianism, out-of-the-way investigations and research, as well as for hunting-up obscure details and statistics. He may well have had journalistic ability.

Middle: Charles was very likely to have adapted his allegiances to lines along which he could have made his efforts count for the most. He knew how to stay abreast of developments within his field so that his career position was reasonably stable. He was alert to subtle changes and he adapted to them, thereby maintaining an even flow in his affairs. Few people were as competent as he was at handling finances, which would have been an asset. Success would have been achieved, being fertile in resource, although lacking in practical enterprise. He may have succeeded more through other people than when acting on his own account.

Charles's dedication to achieving a high degree of competence should have improved his chances of attracting the attention of important people. His gift for conversation should have proved an extra asset here. As soon as he got the feedback, that would have convinced him of his abilities, he would have made his most significant contribution to society and to himself. He would have enjoyed financial rewards, while, at the same time, helping those who required his services.

Charles thought that his work was somewhat beneath him, that he had not got his desserts and that he was fitted for a better position than the one he occupied. His work tended to be unsatisfactory through muddles made and through the two-facedness of work people. In addition, he generally put himself at the mercy of the public's wishes, so it may have become a struggle for him to convince people that he was sincerely concerned about them. But if he had been properly trained, then that would not have been too difficult. Very hard work may have been done for idealistic ends but disappointing and elusive results were obtained because all was too imaginary. Irregular, over-glamorous ways contributed to failure. Thus, the tendency was to find himself constantly thwarted.

Charles had to try to define exactly what he hoped to achieve and to re-examine his goals periodically. Necessity for him had come to be expected as experience. He became preoccupied with getting as much as possible from his available resources. He rarely took chances with risky ventures because he had come to know how difficult it was to recover losses. The tendency was that satisfying his physical desires was fine, but he hadn't to let it become his sole purpose in life. If he had done so, he would have neglected his more important endeavours, to which he should have directed much of his energy.

Probably, he would have changed direction often in his life, which would also have been fine, as long as he had kept to a plan that would have brought him security eventually. He had to have been constantly concerned about the ethical standards that guided him in his ambitions. He had to have examined all of his professional and social contacts with care before he got too deeply involved with them because he could have lost control to forces, which would have exerted very strong pressure. He should not have formed any secret alliances unless he had been fully informed about the people involved. It was also very important to him to have had control over his competitors and to have had the respect of his associates. But he must have remained sensitive to their needs as well.

<u>Late:</u> Charles looked forward to the time when he could have been free of the daily harassment and effort of doing his job. Only determination and persistence would have brought him security during his later years. If he had used all his resources and talents, he could certainly have reached that goal. Knowing that he had done a good job would have given him much contentment when he reflected on it during his later years.

Appearance and Health

<u>Appearance:</u> Charles would have had a middle stature (Wrong! But Pluto was rising in Taurus?); dark and thin, with square build later that inclined to plumpness (along with plump hands and short, broad fingers, also wrong?). He would have had a square face, short, strong neck and a heavy jaw with forehead, nose, lips, cheeks and mouth all full. He would have had round, prominent and dark eyes with hair, possibly curling. He may have had a powerful and possibly discordant voice. He may have stooped often.

<u>Health:</u> Charles was robust physically with good physical and mental health. However, extremism in work or play, could have led to overstrain. His health may have given trouble through his kidneys, throat or bowels and he may have suffered through toxic, hidden causes. Food poisoning and drugs had to have been avoided. Strange fears may have played upon his nerves; his health could have been undermined by these, and by susceptibility to fish poisoning or to harm from impure water. He would have been a good sleeper but with a tendency for it to have become over heavy.

Reference: 'Charles II and the Restoration—A Gambling Man', Jenny Uglow, Faber and Faber, London, U.K., 2009.

James II

*"I shall make it my endeavour to preserve this government
both in church and state as it is by law established."*
February, 1685.

James II ascended the throne upon the death of his brother, Charles II, and was the last Roman Catholic monarch to reign over England from 6th February, 1685 until he was deposed in the Glorious Revolution at the end of 1688. Members of Britain's political and religious élite increasingly suspected him of being pro-French and pro-Catholic and of having designs on becoming an absolute monarch. When he produced a Catholic heir, the tension exploded,  and leading nobles called on his Protestant son-in-law and nephew, William III of Orange, to land an invasion army from the Netherlands, which he did. James fled England (and thus was held to have abdicated) and was replaced by his Protestant elder daughter, Mary II, and her husband, William III. James made one serious attempt to recover his crown from William and Mary, when he landed in Ireland in 1689 but, after the defeat of the Jacobite forces by those of William at the Battle of the Boyne in July, 1690, James returned to France. He lived out the rest of his life as a pretender at a court sponsored by his cousin and ally, King Louis XIV. He died of a brain haemorrhage in September, 1701.

James is best known for his struggles with the English Parliament and his attempts to create religious liberty for English Roman Catholics and Protestant nonconformists against the wishes of the Anglican establishment. Parliament, opposed to the growth of absolutism that was occurring in other European countries, as well as to the loss of legal supremacy for the Church of England, saw their opposition as a way to preserve what they regarded as traditional English liberties. This tension made James's four-year reign a struggle for supremacy between the English parliament and the crown, resulting in his deposition, in the passage of the English Bill of Rights, and in the Hanoverian succession.

James was the third, but second surviving son, of King Charles I of England and his Queen, Henrietta Maria of France. James was born on the 24th October, 1633 NS, at 23:15, in London, England (see Appendix 1, Figure 20). His Epoch occurred on the 20th February, 1633 NS, at 15:54 (see Appendix 1, Figure 19).

Character Portrait

<u>General:</u> The most important person in James's life was James. He insisted on his right to do what he wanted and he didn't really care if others didn't like it. As a result, he didn't feel that he was in the mainstream of activity (where he wanted to be!) but unless he had been willing to join in, the world would have left him alone.

James's self-expression was shown energetically. He was bold, strong, forceful, brave, initiatory, hard-working and quick. As an ambitious power seeking, fond-of-power-and-of-attaining-it personality, James would have burned for success. Proud, arrogant and with ardour, James had a love of grandeur, pomp and ostentation, all with considerable, dramatic feeling. His nature was strong, commanding, firm and self-directed even when at his most emotional. He expended his energy with heart, strong purpose and with creativity but with hot temper also. Unfortunately, he had a tendency for a dominating insistence on being over forceful. He could be explosive and so was likely to end conditions dramatically with unhappy results. However, changeful happenings, even though violent, could have been turned to good account.

James's emotional nature was keen, but not lacking in reflection and, in part, harmonious. Always highly emotional, with an extremely sensitive disposition, James was acquisitive and fond of 'collecting'. His emotion, energy and ambition would emerge depending on prevailing circumstances, but could have led him to dissipate his energies. James's moods were suddenly changeable, resulting in an ability to throw off the static and start new receptive ways. Although restless, his personality may have been tempered by an easy-going and comfort-loving disposition, in which his inclinations towards art and beauty would have been too irresponsible and lazy. Cheerfully contented with his own surroundings and ways, James was independent, interesting, curious, persuasive, sociable, capable and attractive. Being enthusiastic, persevering, dignified and orderly, James developed a love of travel and change that would have been characteristic from youth to old age.

James's nature was highly hospitable and very sympathetic towards suffering. He actually showed a quivering sensitiveness. He would have benefitted through hospitals and charitable organisations. In return, he was inclined to give support, help and charity assertively, but this proved difficult. He showed economy and carefulness especially in small matters. He would have enjoyed visits and social occasions very much. Finally, he may well have shown an interest in ancient customs.

Mentality: James had a responsive nervous system and an active mentality. He was sensitive, strongly intuitive, original, magnetic and rebellious. However, his mind and mental outlook were eased in so far as charm of speech and pleasantness of manner were concerned. Balance rather than worry was evident. His mind tended to enjoy friendly discussion and all beautiful objects for contemplation. Although it wasn't easy for him to start a conversation, he would have contributed meaningful ideas. But once started, he would have been a fascinating conversationalist, and people were generally attentive when he spoke. His sparkling presentation would have aroused interest in the subject at hand.

James had a great respect for knowledge, knowing that it could have opened doors that his shy nature would have been prevented from opening otherwise. Fond of study, intelligent interests and with a keen love of acquiring knowledge, he would have learned if he had liked the subject but would have been inclined to be lazy otherwise. Communication would have taken place in affairs to do with home, domesticity and any business to do with collecting. Probably, he carried out mental occupations at home.

James showed narrowness but a great tenacity for holding onto an idea and so his mind would not have wandered but would have ordered and controlled in practical, cautious and methodical ways. As a deep thinker, he looked forward to the time when he could express himself whenever he wanted without needing anyone else's approval. This pre-occupation may have given him a feeling of inferiority, inclining him to become an introspective loner. However, he had to take care not to slip into a non-productive state of mind and so have failed to apply the necessary energy required to develop his skills. James inclined towards scientific thoughts, to scientific mental interests and to those for-the-good-of-humanity, but also towards linking with other minds similarly motivated.

James's psychic faculties were awakened. His imagination and sensitivity were intense, increasing his economy as well as his receptivity. He would have shown an interest in psychic matters and a readiness to work for research in such ways. However, his vivid imagination tended to be gullible and confused so that his mind was not well-directed. Touchiness induced escapism. His mind would have schemed in an involved way. Action would have been based on intuition rather than on reason. Ideas that had seemed inspirational, would have been better well-scrutinised.

Lifestyle: Because James's inner and outer worlds were quite different, he may have had difficulty making a fulfilling life for himself. Too much loyalty to family concerns may have resulted in some alienation and guilt. Unless he had insisted on greater self-determination, it would have been difficult for him later on to meet the demands of a career as well as those of his relationships.

James would have thought much of public opinion and would have been eager to have been in the swim, while yet timid and retiring in behaviour—a strange contradiction.

At his best, James would have had a capacity for a general worldly interest, and a gift for ordering what to a lesser ability might have seemed like utter confusion. On the other hand, at his worst, he could have got on his horse (figuratively) and have ridden off in all directions. Hence, his activities could have led either to splendid achievement or to bitter disappointment.

James's temperament was that of a self-driving individuality, i.e. an executive eccentricity that was neither queerness nor unbalance, but rather was that of power. In this, he would have appeared to have been moved more by external factors in his environment than by any aspects of his own character. On the other hand, although seemingly impulsive and enthusiastic where his imposed career projects were concerned, this would have been for appearance only, because he was almost certainly self-motivated and very difficult to move by persuasion or by argument, being in reality surprisingly stubborn where his personal enthusiasms were concerned. Thus, he was genuinely impulsive but from within, and not from the result of contact from without.

An important feature of James's life was getting involved in circumstances relating to others' needs, either publicly or privately. But he also had to cope with his own feelings of insufficiency, and it would have required a considerable effort from him to satisfy the demands that others made on him, while also fulfilling his own needs. Until he felt secure, he would have focused primarily on his own interests, but as he matured, he would have realised that doing for others could have proved fascinating and rewarding and then he would have given them the attention they needed. Here, his force could have been directed towards financial matters (as well as towards agricultural affairs?)

James's desire to control and limit, to a certain extent, would have been freed and his scope widened. Freedom of thought and action would have been achieved through long study, application and determination. Gravity and dignity would have increased with age. However, there was disappointment, or frustration, or delay, in what should have brought joys, such as in games, sport, love affairs and children. There would have been seriousness and responsibility over these. Limitation would also have been felt through difficulties that would have been hard to grasp, to come to terms with, or which should have been kept hidden.

Relationships

<u>Others:</u> James expected others to respect his strict moral code. Generally, he was attracted to older people. He also had a tendency to be sensitive to slights and inclined to be subtly perceptive of others' hidden feelings.

James was a kindly, mentally active and useful worker for the good of others. He had a strong desire to exert for others in friendly, self-sacrificing ways. In short, people were the key to fulfilling his destiny. If he had accepted this responsibility, then his efforts on their behalf would have been recognised. As an excellent tactician, he let everyone believe that he had shared their views. He endeared himself to others by indicating that he was attracted to people of quality. Thus, he was well able to influence others to a very large extent, and so control, direct and organise them. It was critical to James's continuing development that he helped others to become self-sufficient. In a sense, he owed that kind of activity to society, because he was so intimately aware of what was needed. He should have invested his creativity in helping others to fulfil theirs.

Communication was expressed in affairs to do with partnership of any kind, or in any matter that implied reciprocity or rapport with others. James listened willingly to people with problems and was equally attentive to their ideas. They appreciated his efforts to help them to derive lasting benefits from their affairs. In return, he could usually count on them to help him gladly when he needed it, for they remembered how instrumental he had been in helping them to plan ahead.

Friends: James had a vital need for friendship, needing people with whom he could share his emotional highs and lows, and new friends were often made. Through his friends, he could have learned to become more self-confident in social situations. However, he tended to be suspicious of his friends, assuming that they wanted his friendship only because he was willing to do favours for them. He capitalised on his friends when necessary, but in these cases, he was willing to reciprocate when they needed favours.

Family: Generally, James experienced harmony at home, which he loved, along with his family. Affection, sympathy, kindness and companionship were marked. His relations with his siblings were happy, and they were likely to have been good-looking. In fact, his family ties may have been so strong that they would have deprived him of a life of his own. Because he identified so closely with his parents and siblings, it may have been difficult for him to act independently without having to refer to them for approval. Although strongly attracted to his mother, with a resemblance to her and a long association with her, his relations with her were not easy. However, there was possible benefit through her side of the family. Additionally, he hadn't to be intimidated by what his father had expected of him, or by comparison with others' accomplishments. That was slavery, not loyalty. He would have had to have been true to himself.

At first, it wasn't easy for him to express himself except in ways that would have offended his parents. Later, he realised that unless he had resisted his family, he would never have got an opportunity to make a life of his own. If his parents had disapproved of his goals, he might well have encountered problems. If they hadn't approved of his chosen partner, he may have had to make a painful choice. He could have experienced deep anxiety about this, but making a life of his own depended on it. He should have lived apart from his parents to learn how resourceful he could have been.

Possibly, there were peculiar happenings regarding his children. However, he created a similar enthusiasm in them as his own, so that they would have fulfilled their own identities. Nevertheless, his children may have disappointed him.

Lover: On the one hand, James's affection was cool, undemonstrative and critical with a tendency to fuss. However, there was intuitive understanding when in love. Additionally, there were muddles over love affairs through idealisation of the loved one, without enough commonsense evaluation. Deceit was possible. The tendencies were that confusion would have occurred, that secret partnerships may have been formed and that affections and partnerships would have been subject to disclosures and upheavals with trouble and unpleasantness. Disappointment occurred when realisation came. A sense of lack came to intensify James's shyness and prevented an easy response to what could have brought happiness. James's relations with women were not easy. However, limitation of affection, or of a happy social life, could have had its reward in a serious, one-pointed direction. Love may have meant sacrifice or a life lonely except for the chosen one. Partnerships would have been a serious matter but successful in a practical way.

On the other hand, a powerful, sexual drive was allied with a desire to be the dominant partner in all relationships, whatever their nature. He had a strong desire nature that he often expressed in extreme ways. His mind was inclined to romance and to love affairs of an intense, emotional nature that stimulated passions and desires that made his feelings very intense and very acute. He didn't hesitate to tell people he liked that he found them very attractive. Although his affection was strong, keen and ardent, it tended to be self-seeking. When the object of his desire was not immediately available, he bided his time patiently until it was, and then he didn't accept rejection gracefully. He tended to have many vicissitudes in his personal affairs and to have been easily changeful. Similarly, partnerships tended to be disappointing and lacked dependability and, if in business, should have been made as fool-proof as possible.

Any difficulties that James had, had probably stemmed from his parents' suggestions that he could have made a better selection. This could have gone on and on. He may have married early to escape from conditions at home, but if his identity had been intact, then there was no reason why it shouldn't have been a happy marriage. He had to have asserted his independence by having picked his own mate.

When thinking of marriage, he was attracted to people who were mature and straightforward. He was not especially romantic, preferring a partner who would have been a dutiful friend rather than a lover. He may have married a foreigner, or have lived abroad after marriage, or may have gone into such partnership for business or profession. There may have been disappointments here. A partner, who understood how difficult it was for him to assert himself, would have reassured him of his ability to succeed. For her part, she would have admired his poise and skill in handling people, which would have helped them both.

Career

<u>Early:</u> James's destiny lay not only in his own hands but lay also in the hands of others as well as depending on prevailing conditions. Prominence in life was indicated at certain times. He would have had plenty of fortunate opportunities in life, a lucky journey through it

and a feeling that, in general, good luck was to have been expected. There was success through foreign countries and through people from abroad. In addition, there would have been considerable gain through others' house property, or through their investments.

There was likely to have been a cleavage in James's life relating to his parents or to early childhood. The resulting disharmony in his nature could have urged him to accomplishment. James's early environment may have been somewhat austere and he may have felt that he had been denied some advantages that others had had. This may have caused him some bitter feelings about his family. Additionally, his early training may not have helped him when he applied himself to achieve his objectives. However, he would have attained his important goals mostly because he was so determined. Unfortunately, family obligations may have delayed the time when he could have done this. He may even have encountered problems if his parents had disapproved of his goals.

With training James could have learned to appreciate just how creative he was, which would have allowed him to succeed in professional and personal relationships. Developing his creativity would have helped to raise his credibility. He needed to learn a skill and become so competent in it, that he would never have had to fear the challenge of competition. He adapted, willingly, as needed, to exploit his creativity fully. If necessary, he would have had to start at the bottom, and have re-educated himself as opportunities came along, so that he would have been ready when a promotion was offered.

James should have thought about becoming independent, so that he could have reached the goals he had chosen. He owed it to himself to invest in his own development. When he was on his own, he would have learned to assert himself, to have accepted occasional setbacks and to have taken on the challenge of competition. He could have become independent and secure but only by accepting his responsibilities.

Self-analysis would have shown James that sacrificing selfish, personal desires could have motivated him to fulfil his destiny. He over-valued the practical and had a tendency to meet hardships. Possibly, willing acceptance of necessity would have strengthened his character and eventually, would have brought good results. James looked for a career with a future so that the investment he had made would have yielded enduring possibilities for growth and for expanding his services. He felt a strong sense of lack, or of a need, or of a problem to be solved, or of a task to be achieved, in the social and intellectual world around him. His desire was directed to achieving good through unusual objectives. He would have had to use his creativity to cope effectively with the demands of the real world. He tried assertively to push support, help and charity forward as the basis of his career.

James's self-doubts about his abilities would have faded as he grew increasingly successful in meeting the challenge of competition. Avoiding public exposure would have denied him the opportunity to exploit his skills and acquire self-reliance. As he preferred to avoid great physical exertion, he might have sought a career that involved him socially with the public. Others may not have considered him to be a hard worker, but his superiors knew that he was thorough and responsible. However, he didn't have to give in when superiors asked him to do more than his share. On the other hand, he hadn't to be content either with only moderate gain, for apathy and indolence were signs of failure. Above all, he had to have believed in himself, and to have known that he could well have succeeded.

Vocation: James could have succeeded in a career in serving the public and have enjoyed a comfortable income without anxiety about material security. If his efforts had been appreciated, then it meant that he had developed worthwhile skills and would have been making a valuable contribution to society. Surgery and psychology would have attracted his mind. Religious and charitable influences would have been congenial. As a writer or speaker, he would have benefitted but ease rather than strength would have been gained. Medicine, financial and investment counselling, insurance and retirement programs could have comprised examples of the many careers that would have been suitable for him. Investments in mercantile affairs, in oil or in business to do with art could have been favoured but, possibly, investments should have been left alone.

Middle: James always had a goal because he never felt that he had acquired all the comforts that life had to offer. He tended towards a willing acceptance of duty, and success through orderly and practical ways that may have caused some personal limitations as well as a lack of gaiety. A further tendency was that practical planning and determined self-will could have united in an unusual way to produce brilliant results. To help here, his ideas and imaginative intuitions were kept in bounds and given shape so that they could have become useful in the material world. He was an admirable worker and when allowed to go his own way, managed things excellently, putting his heart into all he did, and did everything in a way that could only be described by the word 'thorough'. He got along with his superiors because he didn't threaten them, and he did help them to achieve their objectives. He was ambitious and he knew how to cultivate friendly relationships with important people to win promotions and increased earnings.

There was a necessity for James to deal with finance for others. Financial work was carried out assertively for support, help and charity in his career affairs. This extended to include intangible and sympathetic work done forcefully yet harmoniously for support, help and charity matters, but nevertheless with difficulty. Although generally successful, unfortunately he tended to fantasise about successes before he had actually shown that he had achieved them.

Late: James dwelt on the future and worried about whether he would be financially and emotionally secure during his later years. His need for security later bothered him more than he cared to admit, and so he strove to earn as much as possible from his efforts. He should have been independent so that he would have been able to sustain himself later. He may have had to mobilise all his resources in a conservative plan of action to reach his goal of freedom from want. Knowing that he'd made an important contribution to serving people's needs would have enriched his later years with contentment.

Appearance and Health

Appearance: James was moderately tall with large bones and muscles and a long back. In middle age he would have had a square build inclined to stiffness. His head was full-sized with a relatively small face, full cheeks and round, open, grey, or light blue eyes. He would have had a pale skin but ruddy complexion, and possibly a double chin. His hair would have been light in colour with a tendency to baldness. Mostly, his speech would have drawled slightly but would have been soft and attractive. Occasionally, it would have been powerful and possibly discordant. He would have had an upright walk that sometimes would have appeared to be heavy or awkward. His air would have been enthusiastic and convincing with agreeable and entertaining manners. Although he had a fearless demeanour, he may well have lacked combativeness.

Health: Generally James had good health and a vitality of spirit that could have been almost too intense. While physically robust, his constitution would have been soft. Although he benefitted from an harmoniously working nervous system, nervous tension was likely since freedom and limitation do not easily go together and are apt to alternate. James may have had a tendency to dropsical complaints and possibly to chronic irregularities of his alimentary canal. He was apt to take on other people's magnetic conditions and so tended to absorb disease from them. There may have been a danger from accidents of the falling, crashing, limb-breaking kind.

He may well have suffered a relatively quick death.

Reference: 'James II', John Miller, 3rd Edition, English Monarch Series, Yale University Press, Conn., U.S.A., 2000.

Mary II

*"I thank you, gentlemen, for your address. I am glad that
I have done anything to your satisfaction."*
On receiving the congratulations of the country, at the Houses of
Parliament, September, 1690.

Mary II was joint sovereign with her Dutch husband (who was also her first cousin), William (of Orange) III, from 1689 until her death from smallpox at the start of 1695. William and Mary, both Protestants, became king and queen regnant, following the Glorious Revolution, which had resulted in the deposition of her Roman Catholic father, James II. Mary wielded less power than William, when he was in England, ceding most of her authority to him, though he relied heavily on her. She did, however, act alone when William was engaged in military campaigns abroad, proving herself to be a powerful, firm and effective ruler.

During her reign, in December, 1689, Parliament passed one of the most important, constitutional documents in English History, the Bill of Rights. Additionally, the Bank of England was founded in 1694.

Many of Mary's proclamations focused on combating licentiousness, insobriety and vice. Mary was extremely devout and attended prayers at least twice a day. She patronised the composer, Henry Purcell.

Mary was the elder, surviving daughter of King James II of England and his first wife, Lady Anne Hyde. Mary's uncle was King Charles II, who decreed that she should be brought up as a Protestant. Her maternal grandfather was Edward Hyde, who served for a lengthy period as Charles II's chief advisor. Mary was born on the 10th May, 1662 NS, at 02:16 in London, England (see Appendix 1, Figure 22). Her Epoch occurred on the 30th July, 1661 NS, at 05:43 (see Appendix 1, Figure 21).

Character Portrait

<u>General:</u> Mary had an ambitious and power-seeking personality that burned for success. As an attractive personality, she liked gay, luxurious comforts, plenty of amusement and a happy social life. She was independent, determined and had endurance. She was also cautious, careful and thorough. This combination of energy and limitation does not usually blend well but it could have been helpful to her for all arduous, rough or pioneering conditions, or for the bearing of personal hardships.

Mary also had a strongly artistic personality with an enthusiastic interest for the arts, dancing, idealism, the affairs of the sea and the psychic. Hence she was mainly subjective rather than objective. She searched for novelty and may well have grown younger the more she aged.

Mary's self-expression was shown energetically in that she was bold, hard-working and quick. She was also cheerful and contented with her own surroundings and ways. There was a sweetness of character and behaviour. Her tendency was to express herself through her affections, beauty, art and gentle ways. Her disposition was good, faithful, magnanimous and courteous to all persons to the utmost of her ability. She was one who was very ambitious of honour. She showed considerable reserve, sincerity, industriousness, perseverance and success but also the power to sacrifice. She had a wide range of interests.

Mary had the presence of a performer, which, simply, was her way of getting the attention she wanted, while, at the same time, of promoting good public relations. In short, she was a ruler indeed!

More negatively, Mary had a tendency to become very self-centred. There was inflated ambition, materialism, secrecy, tenacity and selfishness. The most important person in her life became herself. She would have insisted on her right to do what she wanted and didn't really care if others didn't like it. She would rather have been her own disciplinarian than follow the dictates of others, whom she felt didn't really know what was best for her. Thus, she couldn't have been led by others' advice. At times, she wouldn't have felt that she was in the mainstream of social activity and unless she had been willing to join in, the world would have left her alone.

Mary liked to be spoilt. She found the comforts of the good life particularly attractive, and she enjoyed the material and physical pleasures of comfortable circumstances. Status was important to her and surrounding herself with beautiful possessions helped her to achieve it. Not surprisingly, Mary would have had some delusions about the realities of life through too much living in the clouds, lovely though that may have been. As a result, she showed tendencies to be impractical and to have concentrated on visions of the future rather than on those of the present. Accordingly, she may have neglected to take advantage of her own potentiality by over-indulging in pleasurable activities.

Mary could have been stimulated to seek sensation as well as frittering away her energy, with tendencies to be very critical, anxious and restless. Although she may have been impatient, she was never bored. However, all this resulted in further tendencies to squander gains, to be extravagant and to trust to luck too easily. At the same time, she also had an inclination to let matters remain as they were and put up with them, thereby becoming patiently conditioned to trying circumstances, but with nervous strain. Pent-up energy could have been expressed through hot temper and by a domineering insistence on being over-forceful. Explosive, she was more than likely to end conditions and force new beginnings but with unhappy results.

Mentality: Mary's mind worked in a detailed, sensible, thoughtful yet fussy manner. She was energetically talkative and more than usually lively. There was charm of speech, pleasantness of manner and the generally beneficial results of an harmoniously working nervous system. Balance rather than worry was evident. She showed prudence, honesty of purpose, refinement, authority, invention, control and business acumen. Her communication would have taken place in money-making ways, in which it would have been used clerically, educationally, commercially and rationally. Her interests would have extended to include mercantile and marine matters.

Mary had spiritual energy and an inflated conscience along with the power to contemplate, to concentrate her thoughts and to perfect them. Overall, she would have been allowing her higher mind to correct her previous mistakes. Eventually, she would have found self-respect before her God. She would have begun by trying to read every book, attend every lecture and literally try to grasp every higher thought in the hope that by sheer possession of much knowledge, she would have found what she was looking for. In the end, most of what she had learned would have come to her through more natural means.

Mary's ideas and hunches came easily thereby revealing a strong imagination, but regardless of how intelligent she was, she often felt that it was not what it could have been. Mary did have more wisdom than knowledge. She doubted herself, which caused her to look harder for her understandings than she really had to, but this was only until she had learned that all of the effort she had put in to try to think out solutions to problems was merely a part of learning how to stop thinking. As soon as she had done this, she would have begun to notice that the answers were always there.

Mary's obsession would have been mobility (mental rather than physical) with a compelling need to become too clever. But she would have had to suppress her emotions of the morose and sudden outburst kind, which, in turn, could possibly have led to subversive activities, betrayal and mental ambush. Her speech, thought and nervous energy could well have been used assertively, explosively and cuttingly. Although she showed strong, mental action through revolutionary (if not perverted, fanatical and with blind zeal) thought, her communication would have become too self-willed, independent, disruptive and brusque, so that it would have lost good contact with others. In addition, she went through much difficulty putting what she knew into words. She was able to understand her higher mind but did not always believe that she would have been able to communicate this higher knowledge to others. Moreover, although her ideals were very high, she had difficulty pulling her higher mind out of her intense sexual drive that had developed and increased since birth. Eventually, her addiction to the unusual and unconventional, so strongly and awkwardly expressed, would have led to her becoming eccentric, odd and tiresome.

Mary was keen about any idea or objective (mental, material or personal) once this had been thoughtfully chosen, but, if she had become disillusioned, then she would have become equally decided about a new idea (or friend). Thus, her mind could have thrown off worries and begun thought anew with good relief of nervous tension. Similarly, she tended to throw off inhibitions and conventions of earlier times so that her expression would have become more open and candid. The result would have been a new phase in pursuit of a more frank and healthy attitude. Unfortunately, she may have conducted this rather violently, so less healthily, following a resulting, driving suppression.

Mary sometimes indulged in fanciful daydreams, creating goals that would have been difficult to achieve. She had a creative mind and would have benefitted greatly by developing it through formal training. Her level of awareness could have become unusually high, as the traditions and restrictions of society did not bind her creative imagination. However, she needed to learn how to balance all she thought imaginatively with all she had to deal with on more mundane and practical levels. It was not enough for her to imagine something idealistically wonderful. She had to find the ways through other aspects of her character to convert her dreams into creative reality. In other words, she would have had to learn to focus on attainable objectives.

Mary pursued hidden things with the desire to experiment in new ways. She had a tendency to the intangible resulting in imaginative faculties, visions, ideals and boundless aims, which would have needed her strength to actualise them. However, she tended to be on the impractical side as the scope of her imagination far surpassed the reality of the world around her. Accordingly, she tended to withdraw from creativity by retreating into a dream world that would have become her reality. On the other hand, Mary had a vital need to achieve an understanding of life. She was a seeker of the first order and she was on a mission. She kept adding substance to her philosophical and spiritual beliefs, thereby transforming her collection of opinions into a very real sense of knowing. In fact, she would have become so deeply appreciative of life that creating things for herself would have become far less important to her than experiencing the essence of all that she could absorb.

Lifestyle: Mary's life was built on past principles. From the start, she would have been struggling for honour. She lived in the expectation of creating all the feeling that would have brought her self-esteem. Her life became one of constant transformation, in which her cause, principle or mission was constantly changing but generally she tended to represent man's need to withdraw from whatever traditions had appeared to have outlived their usefulness. She preferred an uncomplicated lifestyle in which everyone participated actively. Her life would have tended towards caution and towards self-conscious preparation.

Mary would have been most comfortable trying to recreate past experiences that offered her feelings of security. She would have been unusually possessive of all past value systems which worked for her. She would have liked to absorb the world around her as this offered her the very security she was used to feeling. She could have been highly materialistic, while seeking to re-establish and strengthen all past feelings of self-worth. Having a strong tendency to repeat all things that she liked, she would have become a creature of many habits. Even though it would have been a struggle for Mary to let go of the past, she would have had to do so in order that her future could unfold. She had excellent prospects for getting everything she wanted out of life because, actually, she tended not to want to live too much in the past. However, because she feared the unknown, she usually stayed within the tried and true, rather than take risks. But really, she knew that her fears were unwarranted because she'd come as far as she had without running into any serious hazards. Yet so great was her need for assurance on the plane of material and physical substance, that it became difficult for her to be overly generous without feeling that she was losing something in the process.

Mary wanted a lot from life so she used her creativity to reach her goals. She had a zest for making her dreams materialise, as she would have wanted them to. However, it would have been unwise for her to attempt too many of them without planning. In fact, she had to have been discriminating in everything she did, to eliminate whatever was non-essential, or had a low priority. Nevertheless, she was confident that she could have achieved her objectives, and so would have enjoyed a comfortable lifestyle.

Mary had tried to internalise all the values in the world. This increased her normal possessiveness. But with all her security needs, she was not powerfully competitive because there would have been a certain amount of laziness involved. Unfortunately, she had a tendency that her outgoing nature concealed the fact that she was rather easily intimidated by competition. She tended to keep to herself any doubts she had about her ability to cope with challenging situations because she would have been ashamed to have people know her weaknesses.

Mary had a specific capacity, or gift, for some particularly effective kind of activity. There would also have been a rather uncompromising direction to her life effort. Her tendency would have been to act at all times under a consideration of opposing views, or through a sensitiveness to contrasting and antagonistic possibilities. Her temperament would have existed in a world of conflicts, or of definite polarities. Although she may have seemed indecisive, when she did make a decision, it would have been well-considered. Yet, although she would have been capable of unique achievement through a development of unsuspected relations in life, she would also have been apt to waste her energies through an improper alignment with various, prevailing conditions.

Mary's true nature may not have emerged until mid-life, after she had tried the conventional ways of living and had found them to be too restrictive. She realised that she had great difficulty living through mundane situations and circumstances. The boredom she usually felt, was not boredom with life or with people but rather an intense boredom with herself. Rather than face and understand this, she often took great pains to fill her life with one distraction after another until she convinced herself that she had nothing to do with her problem. However, the day she learned to like herself, was the day when her whole life would have changed. Very much the extremist, she would have stood for both heaven and hell at the same time. She had a compulsive desire to achieve through violently insisting on breaking away from existing conditions. The results of this often would have caused her further bondage. She felt that she had to have the freedom to explore the unknown reaches of the world that kept calling to her. She also felt that there was a higher music, a more subtle meaning to life and a deeper understanding of what the world calls 'love'. Her somewhat freed control would have helped her to make humanitarian support, help and charity more available. There could well have been a danger that she would have become so idealistic that she would not easily have disciplined herself to her society's standards. She would have suffered great temptation and may have wrecked her life by her conduct. Eventually, she would have learned to make light of things, which had once seemed burdensome. Later on, she may have found herself doing all that she now knew that she should have done when she was younger. She would have tended to have been a pioneer. Possibly she could have become a spokesperson for the literary and religious realms up to the end of the 17th century.

Relationships

<u>Others:</u> Mary could read character. She was very sensitive to other people's conceptions of themselves and when she felt that someone else's negative self-evaluation was likely to rub off on her, she would have run off quickly in another direction. She could have become defensive when she felt others were putting her on the spot. Being

very self-conscious, she constantly concerned herself with what others thought or felt about her. Initially, she focused too much on her own feelings and assumed that others were trying to take advantage of her. Concurrently, there was a tendency for her to advance herself by ruthless behaviour towards others. She could have become angry when she felt others were impinging on her ways of doing things. Additionally, she needed to be informed before saying anything and had to resist the temptation to circulate rumours, otherwise she would have been sorry when finally they got back to her. She became afraid that people may have rejected her so she spent much time alone in self-analysis and assumed that others were more capable than she was. She worked hard to promote her talents because she was anxious to impress people but she needn't have worried unduly because people were impressed with how well-informed she was. In turn, she was impressed by those who had strong religious convictions and whose ethical standards were not easily swayed. She admired people with strong personalities and tended to become interested only in people who had substantial human values. As a result, she had to watch a tendency to judge others, because she could have alienated herself by doing this. Generally, however, she did try to be fair in her inner appraisal of people.

After a while, Mary would have fraternised readily with others. She would have learned from every person she met, and she impressed them as well. Everyone admired and respected her strength. Her readiness to become involved with people and situations added diversity to her life. She had a fondness for children. They positively adored her and considered her to be the image they wanted to emulate. In a sense, she aspired to be the 'wheel' among those in her immediate surroundings, and she developed a gift for handling others so that they didn't resent her aggressiveness. She understood that she may have had to be forceful in getting people to pay attention to her creative ideas in order to get the resources she needed for developing them. As a self-made person, she would rather not have depended on others for assistance, but she would have helped anyone who deserved it. Even so, she may have succeeded better through other people than when working just for her own account. She came to know how to bring out the best in people in everyday situations by stimulating them when they applied their skills, so that they then rewarded her by getting satisfactory results. Thus, at her best, she became a real instructor and inspirer of others. She always tended to rise to the occasion in helping those who needed her skills. She was highly compassionate and often would have sacrificed much for the needs of others. She would have become the sort of person, who would have given generously, not only without expecting something in return, but not even wanting others to know that she was the giver. Hence, cautious support, help and charity were given to others, critically and with detail, yet also with ease.

Mary tended to project what she believed was truth to others, but she was aware that this was not her complete truth, as she would also have had a deeper understanding. In dealing with people, she knew instantly the point she was going to make. However, she would have avoided making it until she was sure that the language she used would have been accepted by the other person. She could have helped to improve the quality of life for many people by sharing her skills with those who wanted to improve their station in life.

Mary was determined to uphold her strong convictions even when challenged by other people. She knew that when she forcefully projected her claim, no-one could have taken it from her without a challenge. She was immediately aware when anyone tried to undermine her or resorted to unfair practices. Her best asset, which would not have been recognised easily, would have been her willingness to take on powerful adversaries. She would have understood her adversaries' limitations and weaknesses. However, she would also have had to examine her motives carefully, for she might have been tempted to deny others their rights, while she struggled to preserve her own. But she would not have had any trouble finding a solution that would have been equitable to all. Her greatest contribution to them, and to herself, would have been to help them in their moment of need, which would have earned her their gratitude.

Mary was working towards overcoming a separation between her own feelings and the collective feelings of others. It was the residue of this subtle alienation from people that kept her running from herself until she realised that her entire construction of attitudes, towards herself and others, was only that which existed in her own mind. Later on, she tended to pull away from people because her individual desires were to experience more and more of her natural environment in place of the sophistication necessary in living up to the social expectations of others.

<u>Friends:</u> Originally, Mary's tactlessness antagonised her friends so that breaks in personal relationships occurred. Friends who made demands could have caused mental strain especially when they tried to capitalise on her talents for their own selfish reasons. Although, earlier, she may have considered herself obliged to help friends when they expected favours, she also knew that when she had realised her goals she would have had the financial security to indulge only those who merited her attention. At the time, she tried not to alienate them, because she might have needed them in the future, but she would rather have gone about her business without interference.

Generally, however, friends were kindly and were likely to have been connected with artistic, maritime and psychic matters. Before long, Mary communicated well and socialised easily, which ensured that she would always have had her friends. She cultivated those who would have gladly assisted her in reaching her objectives and she offered them help in return. She liked to feel needed by her friends because she got much deep feeling from them and she herself showed genuine concern about them. Although she tended to demand too much of friendship, she kept a wide circle of artistic and intuitive friends. Overall, she enjoyed her friends and close associates so that there was always someone available, who could have done favours for her. Harmonious support, help and charity was given to friends (and good causes) impulsively, but with controlled energy and generosity.

<u>Family:</u> Mary experienced a vital, deeply unsettling, parental influence, partly due to the early death of her mother. There had been a strong parental influence during her formative years, which she had responded to, but she was content with her own identity and eventually she could have resolved any family conflicts. However, her powerful, parental overlay may have diluted her own sense of identity. She had to have taken special care that her family obligations didn't interfere with the development of her creativity thereby further

delaying her independence. Only through a break with her family, or, at least, having a separate residence, would she have had the chance to become herself. She had learned much from her parents' successes and failures and this knowledge would have guided her as she pursued her goals. Yet her experience with her parents had also given her a firm base on which to build her future. Probably, she would always have had good relations with her brothers and sisters.

Mary should have been able to enjoy pleasant relationships with all members of her family. Her family was very important to her and she would have been constantly worrying about whether they had everything they needed. She would have wanted the best for her children and she would have encouraged them to develop their own creativity. Her children would have spurred her to extend herself to have given them the advantages she may have lacked. As a result, she would have wanted her children to get a formal education.

Lover: Sexual and social success was likely throughout Mary's life. This success may not only have brought her pleasure but would also have resulted in material gain. Energy would have been expressed in gay enjoyment of love-making, of children, of games and all pleasures, but perhaps harmfully (although there was helpful control here). The tendency was that her ability to love, enjoy sexual life and all things of beauty was made more robust but less delicate. She would have made subtle demands on her romantic partners and she would not have taken rejection gracefully. Yet she would have been capable of warm, heartfelt affection and would have been faithful and generous in love with a liking to be proud of loved ones but she found her affection most difficult to express. She desired emotional outlets, wanted to be loved and appreciated but she may have chosen to remain obscure until she was sure that she wouldn't have been rejected. Possibly, she would have experienced difficulties with the opposite sex as a result of her own possessiveness, or of her fear of being possessed. Hence, she became frugal with her affections, while, at the same time, tending to exaggerate her own feelings. Thus, her deepest emotions could have become very one-pointed. She would have been willing to make sacrifices for the 'right' person, with whom she hoped to share her life, and no gift would have been too costly when she wanted to impress that person.

Mary would have been selective in choosing a lover, and she offered a mature, secure love relationship that would have benefitted both of them. She would have worked hard to find a mate who would have enhanced her objectives, especially if these had been shared. Her mate would have shared her enthusiasm for doing whatever would have benefitted both of them. Her mate was as defenceless to her charm as others she faced in her daily activities. She would have looked for a partner who shared her desire to help people in need. Helping to solve people's problems would have tended to give her a feeling of accomplishment. She would have wanted the best for her lover; she would have enjoyed giving presents to show how much she cared, and sometimes she would have been extravagant in this regard.

However, duty, or some form of limitation, stopped the full expression of love and harmony, but the duty would have appeared to have been less heavy because of some happiness that it brought. Her partner would have been older (but, unexpectedly, her marriage was not delayed).

Unfortunately, explosive temper, wilful impatience and nervous strain did not make for easy partnership in marriage or business. Marriage for Mary would not have been an easy task because a general lack of trust, combined with too much self-involvement, prevented her from experiencing the full richness of another individual on an intimate basis. But any partnership would have brought responsibility. There would have been sorrow, or loss, through her affections. In addition, her partnership may not have been what it seemed. Conditions would have been kept hidden. Her expression could even have become one of dour jealousy. Nevertheless, her marriage should have proved quite satisfactory.

Career

<u>Early:</u> Mary's destiny lay mainly in her own hands. She had inherited great transformations. She would have expected good luck, success and plenty of opportunities in life. She would have been tolerably fortunate for acquiring money and possessions in which partnership,

marriage and legacies would have had a major financial impact—sometimes good and sometimes bad. There was likely to have been a cleavage in her life relating to parents, or to early childhood. The resulting disharmony could have urged her to accomplishment. Despite traditional and conventional influences, she would have been restless in her birthplace; the whole world would have been her home.

Early in life, Mary would have been conditioned to concentrate on her family and to endure the sacrifices required to help them. Probably, she had been overindulged as a child, and she hadn't grown out of it. She had had a lot of growing up to do. Her need to stay close to home while she was growing up may have been painful, if she had had many family obligations. She had come to understand the need to plan for her goals to achieve success. She accepted the lack of recognition during her learning process as a necessary sacrifice and she knew that the rewards would have been worth it. She had plenty of energy and she asserted herself to get what she wanted in her career and in her personal affairs. She wanted to fulfil her dreams and she would have worked enthusiastically to have seen them realised. She would have hoped to achieve many goals, and she would have applied herself to them knowledgeably and with commonsense. She would have become compulsive and magnetic so that her leadership would have been either obeyed or violently broken. This galvanic force pointed to results of an outstanding nature.

Education could well have helped Mary to achieve a more substantial position. Because she was afraid of remaining in obscurity, she would have done anything to get an education. She was attracted to older people. If she could have spent some time developing her mental assets, she would have been rewarded abundantly. Muscles may have been impressive, but brains were more enduring. She realised that the best way to take full advantage of her creativity would have been to get a formal education. She knew that by making the necessary sacrifices, she would have reaped enormous dividends. Her education would have given her the polish she needed to ease into a position of prominence.

Mary would have done quite well if she had been groomed for a family business, but probably she would have preferred to strike out on her own. With her creativity, she could have built her future without relying on others too much. She wasn't afraid of hard work and nothing would have stopped her when she applied herself to satisfy the demands of her career. However, her apprehension about the future may have caused her to resist change and would have limited her ability to take advantage of opportunities. She must have had to plan carefully for whatever she hoped to achieve and not have assumed that everything would have worked out alright in the end.

Mary would have continued to develop as long as her objectives in life related to those of society. She knew that she would have reached her goals and objectives by putting her ideas to work. These could have been inspired by her 'hunches' that usually would have been proved right. She applied herself confidently and with full assurance so that her ideas would have been implemented successfully. Thus her excellent imagination coupled with good business acumen could have been applied to concrete affairs, i.e. castles in the air could have been converted into reality.

Vocation: As a writer or speaker, Mary would have benefitted through charm of speech but with ease rather than strength. She would have been a good, practical worker, who could have accomplished much. She would also have been fitted for responsibility as a head servant, either in public or private life. In addition, her temperament would have been suitable for serving the public and her creativity would have been an asset in public institutions. She would also have been suitable for office work, for appointments, and for work through companies, associations, factories or for large bodies of people. However, Mary was apt to think that her work was somewhat beneath her, that she hadn't got her desserts and that she was fitted for better positions than she occupied. In a professional environment, she would have enjoyed success in law, in social activities or even in the performing arts, perhaps as a broadcaster in radio or television. She would have excelled in any of these, which would have required close contact with the public. Moreover, she had ability, for example, for chemistry and hygiene, i.e. for many such subject combinations where the ideal and the practical were blended.

Finally, she could have become a great artisan, but always she would have been building something from the past. For example, if ever she had decided to earn her living by building chariots for the 21st century, then that would have been just typical of her.

<u>Middle:</u> No matter what Mary's formal training had been, she would have always continued to educate herself. She came to know how to apply her knowledge skills in the real world to solve problems and earn a decent income. While she respected education, and those who were informed, she tended to avoid further education for its own sake because she had developed an aversion to purely mental pursuits. She was eager to assert herself and would always have had whatever information she needed. As a result, there were few who could have matched her in a direct confrontation. She should have directed her efforts towards developing new skills that she could have used when her family no longer required her attention.

Mary was far more talented than she appeared but she would have been happier when left to do as she wanted with her time and energy. If possible, she preferred to work privately and obscurely. She planned for long-range goals rather than for immediate results in which reversals and setbacks would have been acceptable provided the experiences taught her to avoid repeating her mistakes in the future. She would have been interested in a cause, but with little concern over end-results, over herself or over her resources. She tended to adapt her allegiances to lines along which she could have made her efforts count for the most. Unfortunately, she might have had trouble convincing her superiors that her high visibility would have been enough to satisfy their expectations for more action and less promise. Success would have been achieved but was sometimes lacking in practical enterprise, even though fertile in resource. Although fairly fortunate, she could also have found herself constantly thwarted. Again, unfortunately, Mary was subject to upsets and to forced new phases.

Mary understood money and how to manipulate her affairs to get the most financial benefits. Her mind could have calculated the true value of any item before she bought it. She would have been fortunate materially because opportunities arose for the use of her enthusiasm and energy. She disliked financial limitations because they kept her from doing all that she wanted to do. Having sufficient money would have stabilised her anxieties. Careful planning would have given her great returns. Although she kept her affairs in order because she deplored untidiness, she must have had to have learned to be more disciplined in handling her resources, in order to have satisfied her desires.

Late: Mary looked forward to the time when she would have no longer been forced to earn a living, so that she would have had greater freedom to decide how to use her time. She would have needed to look ahead to the future to assure herself of reasonable financial security. She would have wanted to enjoy her friends more fully and to have indulged herself more freely. She would have realised how important it was to sacrifice some of her self-indulgent desires to improve her future security. Additionally, once free from family obligations, she should have invested in her own future, for more security later. She mustn't have assumed that she could have taken care of that problem when the time came, because it was always later than she thought. The investment she made would have rewarded her later in life by ensuring comfortable circumstances. She would have become preoccupied with gaining resources to sustain herself during her later years. But the uncertainty of the future should have warned her to use her energy prudently. She needed to plan to work more efficiently, so that she was not burned out from exhaustion in the future. However, all being well, she would have been responsible, and determined, to achieve the independence of a stable income and to have defined a program for security during her later years.

Appearance and Health

Appearance: Mary would have been tall, good-looking, muscular and strong with a full, evenly-made and well-proportioned structure but possibly with somewhat short limbs. Later on, her full face and person would have become fleshy with a tendency to a double chin. She would have had large, full eyes, a ruddy complexion, becoming pale later, with plentiful brown to dark hair. She could have shown some assertive gestures.

<u>Health:</u> Generally, Mary had physical robustness, good health and a vitality of spirit that could have been almost too intense. But, if she had got involved in too many activities, had allowed people to make unfair demands on her and had not learned to be more restrained in her physical efforts, then her health may have suffered. These tendencies towards extravagance of thought and deed, as well as extremism both in work and play, could have led to overstrain. Her mind would have been overly energised leading to breakdown causing irritability, temper, and carping incisiveness. However, she would have slept well.

There could have been deep-seated, functional and nervous disorders, lingering, invidious and unusual diseases, paralysis and possible accidents to limbs. Psychic tendencies were likely to have been both unhealthy and difficult to understand.

There could have been isolated circumstances at the end of her life.

References: 1) "Mary II: Queen of England", Hester Chapman, Ulverscroft Large Print Books, Ltd., Leicester, England, 1974.
2) "William and Mary", J. van der Kiste, Sutton Publishing, Stroud, Gloucestershire, England, 2003.

William III

"I came into this kingdom, at the desire of the nation, to save it from ruin, and to preserve its religion, its laws and its liberties."
Taken from the start of his unused abdication address, January, 1699.

William III was a sovereign Prince of Orange of the House of Orange-Nassau by birth. From 1672 he governed the Dutch Republic as Stadtholder. From 1689, he reigned as William III over England and Ireland and as the II over Scotland. He is still known informally by sections of the population in Northern Ireland and Scotland as "King Billy". In the 'Glorious Revolution' of 1688, William invaded England in an action that ultimately deposed King James II. In the British Isles, William ruled jointly with his wife, Mary II, elder daughter of King James II, until her death at the start of 1695 from smallpox. This period of their joint reign is often referred to as that of "William and Mary".

A Protestant, William participated in several wars against the powerful king of France, Louis XIV, in coalition with Protestant and Catholic powers in Europe. Many Protestants heralded him as a champion of their faith. Largely because of that reputation, William was able to take the British crowns when many were fearful of a revival of Catholicism under James. William's victory over James, at the Battle of the Boyne in 1690, is still commemorated by the Orange Order. His reign marked the beginning of the transition from the personal rule of the Stuarts to the more Parliament-centred rule of the House of Hanover.

William Henry of Orange was born in The Hague in the Dutch Republic on 14th November, 1650 NS at 20:42 (see Appendix 1, Figure 24). He was the only child of Stadtholder, William II, Prince of Orange, and Mary, Princess Royal of England, who was the eldest daughter of King Charles I of England, and so sister to Kings Charles II and James

154

II. Eight days before William was born, his father died of smallpox, aged 24. Thus William was the Sovereign Prince of Orange from the moment of his birth. His Epoch occurred on the 25th February, 1650 NS, at 15:47 (see Appendix 1, Figure 23).

Character Portrait.

General: Although William's nature was mainly harmonious, it also showed duality. His combination of energy and limitation would not usually have blended well but it proved helpful to him for all arduous, rough or pioneering conditions, or for the bearing of personal hardship. At his neutral centre, William was mainly subjective, utopian and conservative, showing equanimity. Virtues would have been economy, receptivity and tenacity. There was pride, ardour, some love of grandeur and power, arrogance, pomp, show and ostentation, along with considerable dramatic feeling. As a restless personality that may have been tempered by a comfort-loving disposition, he showed a love of travel, home and change that would have been characteristic of him from youth to old age. His nature would have been easy-going, plastic, poetic, suggestible, emotional and self-pitying. His temperament inclined to be particular, yet impersonal in his interests. He would have attempted to adjust to difficulties and to by-pass them, though rarely without nervous strain. There may have been a tendency to gloom, or despondency, during which he may have seemed hard, selfish, reserved, lacking in candour, or secretive. He needed to have understood his fears and anxieties so that he could have put them into proper perspective. This would have allowed him to understand others better and to have realised that he was not alone in his fantasies.

On his energetic side, William had a versatile, ambitious and power-seeking personality that would have burned for success. He was always "on the go". His magnetic leadership, inner assurance and unusual ability suggested that an active life would have been best for him and that he should have been placed in a position of responsibility where he could have taken the lead. His nature was strong and commanding, firm and self-directed even at his most emotional. Possibly, however, he may have come to occupy a position that he couldn't maintain, thereby resulting in failure, but, by the same token, there would also have been a great power for good. Generally, William was a cheerful, generous, persistent, determined, powerful and contented with his own surroundings and ways. But his robust, courageous manner could be over-active at times and over-quick in response. He sought to be practical rather than dreamy. He would have been intent on self-improvement and would have been able to recruit others' support. In fact, he would have become increasingly dissatisfied with himself unless he got himself involved in activities that proved how valuable he was to others.

On his limitation side, William was possibly unstable, unworldly, chaotic and a hypochondriac. Here, he needed to cultivate determination, concentration and the avoidance of stimulants. He had a tendency to have too many irons in the fire, self-will, impetuosity and a frittering away of energies, leading to a drastic ruination of results, yet some control was also present.

William appeared to be arrogantly self-confident, but actually, he couldn't stand to be upstaged by anyone. His disposition tended not at all to be desired, becoming peevish, somewhat malicious and much inclined to fretful self-indulgence that was both irresponsible and lazy. There developed a great love of ease with a tendency to inactivity. Timidity, reserve and mistrust could have resulted in morbid and fanciful conditions with a liability to go to extremes, become somewhat exacting and over-cautious. Additionally, there was a cantankerous insistence on non-essentials, suppressed emotions and morose, sudden outbursts that may have led to subversive activities. Not knowing when to be silent became one of his greatest liabilities. Thus, he could have become wild, rebellious, overly excitable and revolutionary. Hence, when provoked, he expressed himself in an undisciplined way. Although he may not have been a physically violent person, the results were violent when he unleashed his verbal attacks. It was not that he was dishonest, but he did lack tact. Being sensational and emotional, almost all of his misfortunes could have been traced to his emotional and highly sensitive nature.

Mentality: William's conscious aim was to understand, with a strong sense of sympathy and noble thoughts. His mind and mental outlook were good in so far as charm of speech, pleasantness of manner, ability for repartee and the generally beneficial results of an harmoniously working nervous system, were concerned. However, his nervous system was sensitive, so that elation and depression could have alternated quickly.

Communication took place in affairs to do with more profound studies and with foreign interests. His mind was also forceful, incisive and downright. He was good at debate. Thus, he had good commonsense mentality and nervous force. He was also capable of stimulated sensation seeking, inventiveness, some power of synthesis and a search for novelty. He had strong, inspirational ideas and intuitions through heightened receptivity that possibly suggested some genius in science, but these may have been communicated in a perverse or cantankerous manner with nervous tension.

More negatively, William could have become explosive and so was likely to have ended conditions and forced new beginnings with unhappy results. William could also have used bluff and have been inscrutable, incomprehensible, sarcastic and critical. Additionally, he could have been precipitate, eccentric and fanatical, showing blind zeal.

William was highly sensitive though he didn't appear that way on the outside. Introspective and unusually deep in his awareness of life, as it was during his time, he remained secretive because he himself was not fully in touch with his own motives. Yet he saw enough to know that much of his outer life was forced by society that seemed to make him a hypocrite to his inner being. He felt the bindings of society in his inner mind, but he did have the power to break free from them if he had so desired.

William tried to keep the idea of familiarity in his mind. Even when he travelled, he kept identifying each new place with a past that he was already comfortable in. As a result, he could have moved through life with the feeling that he was securely rooted, no matter where he was, or whom he was with. Because he experienced living in a world that seemed to be changing around him, it would have been better, if, instead of trying to make his present fit into his past, he realised and accepted within, the past security he had known, so that he did not have to have sought it continually in the outer world. In this way, he could have fulfilled his ideal state of ever present birth.

William was truly a lost soul, who would have needed much help from others if he was to find himself in the great expanses of his mental wanderings. However, he didn't like to have others impose their thoughts on him, for he was using much of his mental independence to seek the rectification of a past injustice. Earlier, he would have been a seeker, but his meanderings had still not established a central frame of reference within which he could have catalogued his information. But his mental expansiveness scattered and enlarged his fields of information so much that it became impossible for him to do this, yet he still kept trying. He tried to cover so many subjects that he often didn't know where to start speaking, or what was really relevant to talk about. Even when he returned to the present, he tended to exaggerate the importance of all his collected thoughts out of all proportion to the realities they were aimed at. His biggest difficulty was that his mind wanted to comprehend everything under heaven in order to take the information back to some past time, and then apply it to a problem as yet unresolved. The problem here was that the information acquired was usually superficial and scattered to the point where it was too difficult for him to apply it to any one area. Unfortunately, he then kept trying to use his impersonal wisdoms, which had reflected the great world truths of his own personal problems in the past, rather than by rising his own personal self to a more worldly level.

Clearly, concentration was difficult for him because when focusing deeply on a particular topic, his thoughts were always interrupted by external distractions, which made him feel that whatever he was thinking about, was hardly worthy of much attention. Thus, he left many problems in life unresolved—but he was down to Earth.

Hence, there were mental difficulties. There was never the opportunity to experience enough of a stabilising influence to make clear and precise thinking a natural way of life. Ideally, he was trying to find meaning in his soul and through a very hectic process of elimination he would have eventually discarded all that had no meaning for him, so that ultimately, he would have identified with his essence. His journey was into the unknown regions of 'Man and his World', and whereas he might have experienced the greatest of difficulties along the way, his reward would have been the finding of his Soul. Despite all this, however, he became, oddly enough, a very mystical, spiritual messenger to everyone he met.

Thus, he experienced a degree of mental comfort but he still had difficulties getting along with others, particularly in working situations. He often tried to impress his ideas upon others, while, critically, he went back in time to analyse how well or poorly these ideas had been put into practice. Because of others' reactions to him, he developed feelings of obligation to them. To organise his working habits, he had to understand the end result and the back-to-the-beginning steps, which could have led him to where he was going. He could have become overly critical of himself, spending much energy wondering whether he should keep judging his inner being, or focusing his mental energies outwardly in an attempt to overcome his faults through service to others. Yet there were times when others declined his service. Thus he felt frustrations in dealing with people. Eventually, he developed an ideal state of discrimination, through which he was constantly trying to make all things and people fit into his perceived order of the world.

William had the ability to believe, persist, permeate, renounce, sacrifice himself and receive impressions. Although his mind was intuitional with good practical vision, he could have become confused by complex practical issues, showing short-sightedness mentally, but he was also highly receptive to artistic and benevolent ideas. Additionally, he had a tendency to retirement, philanthropy and to day-dreaming, even to the extent of becoming dream-intoxicated. However, his unusual, imaginative ideas were directable and so could have been brought to good compulsive fulfilment. He showed an interest in psychic matters and would have demonstrated a readiness to work for research in such ways.

Lifestyle: There was a particular and rather uncompromising direction to William's life effort. He would have been interested in a cause but with much less concern over end-results, over his resources or over the need to conserve himself. There would have been highly individual, or purposeful, emphases in his life, where his temperament would have stood out in experience according to his own, very special tastes. He made his own anchorage in existence by his robust resistance to pigeon-holing, either in the neat conventional compartments of nature, or in the idea pockets of his associates. He had a 'splay'foot certainty in every approach he made to life's problems. He was an intensive personality, who couldn't have been limited to any steady point of application. He dipped deeply into life and poured forth the results of his gathered experiences with unremitting zeal. His desire for a fulfilling life was in harmony with the emotional satisfaction he derived by being helpful.

William's inner and outer worlds were sufficiently integrated so that his ambition didn't run into any serious conflicts with his temperament. His value-judgement would have been well-developed, so he would have wasted little time and effort on non-productive enterprises. While it sometimes may have irritated him to do so, he made compromises because he knew that, eventually, he would have got his own way. Generally, he was willing to change old habits for better ones, so that he was rarely locked into an attitude that might have interfered with his continuing progress. Because of all this, his success would have been easier to achieve, and he should have gained it fairly early in life. However, he had to reserve enough time for himself, so that he could have unwound and enjoyed some of the benefits that he deserved.

William had a keenly analytical approach to the organisation of his life. But he was far better at organising things than people. One of his biggest problems was that he had a tendency to harness his life to self-imposed restrictions.

A type of non-trusting attitude pervaded his entire identity structure, due to some earlier situation in which he had felt shut out, or closed off from, what he had tried to reach. Later, instead of facing up to that, he tried to be important so that others would recognise him in a way in which he could not have been hurt. As a result, he kept dwelling on emotions which had hindered his past. This tended to slow his progress in life as he felt constantly that he had to be sure of himself. His need for security became high. There may have been an early, strong attachment to a figure, who represented protection and safety. This would have been transferred to an older, authority figure later, as he did not consciously understand how he could live without a protective womb. When he did try to come out of himself, he was not sure that he would have been fully accepted by others. Thus, he tended to wall his emotions in, as if to save them for the one individual he may have met in his future, who would have been symbolic of the past security he had given up.

Great periods of loneliness and despondency were experienced. He felt misunderstood. He would often have liked to see tiresome situations brought to an end, and as a result of this, he could have stimulated destructive forces in those around him. He could have become the most negative person in respect to the positive efforts of others to help to pull him out of himself.

Accordingly, he tried to find an impressive and formidable identity structure that the world around him could vibrate to. He tried to impress his reality outward because he desired feedback. Something in his personality structure was lacking and as such there was a strong tendency for him to compensate. Usually there was a series of barriers between him and the people he would have liked to get close to.

Ideally, William was learning how to stand on his own two feet and because this process was so slow, he would have been highly fearful that anybody might try to knock him down before he had built his own foundation. Most of all, he would have spent his entire life building a castle of rules, which, ultimately, would have been the structure of the identity he had wanted to achieve.

William had a vital need to achieve an understanding of life, but his ideas on the philosophy of life lacked clarity. His obsession would have been mobility, both physical and mental, together with a compelling need to achieve comprehension and/or to be too clever.

Relationships

<u>Others:</u> William had a tendency to advance himself through ruthless behaviour towards others. He may not have cared about others' needs, or wanted to know how they thought, that only suggested that he was as determined as possible to get as much as he could from them to satisfy his own desires.

Alternatively, he may have been motivated by a strong spiritual commitment to serve others, in which case his gains would have become much greater than the sacrifices he had made for them. He understood that to win people's attention he had to let them know that he could have served them better than his competitors could have done. He knew how to win the public's approval by his tactful presentation of himself and his credentials. He looked for ways to show his concern for people, especially for those who had problems. He developed a strong desire to exert for others in kindly, self-sacrificing ways. It was satisfying for him to know that his actions had helped to improve others' well-being, and when they appreciated his efforts, he would have been inspired to continue. Unfortunately, his efforts could have become confused, so that some muddles occurred.

William's desire for harmony in a widespread way resulted in kindly motives in humanitarian ways. He wanted to help others and not offend them, which was admirable. Generally then, William was willing to help others with their problems. He had compassion for them and he asserted himself in ways that served their needs. His success came from his ability to understand people's needs and his sensitivity to people's failings. He understood that everyone had some weaknesses or flaws, which, usually, he could have overlooked if their positive traits had been more outstanding. His upbringing had taught him how to provide effectively the services that people needed. In their turn, they usually sensed that they could tell him their problems and that he would have done what he could to help them to find solutions. He hoped that he was not being naïve when he offered to help others, assuming that later, he would have been repaid for his efforts when he least expected it. This sort of self-expression gave him the opportunity to develop a high degree of skill. He would have learned to become more self-sufficient as he became more experienced in dealing with people. However, in his desire to help people with their problems, he also attracted those who made no effort to help themselves.

William's skills would have become an asset as he sought to make a good impression on others. Previously, his lack of self-assurance had made him put others on the defensive to distract them from his weaknesses. But he had wanted people to consider him to be responsible and trustworthy. And so he became stimulated to match the good judgement he observed in others. He became a real instructor and inspirer of others. He already had a talent for communicating playfully with people in a close social environment. Now, his gift for conversation fascinated people and encouraged them to respond. He would have become well-able to influence others to a very large extent and so control, direct and organise them. The contacts he made could have given him the opportunity to develop and exploit his ideas creatively. Working with other people could well have become suitable for his temperament and his colleagues probably would have been better off because of his efforts on their behalf. It would have become necessary for him to deal with finance for others.

Friends: Generally, William did have forceful enemies. His tactlessness antagonised his friends causing frequent breaks with them. Often he was unhappy because he tended to get from others the repercussions of his own awkwardness as a companion. His lack of self-control could have got him into a lot of hot water, especially with people in his own immediate environment. But they may have thanked him retrospectively for rousing them to action when, otherwise, they could have missed an opportunity. In return, friends may have offered him needed opportunities for success in his career.

Family: William's ability to succeed probably came from his parents, who had taught him to assert himself within the framework of reasonable discipline and responsibility. They would have supported him in his struggle to make his own way. By taking advantage of the opportunities provided by his parents, he could have succeeded in fulfilling his obligations to them and to himself. However, relations with his mother were not easy. Also, the affairs of his brothers and sisters would have called for his attention. He worked to give critically support, help and charity to members of his close family.

Generally, William's own home matters were happy. Home-life was of major importance and did much to enrich his personality. Warmth and enthusiasm entered into relationships as expressed to young people in a family. His children could have been a real catalyst in his life, stimulating him to higher levels of performance in providing for them.

<u>Lover:</u> William's sexual life would have been important. His mind was inclined to romance and love affairs of an intense, emotional nature, thereby increasing all his passions and desires, making his feelings very intense and very acute. He could have been led into, or exposed to, temptation, as well as to perverted, coarse and base desires.

For William, sexual and social success would have been likely throughout his life. This success may not only have brought pleasure but also would have resulted in material gain. His ability to get what he wanted stimulated the opposite sex, who would have found him exciting. However, a sense of lack intensified his shyness and prevented an easy response to what could have brought happiness. The tendency was that his affection would have been most difficult to express. Thus, his life tended to be solitary. His relations with women were not easy. Although warmth and enthusiasm could have entered into sexual life, his love tended to be unemotional and detached. Friendship was preferred rather than emotional ties, so that he was too cool in affection. Although sincere and stable in affection, he was also conventional. Gain and harmonious conditions in sexual relations would not have been obtained peacefully. Breaks in personal relations would have occurred as well as possible scandal.

William could easily have found a mate because he would have expressed his emotions openly. However, it would have been better if he had postponed having a permanent relationship until he had become established in his career. The limitation of his affection, or of a happy social life, would have had its reward in a serious, one-pointed direction. Love may have meant sacrifice, or a life lonely, except for the chosen one. His partnership would have been a serious matter but successful in a practical way. In fact, there was an excellent indication for a happy marriage and for an ability to live harmoniously with others. However, he had to be wary of accepting a submissive role with his partner. Additionally, explosive temper, wilful impatience and nervous strain did not make for easy partnership in marriage. Moreover, on a personal level, he didn't believe that he could have measured up to his partner's desires. Furthermore, he may have had some problems in that he may have attracted a partner who expected a lot from him so that he really would have had to extend himself to satisfy these expectations. On the other hand, his partner would have been the catalyst that made him excel in his efforts. She would have given him support when he met problems and appreciation when he had done his job well. His devotion would have inspired her to assist him so that they both would have benefitted in the life they shared together.

Career

<u>Early:</u> William's destiny was in the hands of others mainly and depended on circumstances. He had plenty of opportunities in life with a feeling that "good luck" and success were to have been expected. Steady fortunes were normal yet sudden and unexpected gains together, perhaps, with a legacy, were possible but there were also tendencies towards unfounded expectations as well as unusual experiences. He had the power to make money. Financial success and prosperity could have come through increased turnover.

William's striving for significance depended on how well he used his creativity. This would have developed fully, if he had established his own roots. Self-development was the key. He could have become a credit to himself by building a sound mind in a sound body. He adapted to job assignments fairly well and learned new skills easily. He took every opportunity to improve his skills when special training was available. He knew that he had to apply himself to get the necessary training to fulfil the commitment he had made to his goals. The sacrifices that were required would have added meaning and value to the knowledge he had sought. Because he was so willing to apply himself in developing his basic resources, he would have derived the greatest possible gains from his efforts. If he could have capitalised on his talents, and have worked diligently at putting his ideas to work, then he knew that his future was bright. By applying his talents, he would have become an invaluable help to those who needed his skill and competence. He should have been motivated to serve his patrons' needs. He could have inspired them to face their problems with courage and optimism, knowing that they would have succeeded eventually.

However, having had to postpone working towards his objectives early in life may have angered him, but it would have been worthwhile if he could have resolved that problem. It was important that he became more self-disciplined in developing his talents in order to improve his competitive position. He realised that others would have done the job if he didn't, so he strove constantly to improve his skills and proficiency.

William had to have examined his motives carefully to determine exactly why he had felt compelled to take the career direction he'd chosen. He had to have been directed by only the noblest of reasons, including the desire to help satisfy pressing human needs. He had to be wary of the temptation to relax his ethics while pursuing his objectives; giving in would have resulted in massive losses of earnings and prestige. Worry could have proved a major obstacle to success and had to have been avoided to achieve it.

<u>Vocation:</u> William had a special capacity, or gift, for some particularly effective kind of activity and/or shown an important direction of interest. He would have been an excellent worker, especially in areas of following previously created procedures. He may have made a very decided figure in the direction of drama or music. There was keenness to work at educational or literary pursuits. As a writer or speaker, he would have benefitted but ease rather than strength would have been gained. He would have showed quietness, sobriety and self-control. There would also have been carefulness, prudence, economy and forethought, which, probably, would have been used in public life. He could have become connected with town councils, parliament, public bodies or with movements of public importance. Possibly, he had business ability with a special inclination for large undertakings or responsible positions. There would have been financial ability about property or investment, with the power for organising, managing, arranging, planning and scheming, so that he would have been well-fitted for official positions requiring these qualities. Surgery and psychology would have attracted his mind. Additionally, medicine, physical therapy, psychological counselling, vocational guidance, ecological enterprises, nutrition and family planning would have constituted some of the many fields available to him.

<u>Middle:</u> William applied himself with purpose and dedication. To avoid having to do just physical labour, William looked for a field in which he could have exercised his mental faculties. The chances were that he would have grown into a staff, or management position on the job. He could have succeeded in earning a comfortable living by using his skills creatively. Although he might have been restricted by the demanding obligations of his daily routine, he managed to use his innovative ability to make his job interesting. He was clever at devising new and better ways to make his job more exciting. It was reassuring for him to know that he always would have found enjoyable ways to satisfy his needs. With greater competence, his earnings could have increased and he would have established his professional credibility. He adapted his allegiances to lines along which he could have made his efforts count for the most. He may not have wanted a position of high visibility but it would have been satisfying to know that he was respected by those in authority for the excellence he showed in his tasks. Because he was aggressive at promoting his skills, his services would have been almost always in demand. He had a talent for increasing the value of his assets. The tendency was that his ability to get what he wanted impressed his competitors.

William overvalued the practical and there was a tendency for him to meet hardships, possibly because there were frequent changes in work. Sometimes he accepted responsibilities that he thought he shouldn't, while shying away from those he thought he should. As a result, there was some undermining of his power of control and of his completion of purpose. His business interests would have become sacrificed for home cares and public convenience sacrificed for private gain. He had many ideas to promote though he may have had to defer them because of more pressing priorities. Very hard work may have been carried out for idealistic ends. The results may have been disappointing and elusive because all would have been too imaginary. Over imagination, or irregular, over-glamorous, escapist ways tended to contribute to failure. He was never satisfied with anything less than perfection in his endeavours and it bothered him when he failed because he had expected too much from himself. His work would have become unsatisfactory through muddles and through two-faced work people. Some of his associates were disreputable. William was unusually vulnerable to the danger of fellow workers conspiring against him on the job. He must have had to have been constantly alert to this problem and completely informed to keep it from happening. He had to learn to become more tolerant of the human factor, so that his high ideals for order and perfection did not lead him into a negative attitude towards the people he worked with. Additionally, he often neglected to ask others for help in making decisions because he didn't want to appear to be incompetent. Consequently, he had had to learn from his own mistakes. One day, he may have come to see that he had a strong tendency to judge himself by his ideals, while, at he same time, he judged others by their actions.

Late: There were no interpretations for this section.

Appearance and Health

Appearance: William would have been of medium height showing a tendency towards large bones, shoulders and muscles. Similarly, his head would have tended towards full-size and round but with a thin-looking countenance and mainly pale complexion. He would have had grey eyes, light coloured hair and a tendency to baldness. He would have inclined to become stout with a square build in middle age and may have developed a double chin. There would not have been much that was pleasing either in the form of his body or in his way of expression, except that walking (that might have seemed awkward, at times) and riding would have been undertaken keenly and with speed.

Health: Generally, William would have had good health and a vitality of spirit that would have been almost too intense. Much may have been achieved, but illness through worry, nervous strain and nervous disorders may have occurred through suppression and then outbreak. Sudden upsets in health may have affected the knee area of his legs. Also, his health may have suffered through hidden, often toxic or poisonous, causes. Food poisoning, drugs, gas, and impure water had to have been avoided. The use of drugs would have been dangerous for him because they would have tended to remove him further from a state of presence in the reality of the here and now.

Accidents to limbs, paralysis and lingering, insidious diseases were possible. There would have been trouble through annoying dreams, visions and mental states. Strange fears could have played upon his nerves and his health could have been undermined by these.

His death through constitutional weakness, although honourable, would not have taken place peacefully. His father would have died prematurely.

Reference: "William and Mary", J. van der Kiste, Sutton Publishing, Stroud, Gloucestershire, England, 2003.

Anne

*"As I know my heart to be entirely English, I can very seriously assure
you there is not anything you can expect or desire from me which I shall
not be ready to do for the happiness and prosperity of England."*
From her first speech to the English Parliament, March 1702.

Anne became Queen of England, Scotland and
Ireland in March 1702. In May 1707, under the
Acts of Union, two of her realms, the kingdoms of
England and Scotland, united as a single sovereign
state, the Kingdom of Great Britain. She continued
to reign as Queen of Great Britain and Ireland until
her death.

Anne was born in the reign of her uncle
Charles II, who had no legitimate children. Her
father, James, was first in line to the throne. His Catholicism was
unpopular in England and on Charles's instructions Anne was raised
as a Protestant. Three years after he succeeded Charles, James was
deposed in the "Glorious Revolution" of 1688. Anne's Protestant
brother-in-law and cousin, William III became joint monarch with his
wife, Anne's elder sister, Mary II. Although the sisters had been close,
disagreements over Anne's finances, status and main friend arose
shortly after Mary's accession and they became estranged. William
and Mary had no children. After Mary's death in 1695, William
continued as sole monarch until he was succeeded by Anne upon his
death in 1702.

As queen, Anne favoured moderate Tory politicians, who
were more likely to share her Anglican religious views than their
opponents, the Whigs. The Whigs grew more powerful during the
course of the War of the Spanish Succession, until, in 1710, Anne
dismissed many of them from office. Her close friendship with Sarah
Churchill, Duchess of Marlborough, turned sour as the result of
political differences.

Anne was plagued by ill-health throughout her life. From her
30s onwards, she grew increasingly lame and corpulent. Despite

17 pregnancies by her husband, Prince George of Denmark, she died without any surviving children and was the last monarch of the House of Stuart. Under the terms of the Act of Settlement, 1701, she was succeeded by her second cousin, George I, of the House of Hanover, who was a descendant of the Stuarts through his maternal grandmother, Elizabeth, daughter of James I.

Anne was the fourth child and second surviving daughter of James, Duke of York (afterwards James II), and his first wife, Lady Anne Hyde. She was born on the 16th February, 1665 NS, at 23:38 in London, England (see Appendix 1, Figure 26). Her Epoch occurred on the 10th May, 1664 NS, at 01:59 (see Appendix 1, Figure 25).

Character Portrait

<u>General:</u> There appeared to be two sides to Anne. At her worst, she would have had a criminal personality, seeking fulfilment of personal aims without regard for the feelings of others. However, if these tendencies could have been resisted, honest success could have been achieved by means of a thrusting, purposeful nature and a capacity for hard work. Vanity, jealousy, self-esteem and pride may have led to her downfall/failure, since there would always have been a considerable amount for good or evil; and unless the latter had been restrained, her nature would have become a very selfish one. Her feelings were very strong and intense. Her appetites and passions needed curbing. Much reserve and concentrated force were combined with a good deal of secretiveness. Her self-expression tended to be shown energetically, i.e. bold, daring, initiatory, forceful, quick and strong with courage, impetuosity and argumentativeness. Her large fund of energy lay behind a keen desire for widespread activity of mind and body. Although her energy was expressed with 'heart', strong purpose and creativity, it was also controlled, thereby becoming helpful for all arduous, rough and pioneering conditions, or for the bearing of personal hardship. Success in life would have come through persistent determination, dogged self-reliance and stubbornness.

At her best, Anne's moods and ways could have been changeful in an acceptable way since new phases in life were liked. There was a tendency for her to free herself from bounds and ties giving her easy elimination of the unwanted. Additionally, she had an inclination to let matters remain as they were, and put up with them, thereby becoming conditioned to trying circumstances. There was equanimity and duality, as well as a search for novelty and sensation—seeking. She enjoyed creativity through art, theatre affairs and happy occupations as well as in any way of being prominent.

Secondly, in a more relaxed way, her nature tended to be unassuming, somewhat retiring, agreeable and sociable. There was also perseverance, carefulness and studiousness, in which her manner appeared cool, cautious and more limited than she really was. Duty, conscience and orderliness would have been important. She seemed to be timid through a feeling of personal inadequacy, perhaps through her father.

Yet she also had a strong, artistic side, with a likelihood of interests in the psychic, the mystical and the occult, so that mediumship could easily have been developed. There was imagination, musical or artistic ability, refinement and sentiment, but also much charitable feeling and sympathy. However, there was a tendency to be impractical and to concentrate on visions of the future rather than on those of the present. In this vein, she was an ideas person basically, which she may well have expressed fluently and effortlessly. At the same time, there could have been too much love of the easy, the beautiful and the pleasant, at any price.

Mentality: Anne's mentality and self-expression would both have suggested possessiveness and conservatism. There was limitation to herself and to her expression. Feelings of inadequacy were possible, e.g. in the areas of short, general communication, basic mental interests and in dealings with siblings, relatives and neighbours. During a rigorous and hard life, lessons of duty and self-control would have been learned. This apart, though, Anne would have had a cheerful, humorous (with ability for repartee) and witty mentality with success through its exercise. She satisfied her urge for creative expression by using her skills in effective communication. She was eager to know as much as possible about a variety of subjects, despite being easily distracted and with an attention that tended to wander. Yet little in life went by her without her clinically studying it and not knowing something really bothered her.

Anne's mind was forceful, incisive, downright and good at debate. It was also acute, but restless and even acrimonious. Though conducive to strong mental action through revolutionary thought, her communicativeness in every way could have become too brusque and independent so that it lost good contact with others. Her addiction to the unusual and unconventional may have become so strong and so awkwardly expressed that she could have become eccentric, odd and tiresome. Her actions tended to come from intuition rather than from reason.

Anne's mind could have been useful for the study of hidden matters. Her tendencies to the intangible derived from a strong imaginative faculty that contained visions, ideals and boundless aims. These could have been of the most ethereal and inspirational kind but she would have needed strength to actualise them (which she had). All imaginings and subtle impressionability would have been strong. Psychic ability was developable. Being highly imaginative, her psyche was opened through her unconscious so that much may have been given out through the reception of ideas and influences. All this may have been used in art, music, dancing, acting, or more practically as love of the sea and all its affairs. Her awakened sensitiveness gave her a keen, internal aspiration to become a channel through which good things could flow. Emphasis would have been on everything summed up as 'the values' and 'the intangibles', e.g. rhythm and colour harmonies as well as kindness and philanthropy. Over-idealism would have been indulged in, and this would have occurred in art, work and/or religion. There would also have been a tendency to day-dream. Her vivid imagination could have become gullible and confused so that her mind was not always well-directed. She could have schemed in an involved way. Resulting touchiness could have induced escapism.

Anne liked pondering on all she had already lived through. She was most comfortable when she could have absorbed all that had presented past memories of security. Her least amount of comfort occurred during the actual living-out of all that she had already had past glimpses of. Thus, she spent much of her time in the backward, introspective, absorbing place, where she felt the safest. It seemed that she herself was afforded the poorest opportunity to express her imagination and creativity.

Her childhood would have been important as many of her thoughts later on would have centred round the feelings she had experienced during those early years. She may have thought that the needs of others were holding her back, particularly those of her own family, but actually it was her own need most of all to express herself in an environment where she was particularly sure of herself; her outer world did not present such an opportunity. Thus, she didn't always express the uniqueness of her identity and purpose through the right channels, but, instead, had a strong tendency to linger in child-like stages of complaining about why her life was not blossoming as she thought it should.

Anne was holding her mental processes in ideal, earlier stages of her emotional development. She experienced much confusion in her conscious mind. She kept thinking that she was lost, but couldn't readily put a finger on the keynote of her feelings. Earlier, she had experienced a great desperation in her thoughts. Later, she kept recreating these same circumstances and events to allow her to re-enact this desperation so that somehow she might finally find the solution to it that she had been seeking.

One of her difficulties consisted of the trouble she had separating her mental energies from her intuition. Losing herself in imagination, thoughts and fantasies, could have kept her out of contact with the sharpness of reality. Often she thought that others did not understand the scope of her ideas that she was trying to express. She may have known and understood things that were simply beyond words, but when she tried to express these in everyday language, she felt that, literally, she lost the very essence of the ideas themselves.

She also experienced confusion between dominance and submissiveness, while, at the same time, she was so emotionally immature at expressing herself outwardly that she tended to take the entire conflict inside herself. In this way, she closed off her own expression, except for more limited forms that did not entirely make her happy. This was a very difficult situation for her because it coloured her entire character with past emotional thoughts, which, dependent upon their nature, would either have allowed, or impeded, the rest of her character from expressing itself. It was only by being raised to newer and higher emotional levels that would have afforded her the security to express herself adequately on the mental plane.

For Anne, depth would have been emphasised. She sought to understand the deepest mysteries. Whether she expressed her drive physically, or transferred it to mental regions, it powered all she sought to understand in the world. She developed a sense of worldly idealism that she found difficult to explain. She experienced just conflict between joining the world as she saw it and desiring to escape it. She did not think of herself as being truly worthy of others' acceptance, and yet, at the same time, she wondered if the values of social acceptance represented any worthwhile reality at all. She aggressively created constant destruction in old, traditional habit patterns so that ultimately she could have gone through a rebirth within herself on the very deepest of levels. Through her inventiveness, she delivered power for change, yet the more she grew discontented with the world around her, the more she began to fathom the mysteries within herself.

<u>Lifestyle:</u> Anne expressed elimination, renewal and regeneration impulsively, in versatile ways, e.g. concerning the possessions of and from others, shared feelings and in the life-force in sex, birth and death (as well as in the after life). Here she was likely to have been explosive, to end conditions and to force new beginnings but with good results after a crisis. Understandably, she had to have learned to withdraw occasionally for quiet moments to allow her imagination and inspiration to flow more freely. Although Anne's methodical tendency would have been less than expected, her inclination towards economy and usefulness would have been more so, giving her persistency and the ability to use her virtues without passing through vices. Additionally, her ambition would have become strong with the internal power necessary to rise through merit and adaptability.

There would have been a particular and rather uncompromising direction to her life-effort. She would have been interested in a cause but with little concern over end results, over her resources or over herself. She would have dipped deeply into life and would have poured forth the gathered results of her experiences with unremitting zeal. Her inclination would have been to act at all times under a consideration of opposing views or through a sensitiveness to contrasting and antagonistic possibilities. She would have existed in a world of conflicts, or of definite polarities. Yet she would have been capable of unique achievement through a development of unsuspected relations in life but was apt to waste her energies through her improper alignment with various situations. Although she may have appeared to have been indecisive, when she had arrived at a decision, it would have been well-considered.

Anne had excellent prospects for getting everything she wanted out of life, because she didn't actually live in the past. Apprehensive about the future, she was usually prepared for anything. Her obsession became mobility (both mental and physical) with a compelling need to achieve comprehension. Accordingly, she undertook a vital search for the meaning of life.

Anne's ideal state was based on past dreams. This usually made her idealistic to the point that she did not easily discipline herself to the standards of society. She always felt that there was a higher music, a more subtle meaning to life and a deeper understanding of what the world called 'love'. Her level of awareness was unusually high, as the traditions and restrictions of society did not bind her creativity. She tended to be on the impractical side, as the scope of her imagination far surpassed the reality of the world around her. As a dreamer and as a seeker of intuitive awareness, she had to try to learn how to balance all that she felt with all that she must deal with on a more practical level. Thus, it was not enough for her to imagine something idealistically wonderful. She had to find ways to impress her dreams into reality.

Later on, she tended to withdraw from the creative process. She then spent much of her time in retreat into a dream world that had become her reality. She became so deeply appreciative of life itself that creating things for herself was far less important to her than just experiencing the essence of all that she could absorb.

Relationships

<u>Others:</u> Anne would have been popular with an ease of attracting others, or the public in general, by her sheer, innate charm. This easy charm would have been intense and so may well have been overdone.

Anne tended to assume that she was the subject of any conversation that didn't include her. She had the mistaken idea that others knew more than she did, as she was overly cautious in asserting herself in challenging situations. Thus, she was guarded in expressing herself because she wanted to avoid antagonising anyone. She always gave others the benefit of the doubt. She might have been surprised to learn that others considered her to be a walking encyclopaedia, who would have been qualified to discuss any topic. In fact, she was a real instructor and inspirer of others. She had a strong desire to exert for others in kindly, self-sacrificing ways. She would have been highly compassionate and often would have sacrificed much for the needs of others. She was one who would have given generously, not only without expecting something in return but not even wanting the receiving person to know that she was the giver.

Samaritan work was extended to others (but also could have been received). However, her efforts could have become confused and muddles made.

But Anne could also have been selfish with others. She would have been constantly questioning their values. She was so linked with others' values that whether she liked it or not, she was strongly influenced by public consciousness. She was restless too, and uneasy when forced to submit to others' demands. She had a strong desire to be independently secure and free of obligation to others.

Anne's pre-occupation with financial security gave people confidence that she could have helped them in their business affairs. They believed that she would have served their interests well, because she showed a great deal of self-confidence.

Friends: Anne responded playfully to immediate contacts. Friends were kindly and likely to have affinity with 'the values', 'the intangibles' and/or maritime pursuits. She liked to feel needed by her friends because she got much deep meaning from them. In return, she was well-liked by her friends because she didn't threaten their egos. There was never a dull moment when she was around because she lent sparkle and wit to any gathering. She gave and accepted help from close friends. She helped them when they needed it, probably because they had helped her previously. However, she had to invest as much effort in securing her own future as she did in helping her friends when they asked for favours from her. On balance, she would have benefitted through friends and patrons—or even by charity, if it had been needed.

But Anne didn't want to feel obliged to anyone, so she maintained a certain distance from even her closest friends. She was sociable and charming but she wouldn't have tolerated anyone who made demands on her.

Family: There was likely to have been a cleavage in her life relating to parents or to early childhood.

Her parents had provided her with many opportunities to promote her creativity and they were willing to sustain her in developing them. Yet she mustn't have waited for parental approval before exploiting her talents. It was highly likely that her parents' enormous influence during her early years would have been the deciding factor in whether she could have risen to fulfil her creativity. But she alone would have had to make the choice. Her parents may have resisted her efforts to make a life of her own, which could have strained their relationship. However, she knew the importance of thinking for herself, even though she had been strongly conditioned to pattern her thinking after her parents' beliefs. Later on, she may have resented their intrusion. For example, she would have hated to have been told that it would have been risky for her to leave home because she would have wanted to make up her own mind, even though she would have had to have learned the hard way. Even if she had moved away from her birthplace, she would have returned often to renew old ties because those to her family were so strong.

Although she would have enjoyed favourable relations with her brothers and sisters, she easily quarrelled with loved ones. There may well have been some harsh conditions and quarrels at home.

Anne would have been a good parent and partner because her youthful joviality was immediately disarming. Her children would have adored her, and her partner would have known that she would have wanted a comfortable lifestyle with an abundance of happiness and contentment. She may even have chosen to sublimate her dreams for those of her children so that they would have had a chance to succeed when she either couldn't or wouldn't. However, at times, Anne's tendencies towards moodiness, quarrelling and subsequent uneasy expression of affection, could have led to lack of harmony at home.

<u>Lover:</u> Anne had a very strong and romantic sexual nature. This often distracted her from more important issues and kept her from capitalising on her gifts. She was not accustomed to having her desires frustrated and she became very impatient when her lover was non-committal about their relationship. To her, sexuality represented the most unfathomable question of all.

Sensuous, her affection was keen and ardent but self-seeking. Love affairs would have been numerous and very happy. Partnerships would have been beneficial and successful. However, troubles may have been caused by too many love affairs. Her desire for partnership may have been overdone with a restless lack of ability to be happy alone. Partnerships could also have been disappointing and have lacked dependability (and if in business, should have been made as foolproof as possible). There was confusion in love affairs and even deception. Secret partnerships may have been formed. Unusualness in her expression of love, or in artistic accomplishment or in any kind of partnership, would have been delightful, intriguing and fascinating. There would have been an easy slipping away from one attraction and the quick forming of another. Partings would have been likely, but for good reasons, with pleasant replacements or reunions.

But Anne quarrelled easily with loved ones. Her more serious affection could have become most difficult to express. Life could have become solitary. Any serious partnership would have brought responsibility so that there would have been sorrow or loss through her affections. Yet her partner and her children would have meant everything to her and she would have more than satisfied their expectations. Success would have come more readily if her effort had been shared with a sympathetic partner, someone who understood her shortcomings and anxieties and who could have supported her in making the most of her creativity. If their careers had been parallel, then this would have stimulated them to grow together.

Career

<u>Early:</u> Anne's fate was likely to have been unfortunate and possibly disastrous. However, owing to her good environment, she may have succeeded in raising herself above mediocrity. To help here, she had plenty of successful opportunities, a feeling that 'good luck' was to have been expected and a fortunate journey through life, meeting helpful people. Disharmony in her nature could have urged her to accomplishment. In addition, her parents gave her the training she needed to achieve her objectives by using her creativity.

It was urgent that she acquired as much training as possible in order to deal with competitors. With education, her ability to meet challenges would have been improved so much that no-one would have been able to intimidate her with claims of great competence. She mustn't have been embarrassed because her competitors were better informed. Although she was well-read and would have learned easily, a formal education would have been essential for her success. It would have been fun to ask questions but it was the answers that counted. She had to be sure that she didn't overstate her own abilities, because making claims about her qualifications that she couldn't possibly have lived up to, would certainly have ruined her image. She might have been tempted to do this because she was repelled by the idea of being forced into an obscure position. But this needed never to have happened, if she had used her natural talent for learning. A good education was very necessary, otherwise there was a tendency for her to be too easily influenced by surrounding conditions. Because she was very conservative except when opposed or angered, she would have got into a groove. If she had developed great expertise in her career, then her credentials certainly would have been recognised. However, she may have found it difficult to satisfy her family obligations and still have devoted enough time and energy to getting an education. She must have been as determined to find answers as she was to ask questions, or she would have been poorly equipped for open competition. Once she had understood that achieving depended on being competent, she might have considered getting more training through formal education.

Anne's most urgent priority, despite limitations imposed by other people, should have been making her own way in life. Her objectives would have been inspired by 'hunches', which, usually, would have been proved right. She knew how to use her talents and resources to plan for the future. Satisfying her ambitions honestly would have been important to her. However, she underestimated her potential so that she may have hesitated to apply herself as she should. Although hard-working, she often day-dreamed, when a more decisive approach would have given her the yield she had wanted from her efforts. She knew that in order to develop and achieve her goals, she must have been allowed to think for herself, uninfluenced by anyone else, although she may have kept close ties with her parents. She knew that, in the long run, she would have stood strong on her own merits. Her good memory, coupled with her store of knowledge, would have served her well.

<u>Vocation:</u> Purely physical work was not for Anne because it wouldn't have allowed her to extend herself to the fullest. Solving her own day-by-day problems, and helping others with theirs, would have added much meaning to her life. Although change would have been important to allow her to grow, she tended to resist it, fearing that she wasn't ready for it. She would have been most secure and comfortable working at home, or at least in familiar surroundings. She was not basically an optimist, but she would have become more so with each success. Finding the proper vehicle for putting her ideas to work would have been a matter of great concern for her but there was a strong possibility that she could have expressed her gifted

imagination through writing. She had a good blend of feeling and the ability to express it.

Anne's career should have brought her into close contact with the public. She had an obligation to bring her talent before the public. She never had to assume that she knew everything there was to know about people, because dealing with the public required her to be at least one step ahead of their demands. Public response, however, would have motivated her more than she would have expected. Through a career in communications, she could have applied her ideas effectively and gained greater self-confidence in her abilities.

Anne would also have been suited for some quiet, or unambitious, occupation than for one involving publicity, responsibility or conflict. Yet she would also have been good for martial occupations (!) and some kinds of businesses. Her quiet temperament would have been suitable for a career working with young people or children.

Anne was fond of money. She liked to make it by pleasant ways to do with art, beauty, lovely clothes and flowers. She would have been diplomatic and pleasant over money-making and would have enjoyed it for the sake of the lovely things it brought. She would have been successful and happy in this depending on circumstances.

Anne's mind could have become that of a visionary, artist, poet, mimic and spiritualist. Similarly, interest in the sea, in mysticism and in hidden things would have been pursued with energy and with desire to experiment in new ways. She may well have shown enthusiasm for dancing, psychic sensitivity, or in any form of idealism such as in art, work or religion. She may have enjoyed the performing or graphic arts as a medium for expressing her creativity, although she realised that either of these would have required considerable training.

Middle: Anne had executive drive and was apt to adapt her allegiances to lines along which she could have made her efforts count for the most. Knowing that success required determination and hard work, she tended to over-extend herself physically. She expended energy in hard and unstinting work and she expected the same from others. She had always wanted to be an active participant, and she abhorred those who lacked the backbone to get involved with important issues.

Anne's ability to learn and to find ways to use her imagination was a strong point in her favour, and her resourcefulness allowed her to achieve security through her endeavours. Her imagination worked overtime, dreaming up new goals and objectives to turn her attention to. She never felt that she had exhausted the available opportunities. She applied her excellent imagination to concrete affairs. As a result, 'Castles in the Air' would have been converted into reality. Very hard work may have been done for idealistic ends. Her results may have been disappointing and elusive because all was too imaginary. Irregular, over-glamorous, escapist ways could have brought about failure. Her inspired imaginings had great potential but she had to have believed this to make them happen. It wasn't always easy for her to put her ideas to work because she doubted sometimes that they would have succeeded. Her only alternative would have been to promote her ideas at every opportunity. More often than not, her suggestions would have been accepted.

Anne's superiors admired her for doing more than her share of tasks. But she tended to have too many irons in the fire. Also, she was somewhat subject to upsets and to forced new phases. She knew that she would have succeeded in winning public respect for her accomplishments because she considered it a moral responsibility to do her best to serve the public interest. She would have been attracted to situations in which she must have had to extend herself before the public, but her early conditioning made her have misgivings about doing this.

Anne would have developed the skills required to earn a good living because she had a great need for security. She knew that she had to apply herself diligently to achieve security for herself and her family. Her parents had taught her this and she would have been grateful to them for encouraging her to accept responsibility. Energy was expressed in home affairs in quick and able ways. However, her desire for the finer things of life made her careless about financial resources. She found it difficult to hold onto her money when she was tempted to splurge on buying things she wanted rather than on those she really needed. She wanted to accumulate enough money to make investments so as to assure her future financial independence. She felt that when she had developed her talents and ideas, they would have adequately provided for her needs. But she would have had to use her financial resources wisely if she had wanted to satisfy her material needs and still have had sufficient funds to develop her creativity. And so, she became increasingly concerned about her resources.

<u>Late:</u> Anne tried to hold on to what she owned to provide security for her later years. She would have found it shattering to have been without any means of support, so she made sure she could always have converted some of her assets into cash, if necessary. The energy she put into her endeavours ensured her of a substantial return later in life when security would have been more important than previously.

Appearance and Health

<u>Appearance:</u> Anne would have been of average height with a square, fleshy build of body and face, leading to stoutness later, with perhaps small and short limbs. She would have had a pale complexion, full eyes, prominent brows, an aquiline nose and profile with a tendency to a double chin. Her hair would have been plentiful, dark and probably thick, curly and waving.

Her bodily communication, i.e. walking, would have been undertaken keenly and with speed.

<u>Health:</u> Anne had good, strong health and vitality but her nervous system tended to be poor. She tended to overextend herself physically but she would have been a good sleeper. By being more moderate, she could have avoided exhaustion and anxiety. However, there was danger of accidents, some liability to feverish complaints, fits and apoplexy. Strange fears would have played upon her nerves; her health could have been undermined by these, by susceptibility to fish poisoning or by harm from impure water. Her death would have occurred in a public place.

Anne's natal charts do not show any strong indicators for eye troubles (like her elder sister, but both have closely similar Morin

Points around 20^0 Pisces, c.f. Henry III, Edward I and Richard II) gout or pregnancy problems but one possible root source of trouble for Anne could have derived from dyspepsia, indicated by the significantly strong opposition of the Sun to the Moon at Epoch.

Reference: 'Queen Anne', Edward Gregg, Yale English Monarch Series, University Press, New Haven, Conn., U.S.A., 2nd Ed., 2001.

Appendix 1

Presentation, Discussion and Comments on the Natal Charts of England's Rulers (1456-1714)

King Henry VII

For his Epoch chart, the planetary distribution is mainly North, indicating Henry's subjectivity, whereas the overall chart shaping is a 'Bucket' with the Moon and retrograde Saturn as the clockwise handles to Neptune (retrograde) in weak opposition to the Mars/Venus conjunction, as the bucket's 'rim'. This suggests that there would be a particular and uncompromising direction to Henry's life-effort. There are two major Specific Interplanetary Aspect Patterns present in this chart. Firstly, notice the Grand-Trine-in-Fire kite having Saturn (retrograde) in Sagittarius in the 9th House as its focus (it's also one of the "Bucket's" handles) in opposition to Mercury in Gemini, which Mercury rules, in the 3rd House. Simply, this indicates accumulated wisdom, but also dreary discipline leading to mental loneliness. However, there is ample, favourable mediation here. Secondly, there is a mutable T-square having the Venus/Mars conjunction as its focus, bi-square to Jupiter and to the Moon but also is favourably mediated by trines and sextiles to the conjunction. Overall, this suggests an adjustment to difficulties and attempts to by-pass them but rarely without nervous stress. The Sun in Taurus—Moon in Sagittarius sign polarity indicates that Henry's determination inclined him to go to extremes, whereas the Sun in 3rd—Moon in 10th House polarity shows that he preferred activity that brought him before the public even though he was wary of potential, personal abuses, as he was easily unsettled. The Sun semi-square to

Figure 1: Epoch Chart for King Henry VII of England.

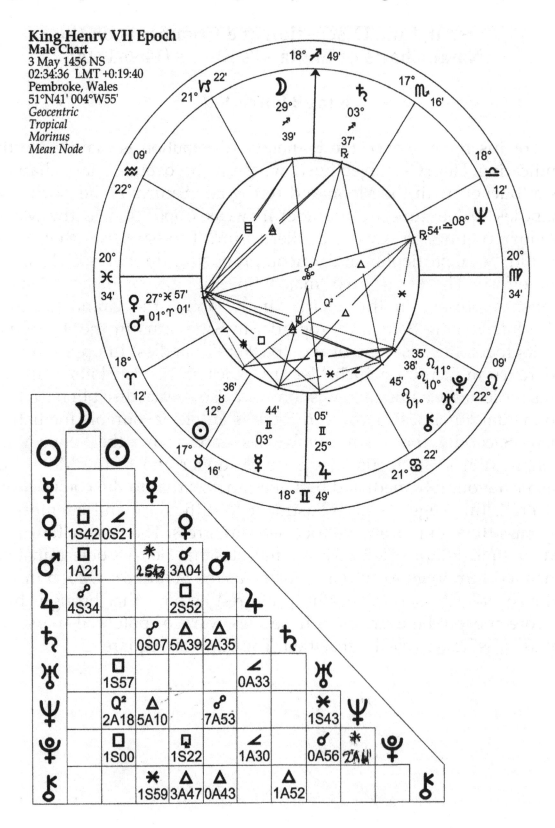

Venus shows an irresponsible tendency to beauty and ease, whereas its square to the Uranus/Pluto conjunction suggests strong self-will and a tendency to advance himself ruthlessly at others' expense. The Moon square to the Venus/Mars conjunction shows moodiness and a lack of harmony at home. The Moon's opposition to Jupiter indicates extravagance. The Morin Point in the 3rd Pisces decanate reveals a strongly artistic personality with an interest in psychic affairs. Conventionality and the material side of life would have been cultivated resulting in hardness. The ruler, Neptune retrograde in Libra in the 8th House shows that Henry's capacity to receive impressions would have added to his gentle charm. The sextile of Neptune to Uranus suggests that he could have transformed his ideals into actuality but probably that he would have been suspicious of others' motives. Pluto (sub-ruler) in Leo in the 6th House indicates self-confidence and an ability to mobilise his resources. Its conjunction with Uranus shows his ability to solve difficult problems.

The Epoch chart generates Henry's Ideal Birth chart (see Figure 2). Notice that in both charts there are six quintile aspects altogether to support an interpretation of good intelligence. For the Birth chart the planetary distribution is mainly South and West indicating that Henry was objective but that his destiny lay mainly in the hands of others and depended on prevailing circumstances. The overall chart shaping is 'See-Saw' suggesting that Henry existed in a world of conflicts but would have been capable of unique achievement through unexpected events in his life. He may have appeared to be indecisive but his final choices would have been well-considered. Examination of the chart for Special Interplanetary Aspect Patterns reveals that all the four oppositions in the chart are mediated favourably. In addition, note that Neptune is bi-sextile to Pluto and Saturn and that Saturn is bi-sextile to the Sun and to Neptune. Note also that all five planets in the South West quadrant, as well as Nep-

<u>Figure 2:</u> Birth Chart for King Henry VII of England.

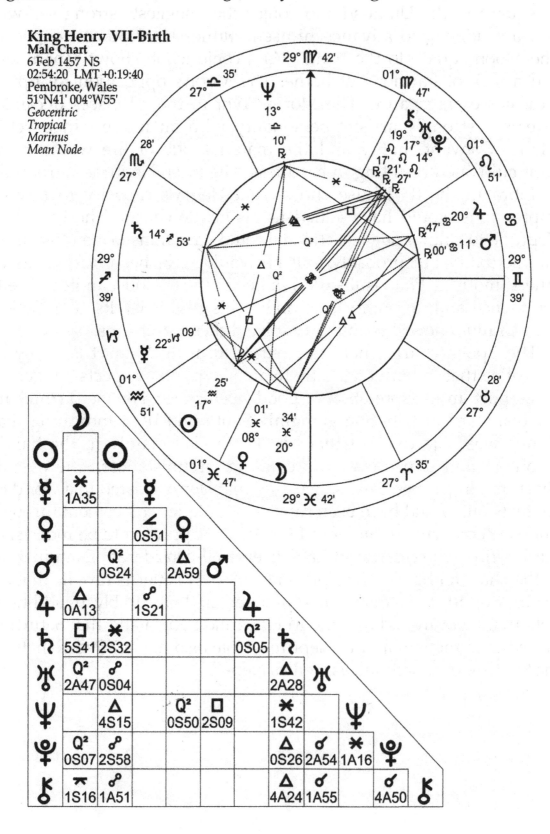

tune near the midheaven, are retrograde. Finally, note that Uranus is exactly opposite to the Sun and at the same time is the central planet of the triple conjunction with Chiron and Pluto, i.e. the main focus of the chart. Neptune's chart situation suggests that certain people could intimidate Henry fairly easily, that secretly, he doubted that he could ever have achieved in life and that he would have been a friend to those in need. Saturn's chart situation shows that Henry's apprehension among competitors caused him to choose mature friends carefully.

The Sun in Aquarius—Moon in Pisces sign polarity shows much perseverance, carefulness and studiousness. In some ways, his nature would have been unassuming; he would have benefitted through friends. The Sun in the 3rd—Moon in the 4th House polarity suggests that he tended to confuse his emotions with his rational thinking. On the other hand, the Sun exactly opposite to Uranus shows self-will, the opposition to Pluto shows ruthlessness towards others and the opposition to Chiron shows support for profound study but with difficulty. Its biquintile to Mars indicates strengthened self-expression. The Moon exactly biquintile to Pluto reveals changeful yet acceptable moods, the strong trine to Jupiter indicates good health and the sextile to Mercury suggests good commonsense and nervous force. The Morin Point in the 3rd Sagittarius decanate shows an honourable character that inspired respect. Travel and outdoor life would have pleased him. Retrograde Jupiter (the ruler) in Cancer in the 8th House suggests a lack of sophistication but sympathetic and protective ways. Probably, his death would have occurred with a feeling of release. Jupiter's trine to the Moon indicates a tendency to a 'do-nothing' attitude about his future goals. Its opposition to Mercury shows that, at times, his judgement would have been poor, whereas its exact biquintile to Saturn reveals his interest in what motivated people to deal with him. Retrograde Mars in Cancer in the 7th House shows his need for protection as well as some disorientation in his relationships with others. Mars trine Venus shows warmth and enthusiasm in affection but its square to Neptune indicates that very hard work done for idealistic ends may have ended disappointingly. Retrograde Uranus in the 9th House in Leo reveals: 1) Henry's independence of others to the extent that he hardly ever asked for outside advice; 2) his hunger for power and 3) his anxious desire to assimilate new philosophy. Uranus trine Saturn shows his skill in management and his faith that he could accomplish nearly anything. Retrograde Pluto in Leo in the 8th House indicates his willingness to overthrow power for the sake of transformation and his constant questioning of others' values. Pluto trine Saturn reveals his ability to concentrate deeply and his almost buried inner-drive to make a contribution to society. Its trine to Neptune implies intensified sensitivity, while its opposition to the Sun suggests that he held strong opinions about unsatisfactory social conditions.

--—--—--—--—--—--—--—--—--—--—--—--—--—--—--—--—--—--—---

King Henry VIII

For Henry's Epoch chart, the planets lie more prominently above the Earth (to the South) showing objectivity, and to the West showing that his destiny lay mainly in the hands of others and depended on circumstances. The Overall Shaping of the chart is a 'Bucket' with Chiron as the perpendicular handle but also with retrograde Jupiter as an anticlockwise handle to the Moon opposition to Mars (ruler) as the bucket's rim. This suggests a particular and uncompromising direction to Henry's life-effort. Retrograde Jupiter in Gemini in the 3rd House indicates that his philosophies of life were based on the ideas of others and that he tended to be abrupt. There is a cardinal T-cross comprising the bucket's rim with the Chiron-Pluto opposition (without mediation, suggesting elimination of support, help and charity) with Mars (ruler) as the cross's focus. This reveals Henry's intention to surmount difficulties but not without nervous stress. Notice that Uranus on the Midheaven, is almost unaspected save for the medium to weak conjunction with Saturn, suggesting a changeful career with some control that may have led to some brilliant results. The Sun in Libra—Moon in Capricorn sign polarity shows musical ability and neatness but also that his emotions and impulses would have been disciplined and regulated. The Sun in the 7th—Moon in the 11th House polarity indicates that he could have had the talent to promote others' ideas to his own advantage. The Sun trine Jupiter shows good luck, good opportunities and contentedness with a gift for conversation and dramatic ability. The Moon trine Mercury reveals a good, commonsense mentality and enjoyment of the world around him; its square to Pluto suggests upsets and forced new phases and its exact square to Chiron reveals a strong, negative response to support, help and charity. The Morin Point in the first Aries decanate indicates an open disposition, a

Figure 3: Epoch Chart for King Henry VIII of England.

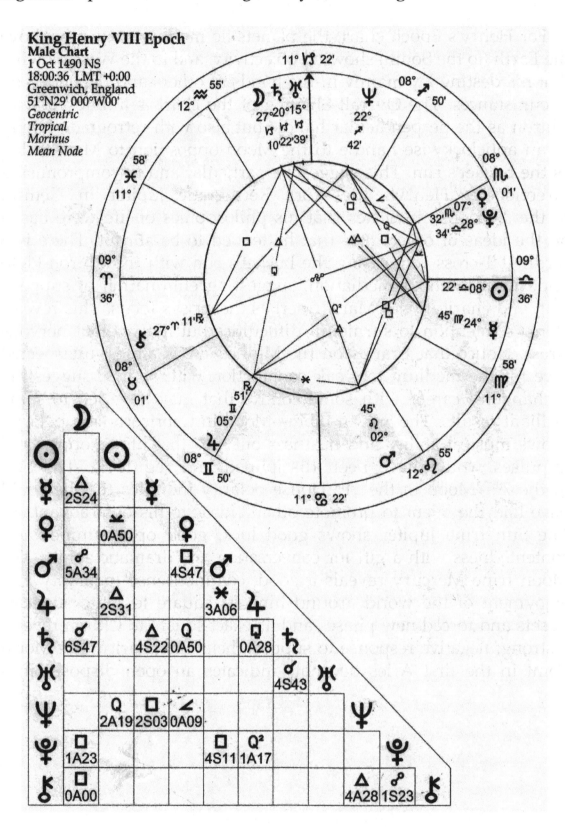

King Henry VIII Epoch
Male Chart
1 Oct 1490 NS
18:00:36 LMT +0:00
Greenwich, England
51°N29' 000°W00'
Geocentric
Tropical
Morinus
Mean Node

tendency to rash action and an ability to work hard, particularly at administration. The ruler, Mars in Leo in the 5th House, shows a dominating insistence on being over-forceful and its medium square to Venus shows that a cutting harshness was likely to have entered into relations of affection.

The Epoch chart generates Henry's Ideal Birth chart (see Figure 4). Altogether, in both charts, there are seven quintile family aspects to support an interpretation of good intelligence. The planetary distribution is mainly to the East but also to the South and West that confirms Henry's objectivity. His destiny was shared between himself, others and prevailing conditions. The Overall Shaping of this chart is 'See-Saw' (containing four oppositions) revealing that his well-chosen actions were the result, at all times, of a consideration of opposing views. Mars is at the focus of a mutable T-square that is mediated favourably by a Grand Trine in earth. In combination, these patterns show Henry's inability to know when to remain silent but also his diligence at putting his ideas to work, both of which were helped by his ability at debate but not by a tendency to a lack of control. Notice that Venus in Gemini in the 11th House is bi-trine (to 3rd and 7th) to Mars and to Saturn showing that Henry focused on achieving a comfortable and abundant lifestyle enriched by his career and good friends. The Sun in Cancer—Moon in Aries sign polarity shows activity, much prudence and a great deal of impulse— his parents would have affected him considerably. The Sun in the 1st—Moon in the 10th House polarity indicates the conflict between his early development and his drive to achieve in life and that he needed to be very careful before committing himself to marriage. The Sun square to the Moon shows a cleavage in his life relating to parents or to early childhood that would have urged him to achieve. The Sun strongly bi-quintile to Mars and to Chiron shows boldness but that any support, help and charity were conservatively directed towards

<u>Figure 4:</u> Birth Chart for King Henry VIII of England.

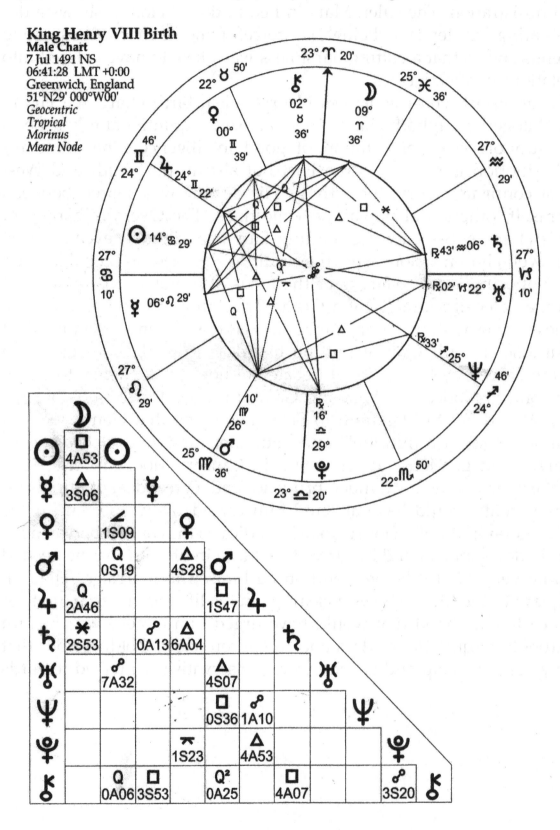

his own career matters. The Moon (ruler) once again trine Mercury emphasises his commonsense mentality and nervous force. The Morin Point in the 3rd Cancer decanate indicates a restless personality that may have been tempered by an hospitable, easy-going and sympathetic, comfort-loving disposition. Retrograde Neptune (sub-ruler) in Sagittarius in the 6th House square to Mars suggests that very hard work may have been done for idealistic ends but that imaginary, over-glamorous ways may have led to failure. His over-sensitivity would also have caused trouble. Yet Henry would also have experienced a heightened consciousness of the world and his place in it, which he could have brought down to a personal level (with difficulty), where it could have been of use. The Sun rising in Cancer shows Henry's fondness for company (particularly female) and Mercury rising in Leo indicates a bombastic nature as well as a lack of concentration on objectives. Mercury's strong opposition to Saturn suggests dreary planning, possibly leading to mental loneliness.

King Edward VI

The planetary distribution at Edward's Epoch is mainly to the West and to the South suggesting that his destiny lay mainly in the hands of others and depended on circumstances; he would have been mainly objective. The overall shaping of the chart is 'Splay' (i.e. planets in groups irregularly spaced around the chart) showing individual, or purposeful emphases in his life. A Yod to retrograde Saturn as the focus, in Virgo in the 2nd House, is the main special interplanetary aspect pattern in the chart. It suggests transformation through trying to re-establish his past ideals. Additionally, the Moon, in Leo and again, in the 2nd House, is bi-biquintile to Pluto and to Neptune showing that being well-informed would have increased his security and helped to stabilise his career. Note also that retrograde Uranus is rising in Leo suggesting that he would have been a high energy loner. In addition, the Sun closely conjoint Mars in Capricorn in the 7th House while indicating a robust, over-active manner also shows that he would still have been dependent on opportunities provided by others. The Sun in Capricorn—Moon in Leo sign polarity reveals that his personal, affectionate instincts would have conflicted with his internal ambitious ones. The Sun in the 7th—Moon in the 2nd House polarity confirms that his success in life would have required focusing on the affairs of others. We have already mentioned briefly the interpretation of the Sun exactly conjoint Mars. The Moon exactly trine Mercury shows a good, commonsense mentality and nervous force. The Morin Point in the 3rd Cancer decanate suggests a restless personality tempered by an hospitable, sympathetic and comfort-loving disposition. Although studious and intuitive, he would also have been anxious and hypersensitive. His sub-ruler, Neptune, well-

Figure 5: Epoch Chart for King Edward VI.

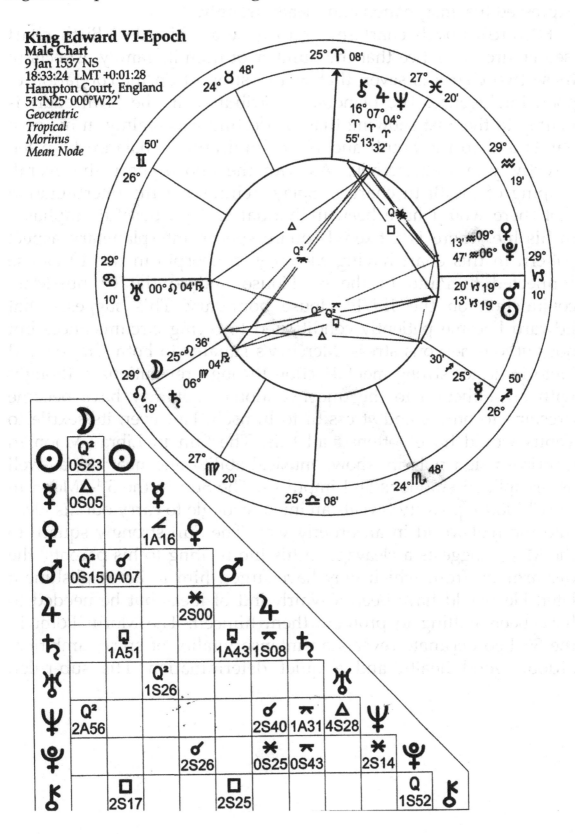

aspected in Aries in the 9th House shows that he would have expressed his imagination and ideals strongly.

Edward's Epoch chart serves to generate his Ideal Birth chart (see Figure 6). Notice that the number of quintile family aspects in these two charts is seven that would support an interpretation of good intelligence. The planetary distribution in the Birth chart is mainly to the East showing that his destiny was mainly in his own hands and to the South and North indicating a balance between objectivity and subjectivity. As with the Epoch chart, the overall shaping of the Birth chart is 'Splay' reinforcing the interpretation that there would have been individual and purposeful emphases in his life. There is a fixed T-square special interplanetary aspect pattern in this chart having Mercury in Scorpio in the 4th House connected to Pluto in the 6th House and to the Uranus-Mars conjunction on the 12th/1st House boundary. This suggests that Edward became patiently conditioned to trying circumstances but not without nervous stress. Mercury's squares to both Uranus and Pluto indicates strong mental action through revolutionary thought with an addiction to the unconventional that may have become tiresome to others and stressful to himself. However, its sextile to Venus would have softened all this. The Sun in Libra—Moon in Capricorn sign polarity shows musical ability and neatness as well as disciplined emotions and impulses. The Sun in the 3rd—Moon in the 6th House polarity reveals an inner struggle to carry out his ideas into the real world in an orderly way. The Sun strongly square to the Moon suggests a cleavage in his life relating to his parents, the disharmony from which may have urged him to accomplishment later. He would have been a whirlwind of ideas but he needed to have been willing to promote them himself. The Morin Point in the 3rd Leo decanate reveals an intense vitality of spirit, ambition, ardour, good health and a quiet determination. His sub-ruler,

Figure 6: Birth Chart for King Edward VI.

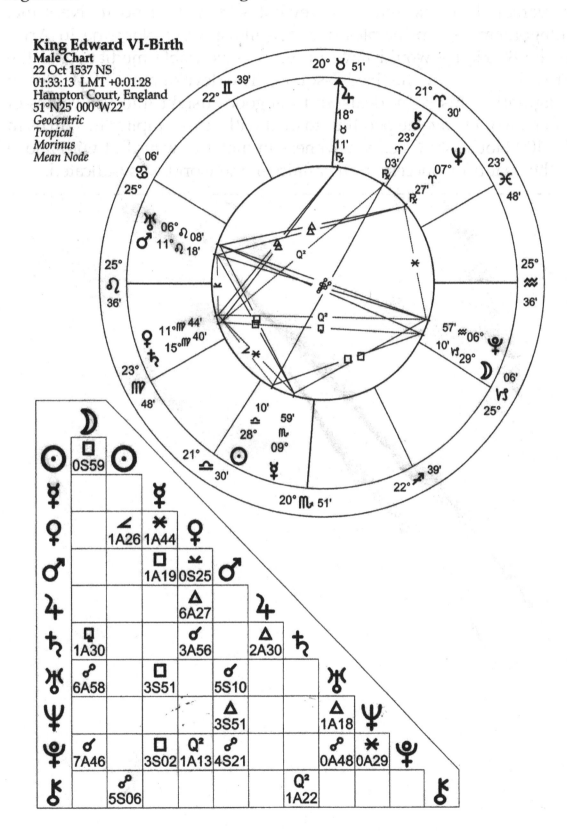

Mars rising in Leo and poorly aspected shows temper, energy in personal affairs and a somewhat softened (trine to Neptune) antagonism. The principles of the well-aspected Neptune in Aries in the 8th House would have provided favourable mediation of the stress imparted by the fixed T-square. The development of his strong imagination, his keen ideals and his good insight into the values of others, would have helped him to deal with stress. Jupiter in Taurus in the 10th House shows expansiveness in material ways but with a love of the beautiful. Success in the affairs of the world was indicated.

Mary I

The planetary distribution at Mary's Epoch (see Figure 7) lies mainly to the East indicating that her destiny lay largely in her own hands; and mostly to the North, indicating subjectivity more than objectivity. The overall shaping of the chart is a somewhat distorted 'Bowl' having Saturn opposition to Mercury as the Bowl's main rim. Here Saturn is the leading planet. All this suggests that she would have advocated some cause; that she would have tried to capture various life phases, that she would always have had something to give to her fellows and that she would always have had something to bear. There are no Specific Interplanetary Aspect Patterns in her chart save some weak, favourable mediation of the Saturn to Mercury opposition by a medium strength quintile to Chiron and a weak trine to the Moon. The Sun in Gemini—Moon in Aquarius sign polarity shows much mental and physical activity and so indicates that she could have received a good education. The Sun in 4th—Moon in 12th House polarity reveals an inner harmony that was reflected in her serene disposition. The Sun trine to retrograde Neptune (ruler) suggests strong, imaginative faculties. However, the Moon sesquiquadrate Jupiter indicates tendencies to squander gains and to be extravagant. The Morin Point in the first Pisces decanate shows a strongly artistic personality with a tendency to look too much to the future. Retrograde Neptune (ruler) in Aquarius in the 12th House shows a good sense of overview and, eventually, of improved tolerance. The quintile to Venus suggests sweetness of character but a tendency to live in the clouds too much. Retrograde Mercury in Gemini in the 4th House reinforces the notion that she was a born student and that she could have been a good communicator, although her thoughts may have seemed disjointed at times. The

Figure 7: Epoch Chart for Queen Mary I of England.

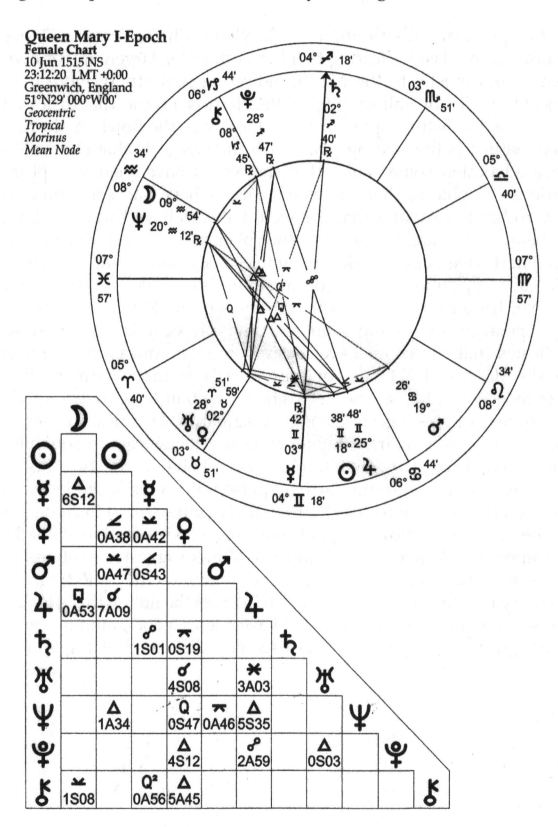

strong opposition to Saturn strongly indicates rigid mental discipline leading to mental loneliness. The biquintile to Chiron reveals that to realise her fondest dreams she would have had to make a deliberate attempt to do so.

Mary's Epoch chart generates her Ideal Birth chart (see Figure 8). Notice that the number of quintile aspects in both of these charts is three, which gives support to an interpretation of intelligence. The planetary distribution of the Birth chart is mainly to the East thereby reinforcing the corresponding interpretation of the Epoch chart that her destiny lay mainly in her own hands. The North-South distribution is roughly equal indicating a mixture of subjectivity and objectivity. The overall shaping is a 'Bucket' using the Mars-Jupiter opposition as the Bucket's rim and the Moon as the somewhat clockwise handle planet (the stronger Sun-Moon opposition may have been chosen as a rim but then there would have been two Bucket handles, i.e. Jupiter and Uranus, as well as an unoccupied half of the Bucket's contents). The former choice suggests that Mary adapted her allegiances so that her efforts would have counted for the most and that she would have dipped deeply into life. The Moon handle suggests a somewhat impulsive inclination to be of service, in which she reservedly dealt with detail in her mother's affairs. The Sun in Pisces—Moon in Virgo sign polarity suggests good, all-round ability and a good worker. Additionally, her mentality would have been well-developed, in which imagination and intuition blended with well with intellect. The Sun in the 2nd—Moon in the 8th House polarity shows an uncomfortable, confusing contrast between her active desire nature and her passive, emotional one. The Sun strongly opposing the Moon indicates a cleavage in her life relating to parents or to early childhood but the strong trine to Jupiter provides favourable mediation because, generally, she would have been cheerful, optimistic and contented. She would also have done more

Figure 8: Birth Chart for Queen Mary I of England.

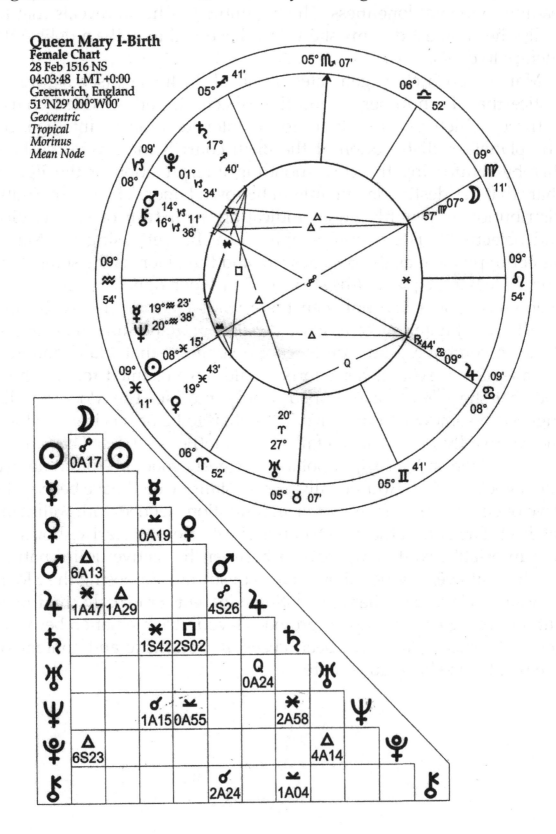

for others than she did for herself. The Morin Point in the 1ˢᵗ Aquarius decanate shows independence, originality and even eccentricity. She would have had some intellectual interests and have been attracted by new and unusual theories. Uranus (ruler) in Aries in the 4ᵗʰ House suggests vehement and assertive expression as well as frequent changes in her home. The quintile to Jupiter indicates excessively expansive ways that could have proved helpful to Mary as the Queen. Mercury strongly conjoint Neptune and rising in Aquarius reveals humanitarian and scientific interests that probably would have been widespread as well as directed inwards towards herself. This conjunction indicates a mind that could take varied patterns as wax takes an imprint but that, although talkative, she would also have needed times of quiet and withdrawal. The sextile of the conjunction to Saturn imparts order, control and practicality to her thoughts, whereas the semi-sextile to Venus indicates balance and ease with clouds of glory rather than any real delusion. However, the square of Venus to Saturn shows that her affection would have been difficult to express, that it would have led to sorrow and to loss, that her life would have tended to be solitary and that any partnership would have brought responsibility.

Elizabeth I

The planetary distribution of Elizabeth's Epoch chart is to the South indicating objectivity. The overall shaping of the chart is a distorted (i.e. without a rim) 'Bucket' with retrograde Saturn conjoint retrograde Uranus in Cancer in the 3rd House as the somewhat clockwise (impulsive) handle. This shows that she had a particular direction to her life, into which she dipped deeply. The handle suggests that practical planning and determined self-will could unite to produce brilliant results but stressfully. Uranus, in particular, indicates that she would have been responsive to the new order of civilisation. The Sun in Capricorn—Moon in Aquarius sign polarity reveals splendid organising ability, with success in large undertakings, probably through careful forethought and steady persistence. The Sun in the 9th—Moon in the 10th House polarity shows that emotional identification with her parents was a powerful force in her life. Perhaps this delayed her becoming established independently. At first, she would have needed a champion. The Sun, almost exactly semisextile to the Mars—Jupiter conjunction in Sagittarius in the 8th House shows that she expressed herself strongly, yet worked hard without annoyance to others. The Moon semisquare to Neptune and quincunx to Uranus reveals that imaginative ideas may have been expressed perversely. The biquintile to Saturn imparts control and shows that duty stopped her full experience of love but that the duty did lead to some acceptable happiness. The Morin Point in the 1st Taurus decanate indicates that a love of pleasure and social life brought popularity but hadn't to be overdone. Venus (the ruler) in Sagittarius in the 8th House indicates that she didn't wish to be enchained but that there would have been gain through marriage. Mercury exactly quintile to Neptune shows a

Figure 9: Epoch chart for Queen Elizabeth I of England

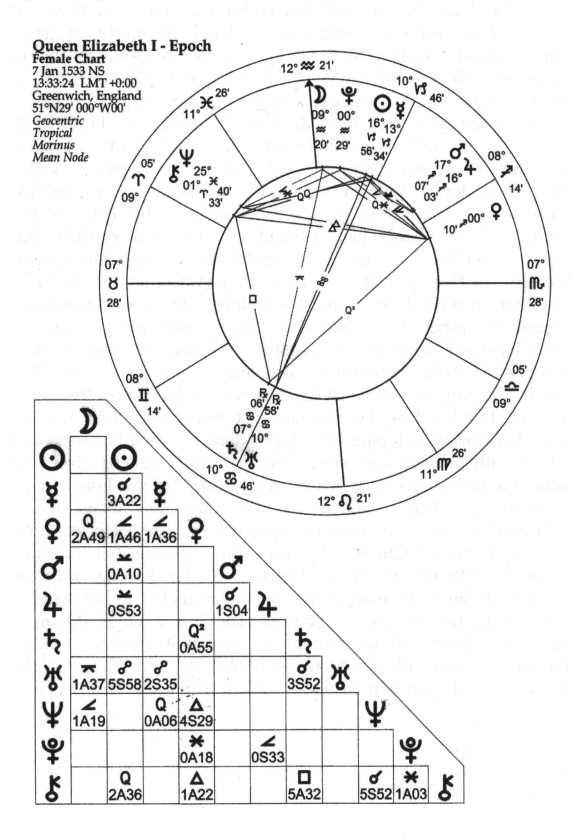

fertile imagination and gentle kindliness; its opposition to Uranus, on the other hand, shows revolutionary, brusque communication that may have lost good contact with others. Mars in Sagittarius in the 8th House reveals enthusiasm for far-flung ideas, but exaggerative and off at a tangent. She would have dealt with finance for others. The close conjunction with Jupiter suggests vastly increased energy.

Her Epoch generates her Ideal Birth chart (see Figure 10). Notice that in both charts there are five quintile family aspects altogether to support an interpretation of intelligence. Notice also that, in total, there are seven opposition aspects in the two charts, reminiscent of those in her father's charts, but hers are less severe. Still, she would have existed in a world of conflicts but would, nevertheless, have been capable of unique achievement through a development of unsuspected events in her life.

For her Birth chart, the planets lie mainly to the North suggesting subjectivity rather than objectivity. The planets also lie mainly to the West indicating that her destiny lay more in others' hands, or depended more on circumstances, than in her own hands. The overall shaping of the chart is another 'Bucket', but this time there are two handles: the anticlockwise retrograde Pluto and the somewhat clockwise Jupiter. The oppositions between Neptune and Chiron with the Sun and Venus comprise the bucket's 'rim'. The bucket interpretations have been given already for the Epoch chart but retro-grade Pluto rising in Aquarius suggests a conservative spokeswoman for a compromise approach towards, for example, the two forms of Christianity prevailing during her lifetime. Jupiter in Sagittarius in the 11th House, the other handle, indicates a somewhat impulsive exaggeration of licentious behaviour coupled with a desire for freedom at any price. The Sun in Virgo—Moon in Taurus sign polarity shows strong practical ability, reserve, caution and secretiveness, all of which could have proved useful to the business world. The Sun in 9th—Moon in 4th House polarity sug-

Figure 10: Birth Chart for Queen Elizabeth I of England.

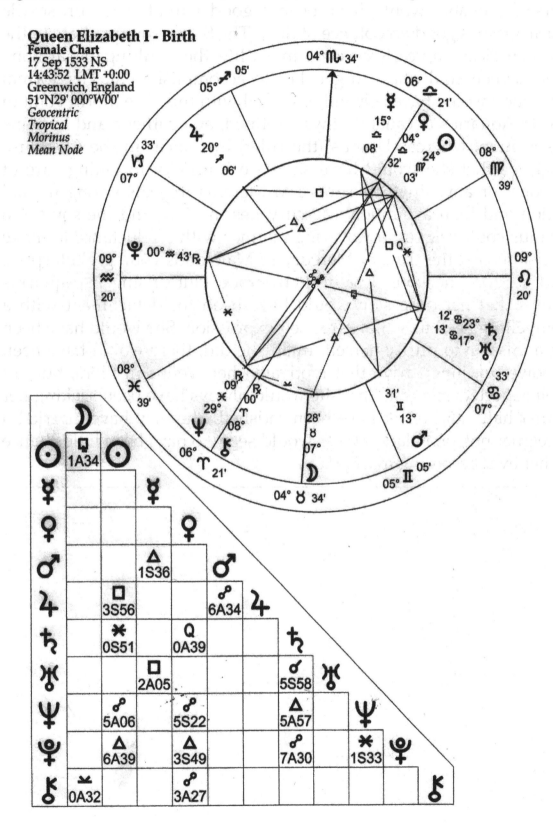

gests that she experienced strong parental conditioning, yet that she herself probably would have been a good parent. The Sun sextile Saturn shows good acceptance of duty. The Sun sesquiquadrate to the Moon indicates an early cleavage in her life, the resulting disharmony from which could have urged her to accomplishment. Her formal education would have helped her to deal with this. The Morin Point in the 1st Aquarius decanate shows a refined, sympathetic and humane disposition, whereas Uranus (the ruler) in Cancer in the 6th House suggests that she would have shown eccentricity in taking care of anyone (or anything). Its square to Mercury reveals strong mental action and high aspiration. Mercury lies in Libra and the square to Uranus could suggest a wavering manner with a reluctance to make decisions. Yet the trine of Mercury to Mars adds courage, enterprise and a strong nervous system. Retrograde Pluto rising in Aquarius shows that her obsession would have been for detachment with a compelling need to achieve free self-expression. She would have been on a mission to purify herself. In all she did, there would have been a powerful, inner drive that motivated her. Venus in Libra, but not well aspected, suggests that she would always have been seeking her "other half" and never have been satisfied. She may have married a foreigner but, on balance, there would seem to have been little chance of her ever becoming married.

James I

<u>Figure 11</u>: The Epoch Chart for King James I of England

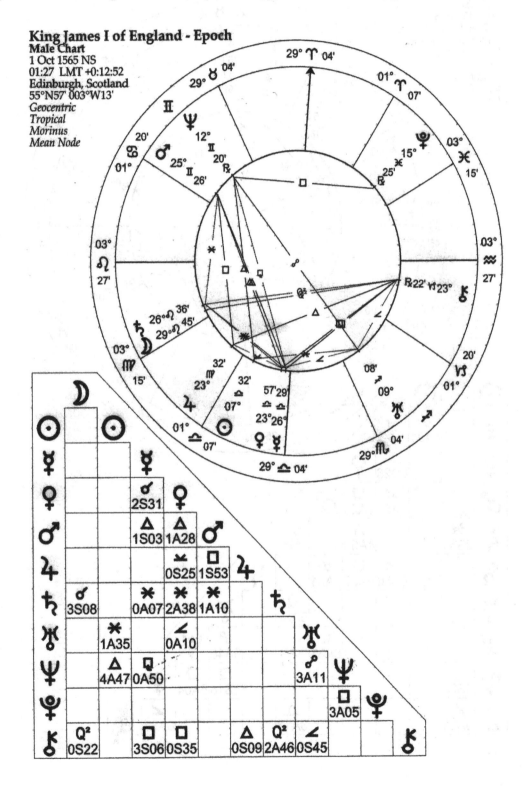

Figure 12: The Birth Chart for King James I of England.

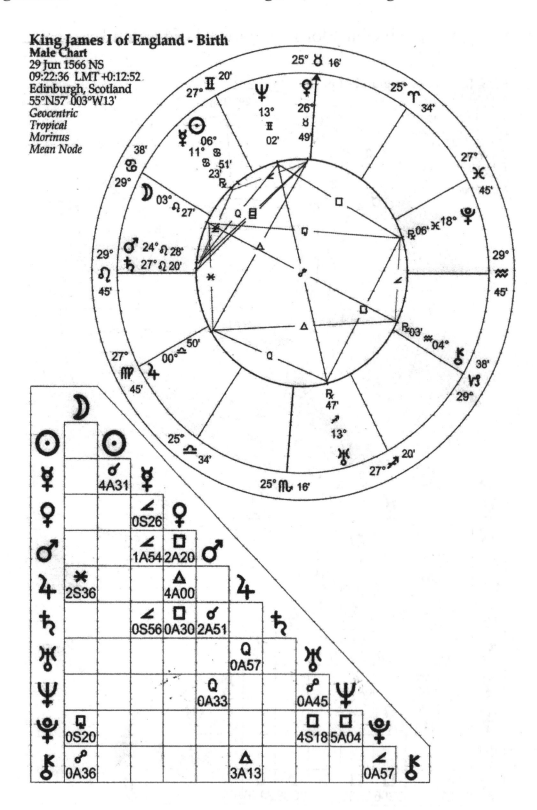

Comments on the Natal Charts of King James I of England

Two points about James's Birth chart are worthy of note: Firstly, his Sun in Cancer, in the 11th House, is unaspected save for a relatively weak conjunction with Mercury. An interpretation for this would be that his inner-self felt fragmented, or disconnected, from the rest of his character, implying independence, detachment and a law unto himself. He would not have been close to his father. All this could well have been true for James. However, closer examination shows that there is an essentially exact nonile (40°) aspect of the Sun with Venus. Additional close aspects to the Sun include a decile (36°) to the Moon and a tredecile (108°) to Pluto. Moreover, there is a septile (51.43°) within one degree as well as an almost exact 15th aspect (24°) to Neptune.

The nonile of Venus to the Sun suggests that his marriage partner would have been required to complete an ideal state for James.

Secondly, Mercury in Cancer, in the 11th House, is retrograde. This tends to reinforce his emotional sensitivity and to render his thinking less practical but more free (see the text, small print, under the Mentality section).

Note also that in James's two natal charts there are four quintile family aspects altogether to support an interpretation of good intelligence.

Charles I

Figure 13: Epoch Chart for King Charles I of England.

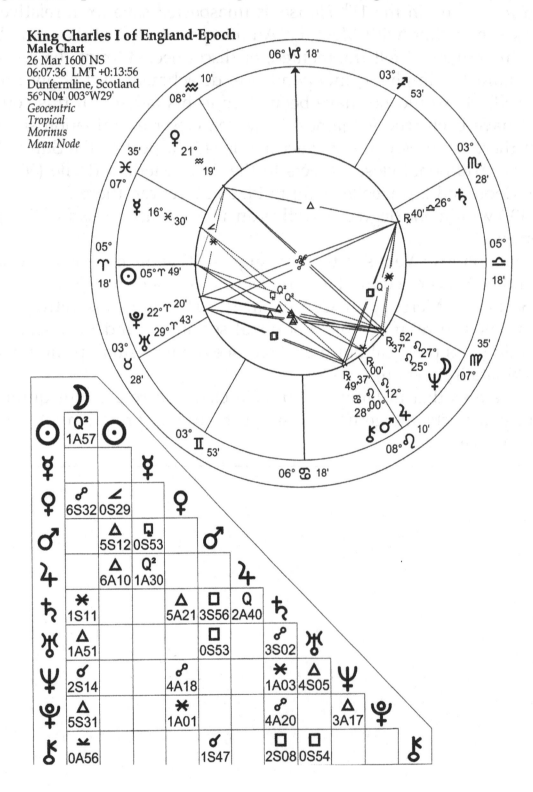

Figure 14: Birth Chart for King Charles I of England.

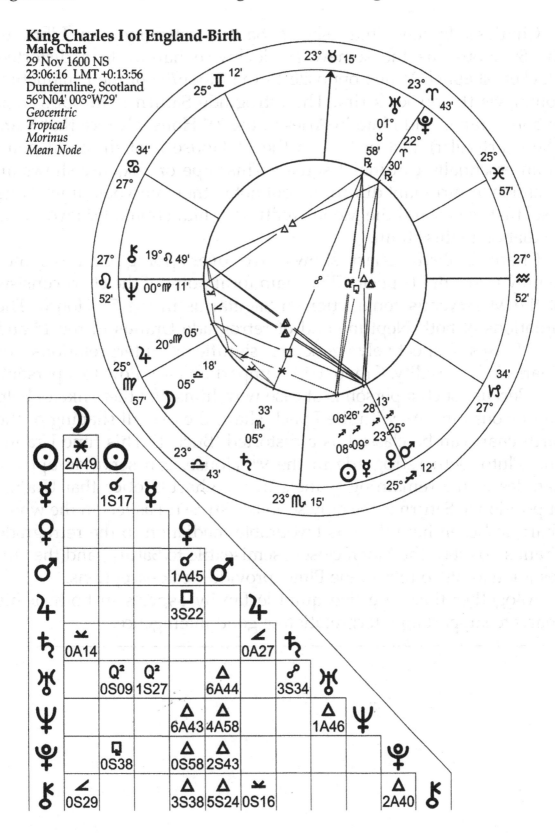

Comments on the Natal Charts of King Charles I

Charles's Epoch Chart shows Saturn retrograde in Libra in the 8th House as the somewhat clockwise handle to a distorted 'Bucket' shaping. Venus opposite to the Moon/Neptune conjunction comprises the bucket's rim. The retrograde Saturn is in opposition to both Uranus and Pluto in Aries in the 2nd House. Notice that Mars (the chart ruler), just in Leo, in the 5th House is at the focal point of an essentially cardinal T-square. This type of T-square shows an intention to surmount difficulties but not without nervous strain. Note also, that Venus and the Moon/Neptune conjunction offer favourable mediation to this strain.

Charles's Birth Chart shows two overlapping Grand Trines mainly in the fire triplicity. The main focal point of the chart consists of the Mars/Venus conjunction in Sagittarius in the 5th House. The situations of both Neptune and of retrograde Uranus in the 1st and 9th Houses respectively, generate significant interpretations for Charles's personality. Grand Trines impart an easy flow to a person's life. Because such a person is at ease with himself, others like to help and favour him. As with the Epoch chart, the overall shaping of the Birth chart can be classed as a distorted 'Bucket'. This time Uranus and Pluto, both retrograde in the 9th House, can serve as upright handles to the remaining planets in the chart. Notice that Uranus opposition to Saturn is the only seriously stressful aspect in the whole chart and even here there is favourable mediation to the retrograde Uranus Possibly, the Moon closely semisextile to Saturn, and the Sun sesquiquadrate to retrograde Pluto, provide weak exceptions.

Altogether there are five quintile family aspects in both of his charts to support an interpretation of good intelligence.

Oliver Cromwell

<u>Figure 15:</u> Epoch Chart for Oliver Cromwell, Lord Protector.

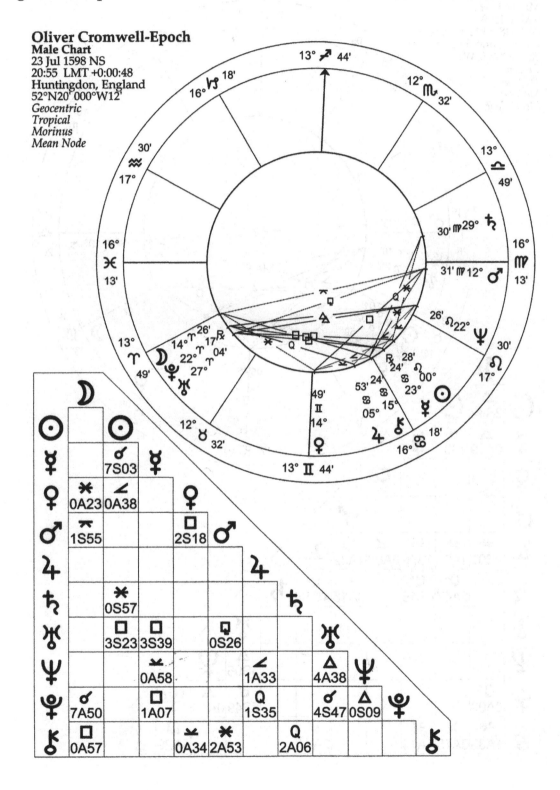

Oliver Cromwell-Epoch
Male Chart
23 Jul 1598 NS
20:55 LMT +0:00:48
Huntingdon, England
52°N20' 000°W12'
Geocentric
Tropical
Morinus
Mean Node

Figure 16: Birth Chart for Oliver Cromwell, Lord Protector.

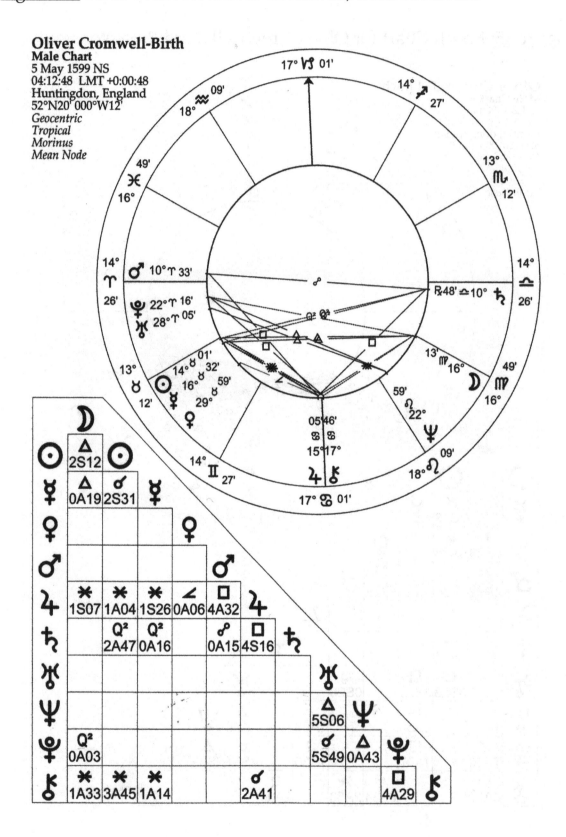

Comments on Oliver Cromwell's Natal Charts

Both of Oliver's charts are 'Bowl' shapes of the 'scoop-up' and 'give-out' type. They show his capacity for mobilising and conserving the resources of the Puritan way of life. The horizontal position of the rim of the bowl of the birth chart is the one that indicates pure conservation, or Oliver's supreme skill at preserving the values for which he fought. Here also, self-containment is at its most intense, or most completely centred in a cause, or sense of mission, to which he responded. His total power of achievement came from his instinctive realisation that there was a complete half of experience from which he was excluded in some subtle fashion, i.e. the unoccupied half of the chart became a challenge to his existence. The leading planet (Mars) shows how he sought to carry out his mission, or his everyday justification for existence. 'Bowl' characters are idealists and Oliver had two of them. At Epoch the rim of the bowl is not as clearly defined as it is at birth. However, the leading planet is the Moon, which indicates that his achievement had to have been public in nature and that it must have been rooted in his sympathy for the situation of men and women generally. Note also that at Epoch Mercury is retrograde in Cancer in the 5th House

Notice that altogether in both charts there are five quintile family aspects to support an interpretation of good intelligence. In the birth chart, note that Jupiter in Cancer in the 4th House, is the focal planet of the chart. It is at the focus of the strong bisextile pattern as well as at the focus of the weaker cardinal T-square one. It also has an exact semisquare to Venus. Its interpretation forms one of the main features in the interpretation of Oliver's birth chart.

Charles II

Figure17: Epoch Chart for King Charles II of England.

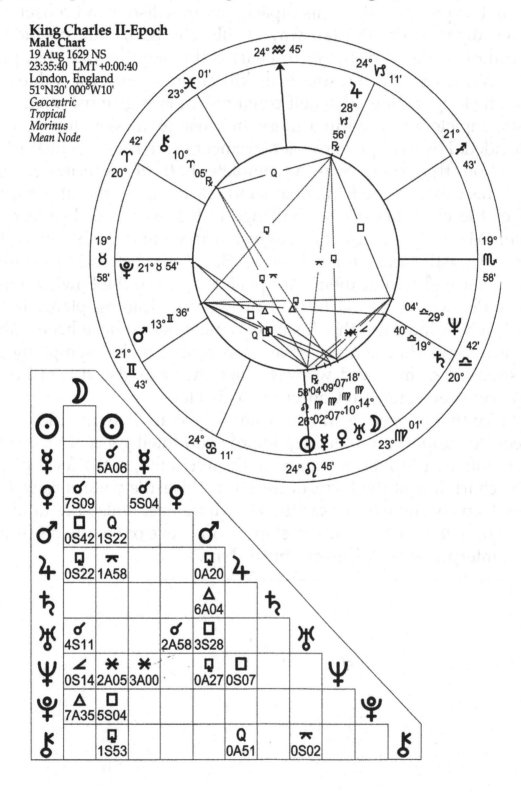

Figure 18: Birth Chart for King Charles II of England.

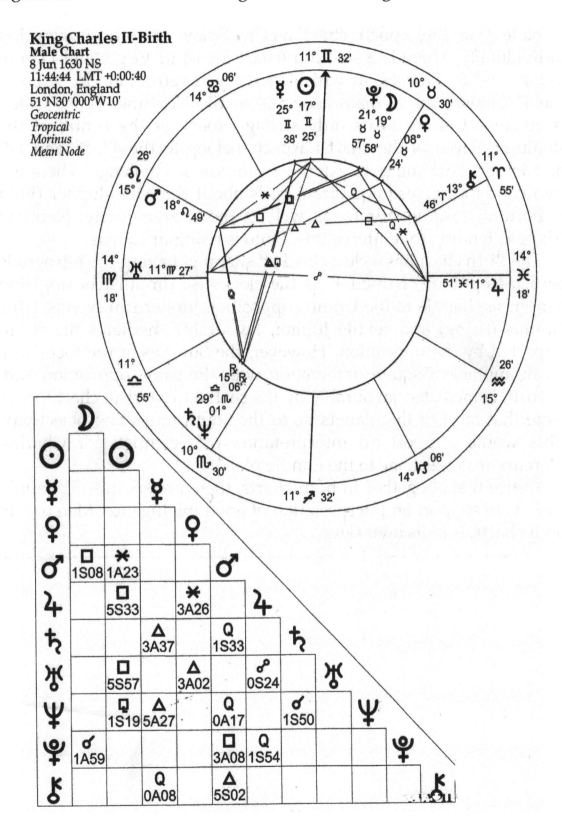

Comments on the Natal Charts of King Charles II

Note that the Epoch chart has a 'Splay' shaping suggesting individuality. There is a stellium (chart focus) in Virgo (and Leo) in the 4th and 5th Houses, in which Mercury is retrograde in Virgo in the 4th House and its main aspect is sextile Neptune. Venus (ruler) is conjoint Uranus as its only strong aspect, at the centre of the stellium. Eleven of the chart's aspects belong to the 4th, 8th and 12th harmonics. This suggests external stimulus or challenge. There are two contiguous, sesquiquadrate yods about the Mars-Jupiter (both important) sesquiquadrate, as well as the Uranus-Jupiter-Neptune triangle, tending to reinforce this. Pluto is rising in Taurus.

The Birth chart has a clear 'Bucket' shaping, having the retrograde Saturn-Neptune conjunction as the clockwise (impulsive) singleton (emphasis) handle to the Uranus opposition Jupiter rim. Venus, trine Uranus (rising) and sextile Jupiter, favourably mediates the strain imparted by the opposition. However, the Sun lies at the focus of a weak, mutable T-square interaction with the same opposition and, in turn, is mediated favourably by the sextile to Mars (a chart focus). Note that most of the planets lie to the South indicating objectivity. This would support an interpretation of 'Scientist' for Charles. Mercury (ruler) is trine to the handle planets.

Notice that altogether in both charts, there are six quintile family aspects to support an interpretation of good intelligence. Mercury, in both charts, is in its own sign.

James II

<u>Figure 19:</u> Epoch Chart for King James II of England.

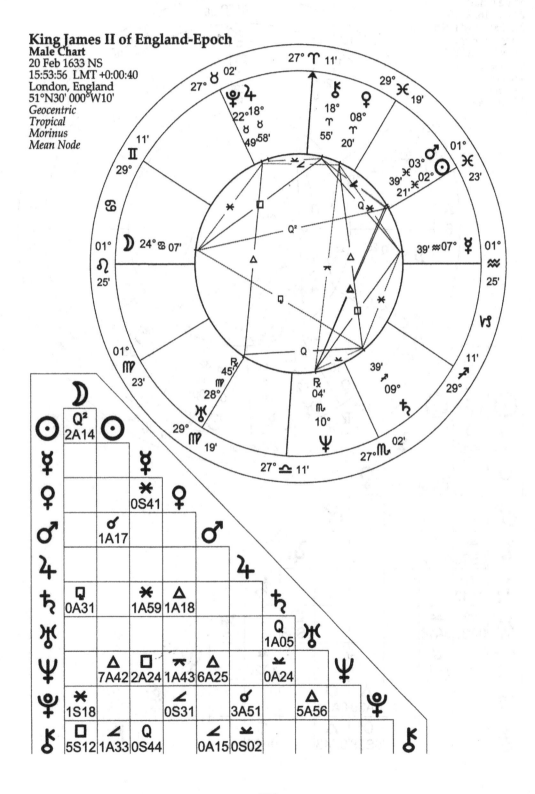

King James II of England-Epoch
Male Chart
20 Feb 1633 NS
15:53:56 LMT +0:00:40
London, England
51°N30' 000°W10'
Geocentric
Tropical
Morinus
Mean Node

Figure 20: Birth Chart for King James II of England.

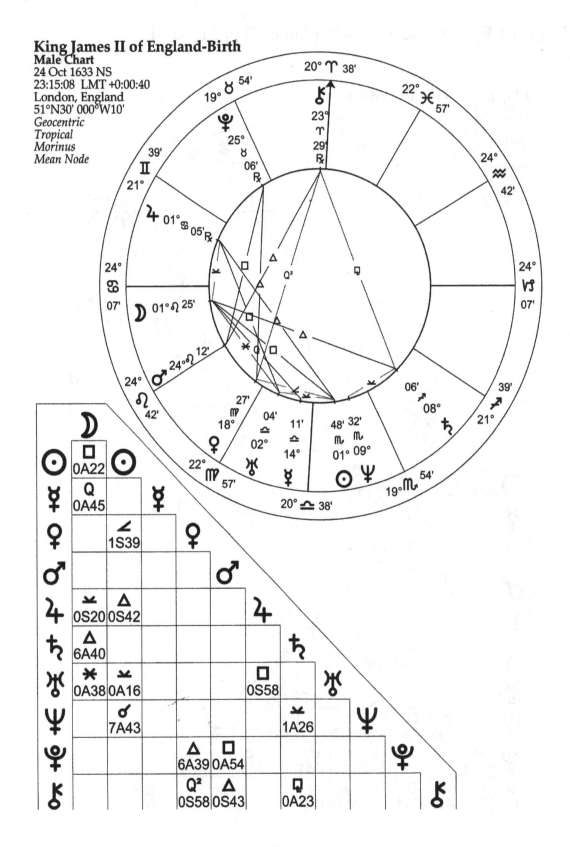

Comments on the Natal Charts of King James II

Notice that James's Epoch chart has a 'Splash' shaping; the planets tend to be distributed all around the chart, indicating scattered activities. 'Splash' people in life are connected with scattered situations. At their best, they have an ordered, general, worldly interest (for which they would need a good memory); while, at their worst, they spread their interests too widely, thereby exhausting their energies.

Notice also that James's Birth chart has a 'Locomotive' shaping, i.e. there is an empty 'trine' in the chart. This sort of person senses that a task needs to be accomplished in the social and intellectual world surrounding the person and drives forward to complete it. In James's case the leading planet of the 'locomotive' is retrograde Chiron in Aries in the 10th House. Chiron is described as 'the wounded healer', i.e. the person who is completing the task is someone who also needs help, perhaps of another/related sort, and so appears as a flawed problem solver.

The only specific-interplanetary-aspect-pattern in either chart is the bi-sextile to Mercury in Aquarius in the 7th House, at Epoch. This suggests beneficial, if not fascinating, conversation with people and their problems, who, in turn, would be willing to reciprocate later.

Notice that the Moon is rising in both charts, which provides James with a double dose of 'emotional response' but also with a remarkable memory (see above).

Finally, note that there are five quintile family aspects altogether in James's charts, to support an interpretation of good intelligence.

Mary II

Figure 21: Epoch Chart for Queen Mary II of England.

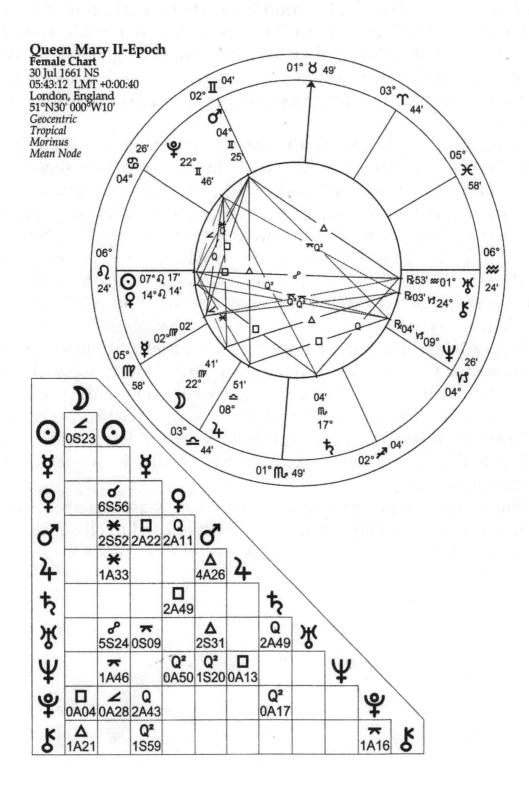

Queen Mary II-Epoch
Female Chart
30 Jul 1661 NS
05:43:12 LMT +0:00:40
London, England
51°N30' 000°W10'
Geocentric
Tropical
Morinus
Mean Node

Figure 22: Birth Chart for Queen Mary II of England.

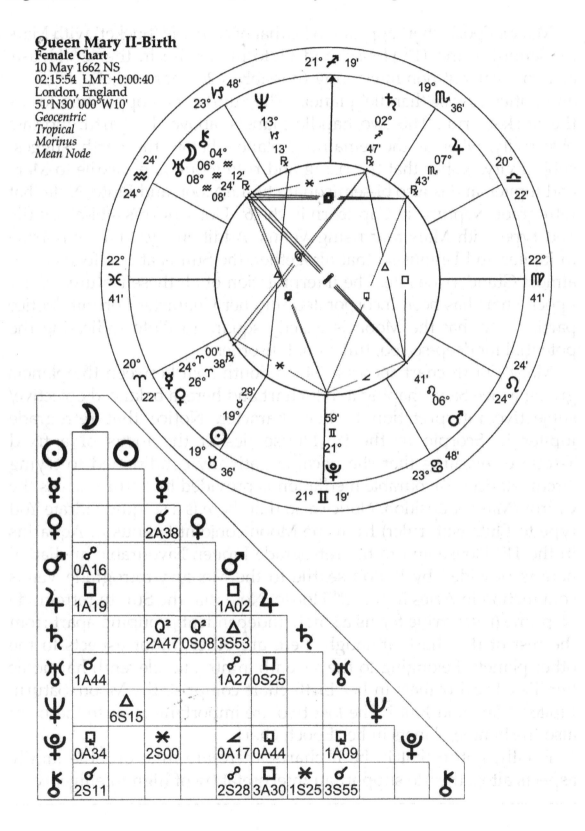

Queen Mary II-Birth
Female Chart
10 May 1662 NS
02:15:54 LMT +0:00:40
London, England
51°N30' 000°W10'
Geocentric
Tropical
Morinus
Mean Node

Comments on the Natal Charts of Queen Mary II of England

Mary's Epoch chart appears to be that of a double 'Bucket' with Mars in Gemini in the 11th House, and Pluto in Gemini in the 12th House, as two focal, but non-interacting (possibly a 20th harmonic?), singleton and anticlockwise 'handle' planets. The Sun/Uranus opposition forms the Bucket's rim. The two handle planets, above the Earth, indicate objectivity, whereas the remaining planets below the Earth, suggest subjectivity. Notice that the rising and ruling Sun is bi-sextile to Mars and Jupiter, and is also bi-semisquare to the Moon and Pluto. Note that retrograde Neptune in Capricorn in the 6th House forms a bi-biquintile Yod type with Mars and rising Venus. Additionally, Mars is bi-trine to Jupiter and Uranus so that altogether, the Sun is at one focus of an almost Grand Trine kite. The interpretation of all these features of her Epoch chart has been incorporated into her Character Portrait. Notice particularly that the Moon is exactly square to Pluto indicating the potential for deep-seated, functional disorder.

Mary's Birth chart shows a North-South split between the planets giving a 'See-Saw' shaping to her chart and here, a balanced objective/ subjective interpretation to her character. Notice that retrograde Jupiter in Scorpio in the 9th House lies at the focus of a fixed T-square revealing that she became patiently conditioned to trying circumstances. Favourable mediation is provided by Saturn across the Chiron/Mars opposition. Notice also that there is a sesquiquadrate Yod type to Pluto (sub-ruler) from the Moon conjoint Uranus in Aquarius in the 11th House and to the retrograde Jupiter. Favourable mediation here is provided by Pluto's sextile to the Mercury-retrograde Venus conjunction in Aries in the 2nd House. Note that the Sun to retrograde Neptune (ruler) trine forms a small, independent grouping apart from the rest of the chart, although there are other minor aspects to the other planets, belonging to the seventh, ninth and eleventh harmonic families. Focal planets in her Birth chart comprise the Moon, Saturn, Jupiter, Mars and Pluto. The last two are important because these are also the handle planets in her Epoch chart.

Finally, notice that in both charts, there are nine quintile family aspects altogether, to support an interpretation of high intelligence.

William III

<u>Figure 23</u>: Epoch Chart for King William III of England.

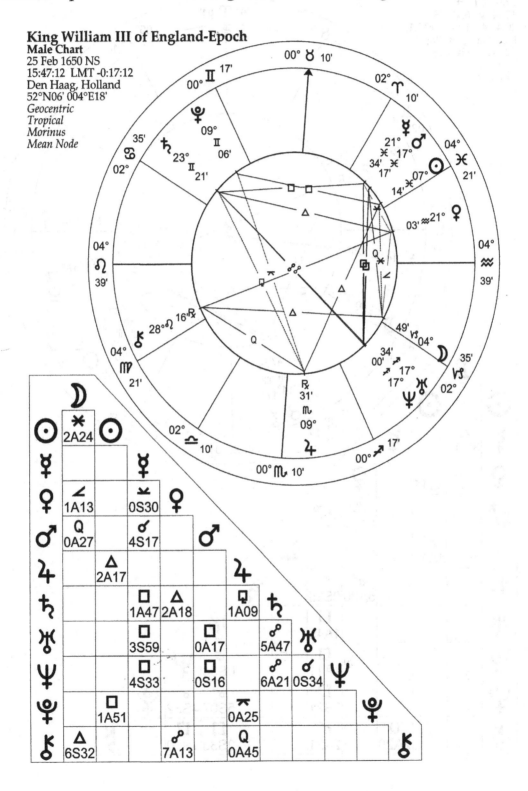

Figure 24: Birth Chart for King William III of England.

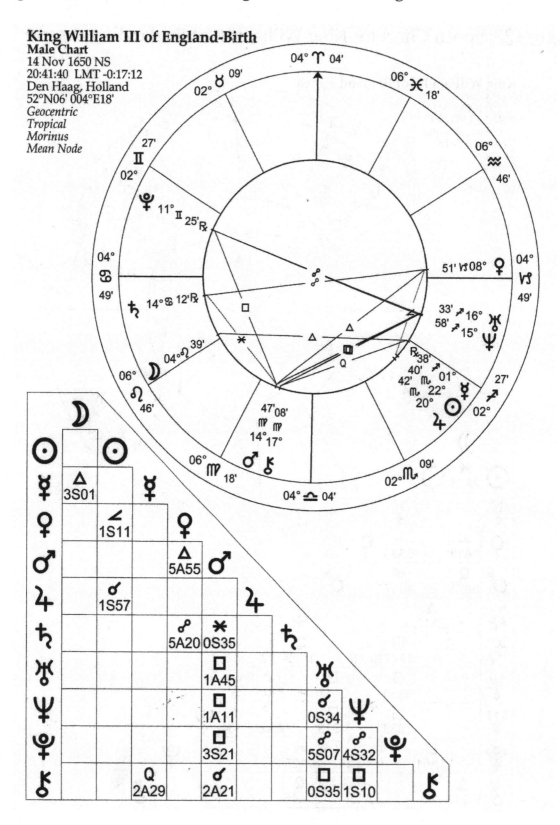

Comments on the Natal Charts of
King William III of England

William's natal charts indicate that his destiny was not in his own hands and that he was mainly subjective. Altogether, in both charts, there are three quintile family aspects to support an interpretation of intelligence.

His Epoch chart has a 'Splay' shaping, suggesting that he had his own particular individuality. A very noticeable feature of his Epoch chart concerns the almost exact conjunction between Uranus and Neptune, the centre of which is precisely square to Mars. This conjunction recurs every 171 years and suggests that William's imaginative idealism and intuition would have been unusual yet directable. In turn, this would have been inflamed by the square to Mars. Saturn completes a fairly weak, mutable T-square (through the medium strength conjunction of Mercury with Mars) that indicates an attempt to adjust to difficulties but here may also have imparted some sort of control. Favourable mediation comes from the trine of Saturn to Venus. Fortunately, William's individuality is supported strongly in both charts by a trine aspect at Epoch and conjunction one at Birth, of the Sun to Jupiter.

A similar (T-square) configuration occurs in William's Birth chart but even though the aspects are less severe, they still remain strong. Favourable mediation in this case occurs by means of the trine of Mars to Venus. The shaping of his Birth chart has been taken to be a 'Bucket' with malaspected Pluto as the anticlockwise (conservative), singleton, handle planet, but the shaping also fits rather well as a 'Bowl' (with Pluto, important as the leading planet), suggesting idealism. Notice that retrograde Saturn is rising in Cancer (probably its least favourable position), which would have had a detrimental impact on both William's appearance and character. Fortunately, it is almost ten degrees away from an exact conjunction with the Morin Point.

We could expect that it would prove interesting to conduct a synastry exercise for "William and Mary".

Anne

<u>Figure 25:</u> Epoch Chart for Queen Anne of England.

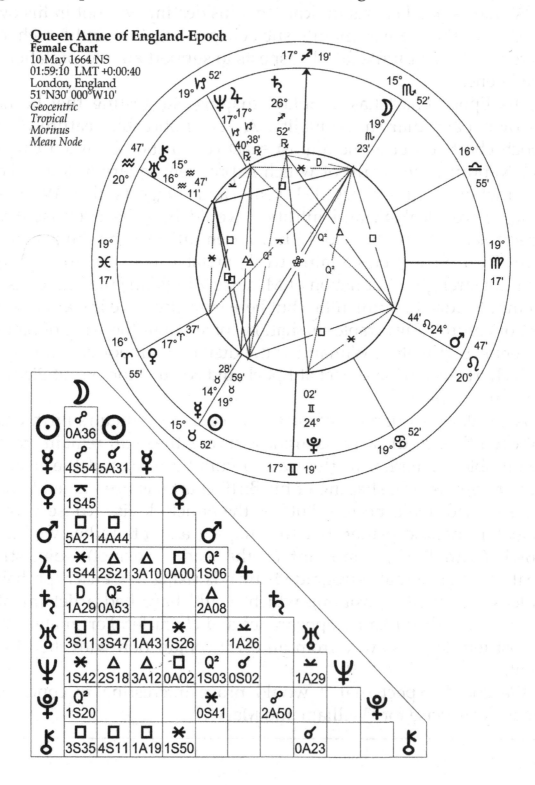

Queen Anne of England-Epoch
Female Chart
10 May 1664 NS
01:59:10 LMT +0:00:40
London, England
51°N30' 000°W10'
Geocentric
Tropical
Morinus
Mean Node

<u>Figure 26:</u> Birth Chart for Queen Anne of England.

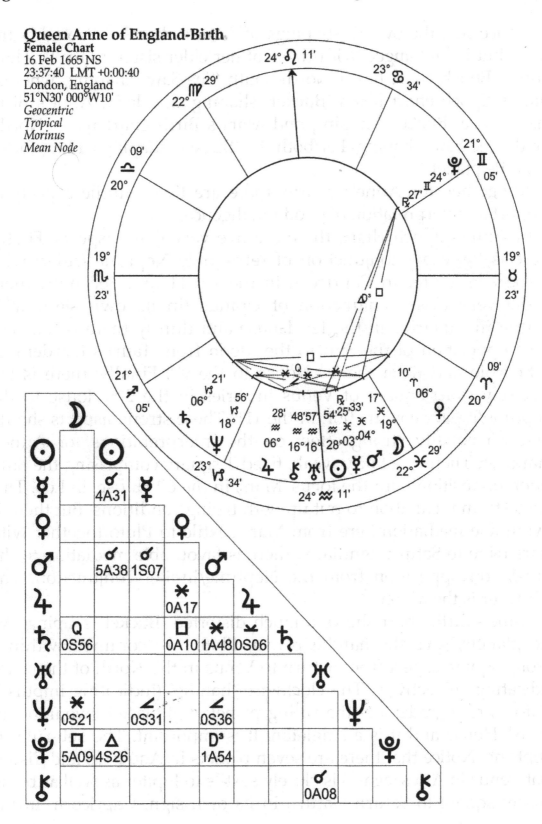

Comments on Queen Anne's Natal Charts

Notice that the overall shapings of Anne's charts are roughly the same, but interchanged with those of her elder sister, Mary II. Thus, Anne's Epoch chart has a North-South 'See-Saw' shaping, whereas Mary's Epoch chart has a 'Bucket' shaping. Similarly, Anne's Birth chart has a 'Bucket' shaping and Mary's Birth chart has a North-South 'See-Saw' shaping. For both the 'Bucket' shapings, Pluto forms a handle planet.

Altogether, for Anne's charts, there are five quintile aspects to support an interpretation of good intelligence.

In Anne's Epoch chart, there are five very close aspects. Firstly, there is the exact conjunction of retrograde Neptune (ruler) with retrograde Jupiter in Capricorn in the 11th House. Secondly, there is the very close conjunction of Uranus (in its own sign) with Chiron in Aquarius in the 12th House and thirdly there is the very close opposition of the Sun to the Moon from Taurus (gardening) to Scorpio and from the 3rd House to the 9th. Finally, there is the precisely exact square of Venus in Aries in the 2nd House to the Neptune/Jupiter conjunction in the 11th. These strong aspects should have an equally strong effect on the interpretations for Anne's character. There is a fairly weak, fixed T-square comprising the Sun-Moon opposition with the focus, Mars, in the 6th House, in Leo. This suggests an inclination to put up with trying conditions. But there is favourable mediation here from Mars sextile to Pluto together with Mars trine to Saturn. Similarly, there is favourable mediation to the Sun-Moon opposition from the Neptune/Jupiter conjunction. The sub-ruler is the Moon.

Anne's Birth chart shows a much distorted 'Bucket' shaping. All the planets, save the handle planet, Pluto, are confined within a strong square aspect from Saturn to Venus in the North of the chart, indicating subjectivity. The clockwise 'handle' (indicating impulse), Pluto, is retrograde; it is the ruling planet; it is placed favourably in the 8th House and it is a singleton. It is important. The sub-ruler is Neptune. Notice that there are seven planets in Aquarius and Pisces, that Venus in Aries (again) is closely sextile to Jupiter as well as being closely square to Saturn. Saturn in its own sign, Capricorn, in the

2nd House, is the leading planet of the 'Bucket' and is closely semi-square to Jupiter. Notice also that Mercury is retrograde in Pisces in the 4th House and finally, that the exact, unaspected Uranus/Chiron conjunction in Aquarius in the 4th House, in fact, is closely nonile to Saturn.

Appendix 2

Natal Charts for England's Tudor, Stuart and Protectorate Nearly Rulers.

Arthur Tudor

Lady Jane Grey

Philip II of Spain

Mary, Queen of Scots

Prince Henry Frederick Stuart (speculative)

Richard Cromwell

James, the Old Pretender

Bonnie Prince Charlie

Figure A: Epoch Chart for Arthur Tudor.

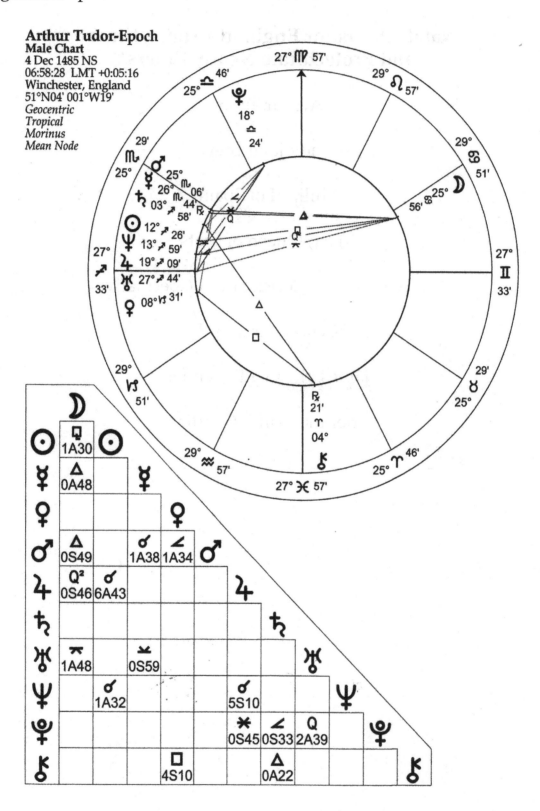

Figure B: Birth Chart for Arthur Tudor.

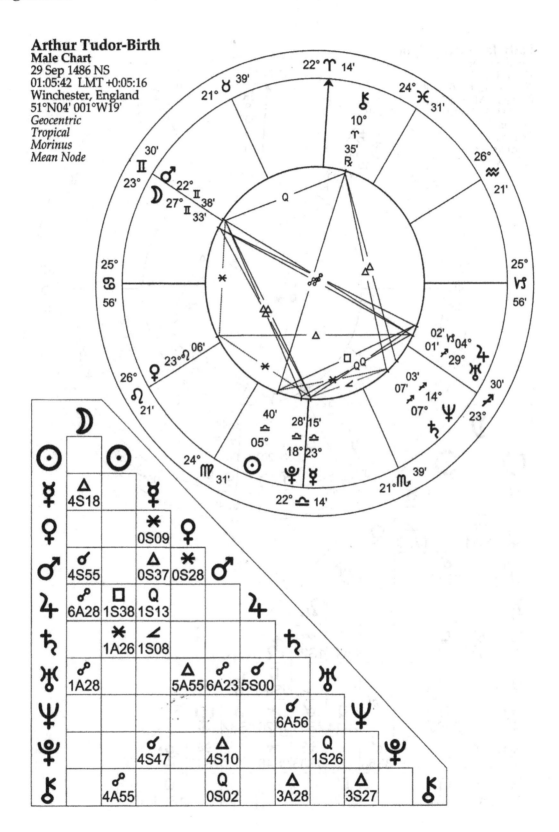

<u>Figure C:</u> Epoch Chart for Lady Jane Grey.

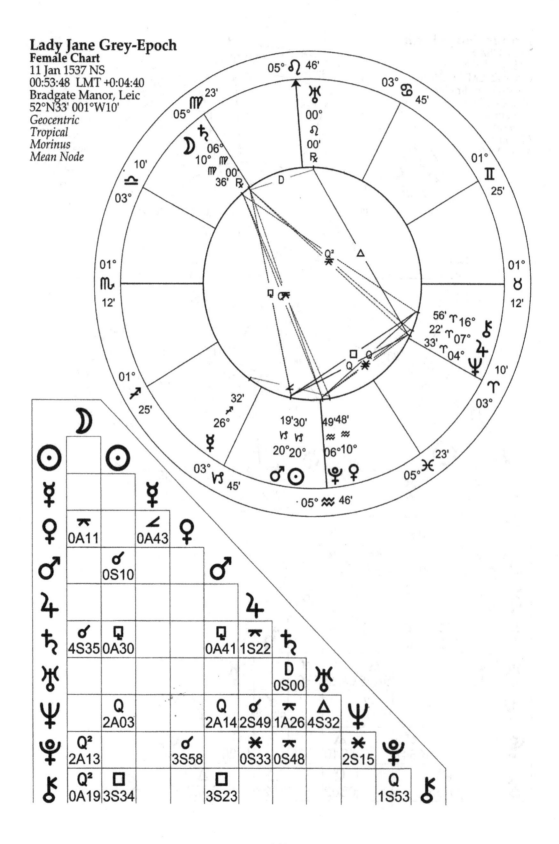

Figure D: Birth Chart for Lady Jane Grey.

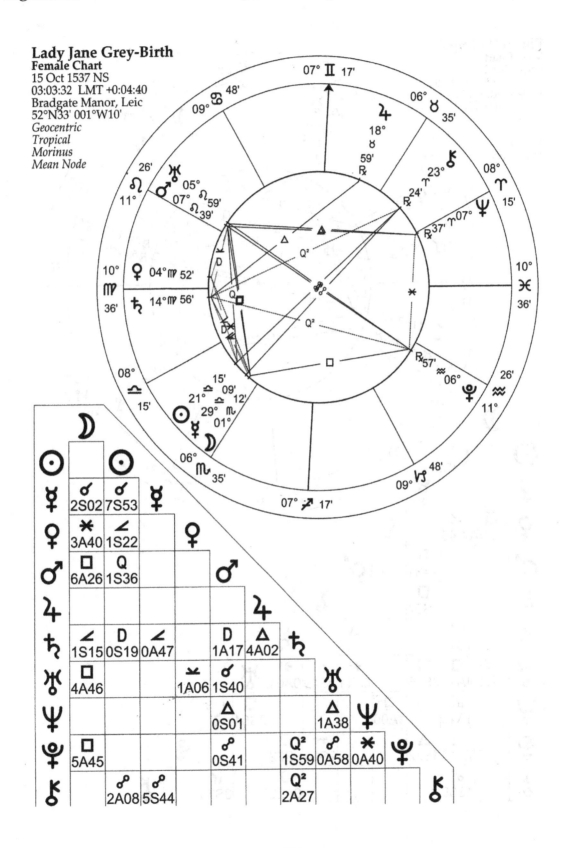

Lady Jane Grey-Birth
Female Chart
15 Oct 1537 NS
03:03:32 LMT +0:04:40
Bradgate Manor, Leic
52°N33' 001°W10'
Geocentric
Tropical
Morinus
Mean Node

Figure E: Epoch Chart for Philip II of Spain.

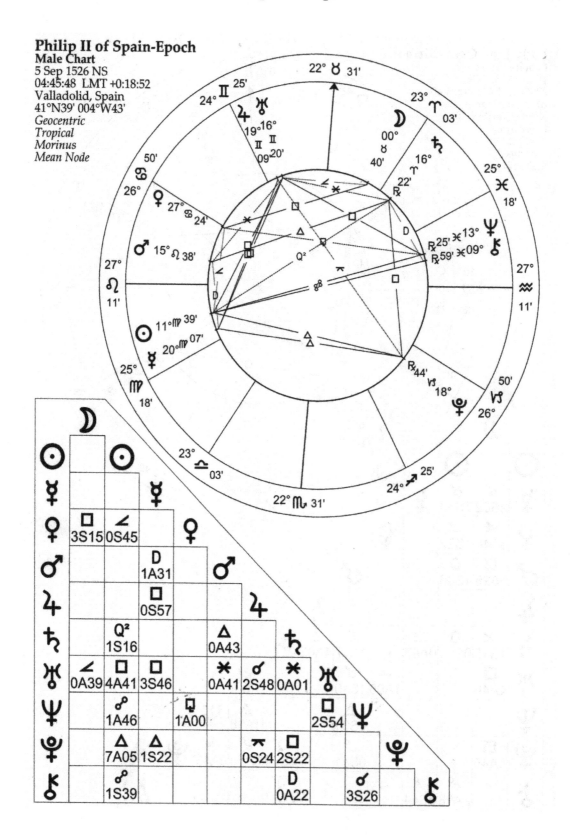

Philip II of Spain-Epoch
Male Chart
5 Sep 1526 NS
04:45:48 LMT +0:18:52
Valladolid, Spain
41°N39' 004°W43'
Geocentric
Tropical
Morinus
Mean Node

Figure F: Birth Chart for Philip II of Spain.

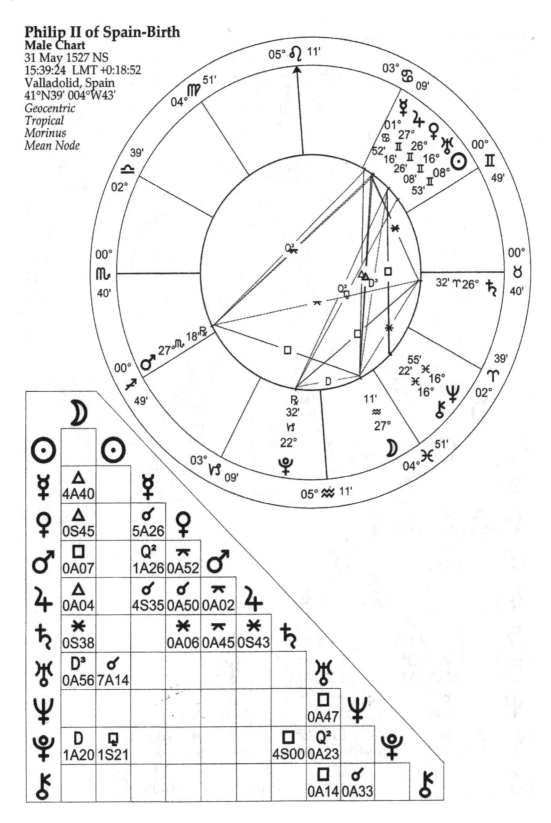

Philip II of Spain-Birth
Male Chart
31 May 1527 NS
15:39:24 LMT +0:18:52
Valladolid, Spain
41°N39' 004°W43'
Geocentric
Tropical
Morinus
Mean Node

Figure G: Epoch Chart for Mary, Queen of Scots.

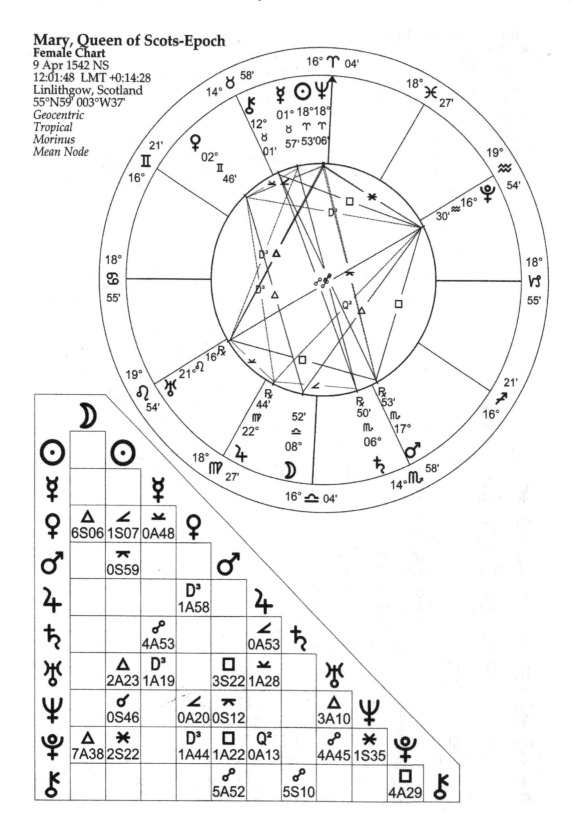

Mary, Queen of Scots-Epoch
Female Chart
9 Apr 1542 NS
12:01:48 LMT +0:14:28
Linlithgow, Scotland
55°N59' 003°W37'
Geocentric
Tropical
Morinus
Mean Node

Figure H: Birth Chart for Mary, Queen of Scots.

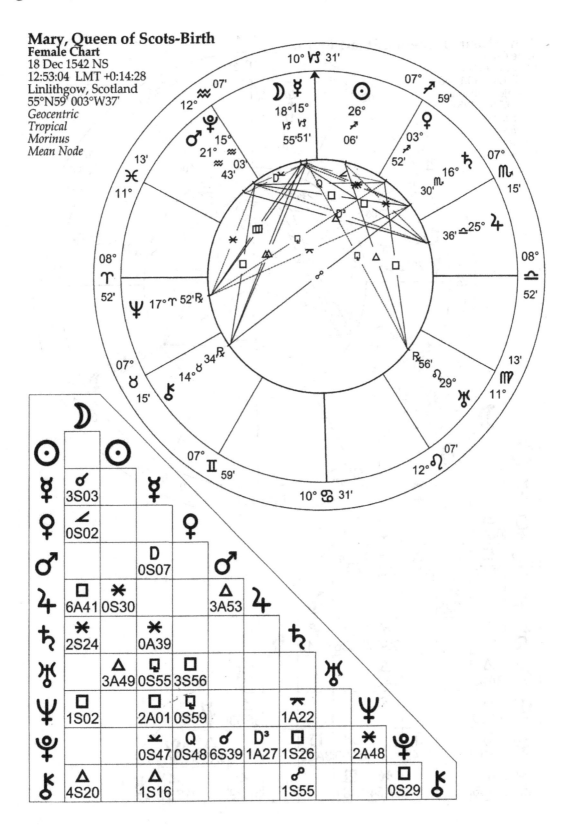

Mary, Queen of Scots-Birth
Female Chart
18 Dec 1542 NS
12:53:04 LMT +0:14:28
Linlithgow, Scotland
55°N59' 003°W37'
Geocentric
Tropical
Morinus
Mean Node

Figure I: Epoch Chart for Prince Henry Frederick Stuart (speculative)

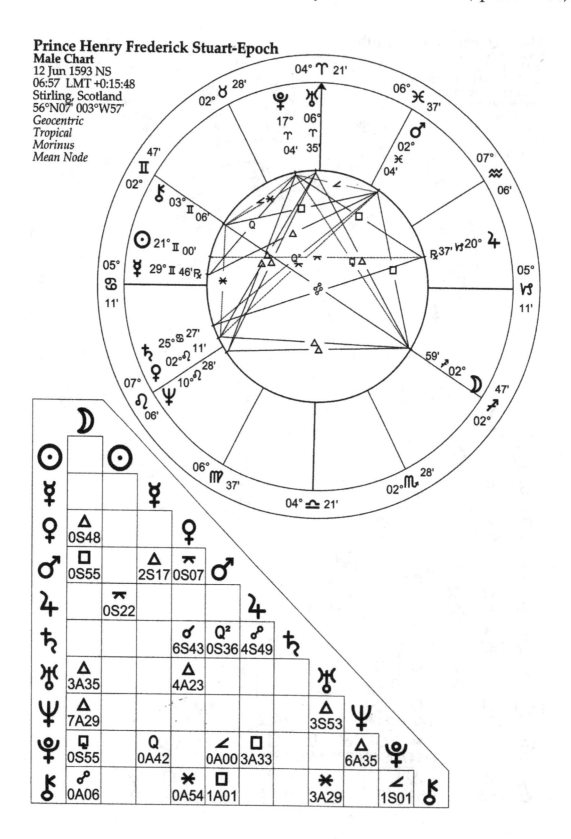

Prince Henry Frederick Stuart-Epoch
Male Chart
12 Jun 1593 NS
06:57 LMT +0:15:48
Stirling, Scotland
56°N07' 003°W57'
Geocentric
Tropical
Morinus
Mean Node

Figure J: Birth Chart for Prince Henry Frederick Stuart (speculative)

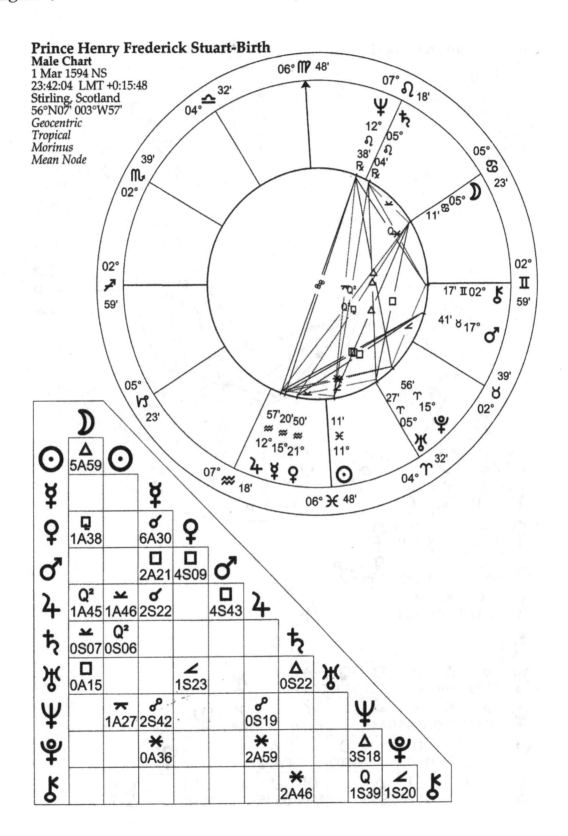

Prince Henry Frederick Stuart-Birth
Male Chart
1 Mar 1594 NS
23:42:04 LMT +0:15:48
Stirling, Scotland
56°N07' 003°W57'
Geocentric
Tropical
Morinus
Mean Node

Figure K: Epoch Chart for Richard Cromwell.

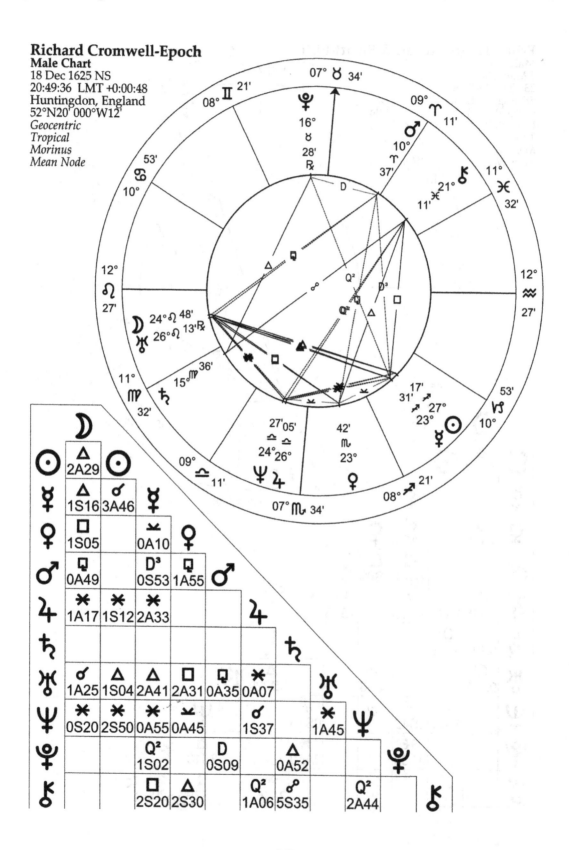

Richard Cromwell-Epoch
Male Chart
18 Dec 1625 NS
20:49:36 LMT +0:00:48
Huntingdon, England
52°N20' 000°W12'
Geocentric
Tropical
Morinus
Mean Node

Figure L: Birth Chart for Richard Cromwell.

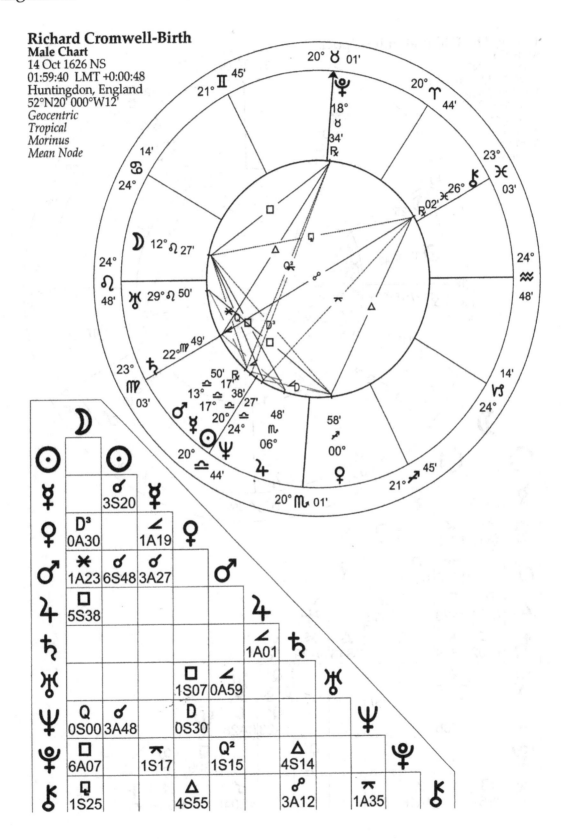

Richard Cromwell-Birth
Male Chart
14 Oct 1626 NS
01:59:40 LMT +0:00:48
Huntingdon, England
52°N20' 000°W12'
Geocentric
Tropical
Morinus
Mean Node

Figure M: Epoch Chart for James, the Old Pretender.

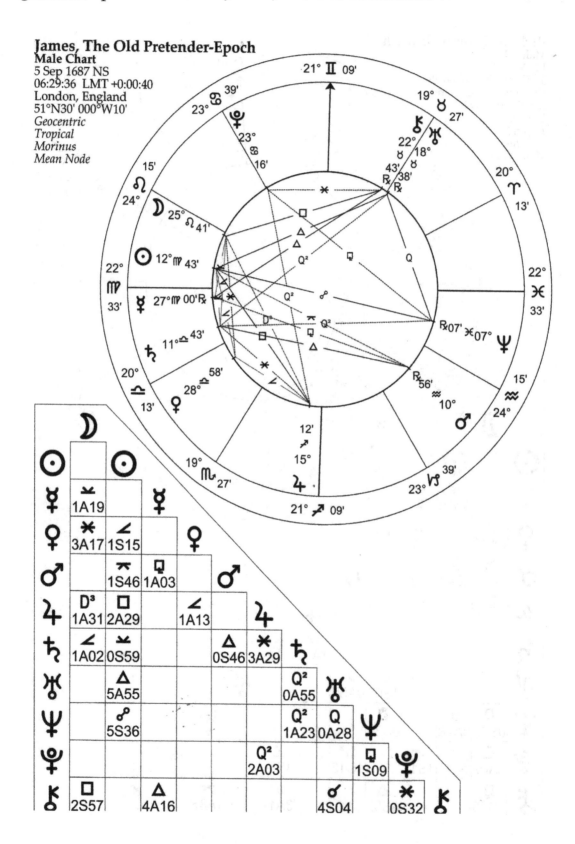

Figure N: Birth Chart for James, the Old Pretender.

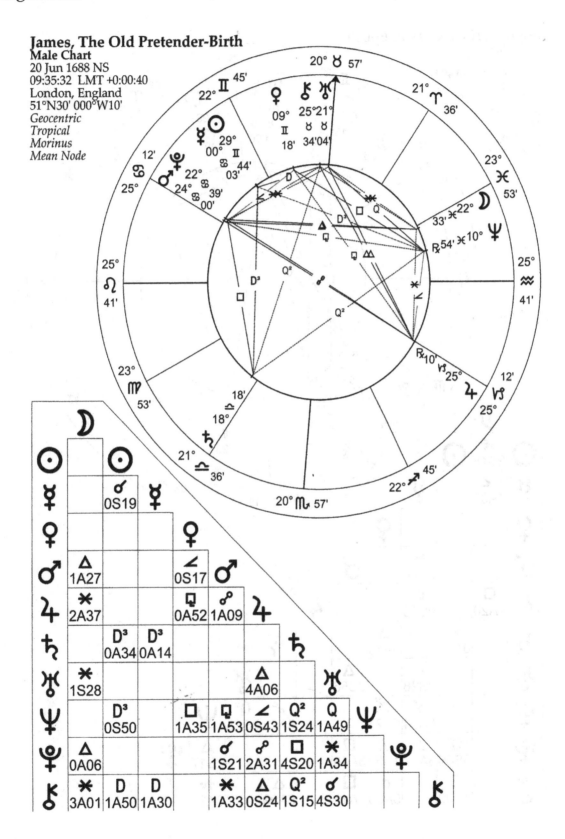

Figure O: Epoch Chart for Bonnie Prince Charlie.

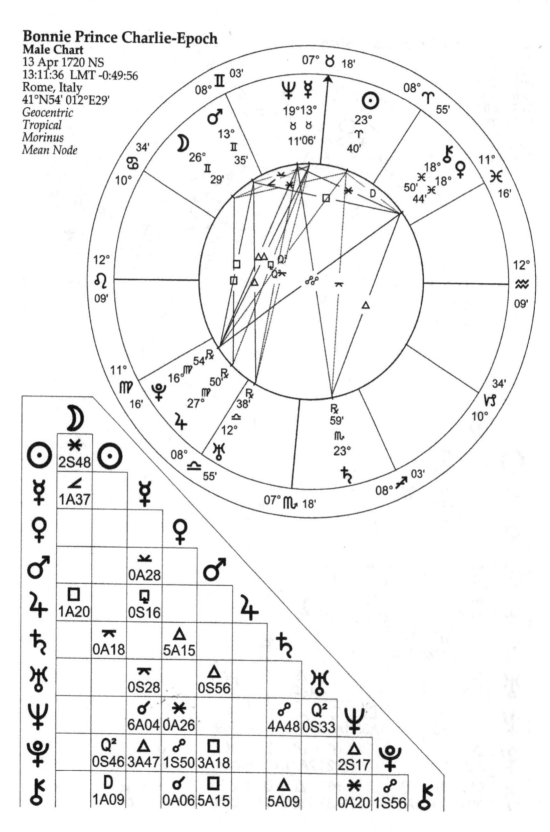

Bonnie Prince Charlie-Epoch
Male Chart
13 Apr 1720 NS
13:11:36 LMT -0:49:56
Rome, Italy
41°N54' 012°E29'
Geocentric
Tropical
Morinus
Mean Node

Figure P: Birth Chart for Bonnie Prince Charlie.

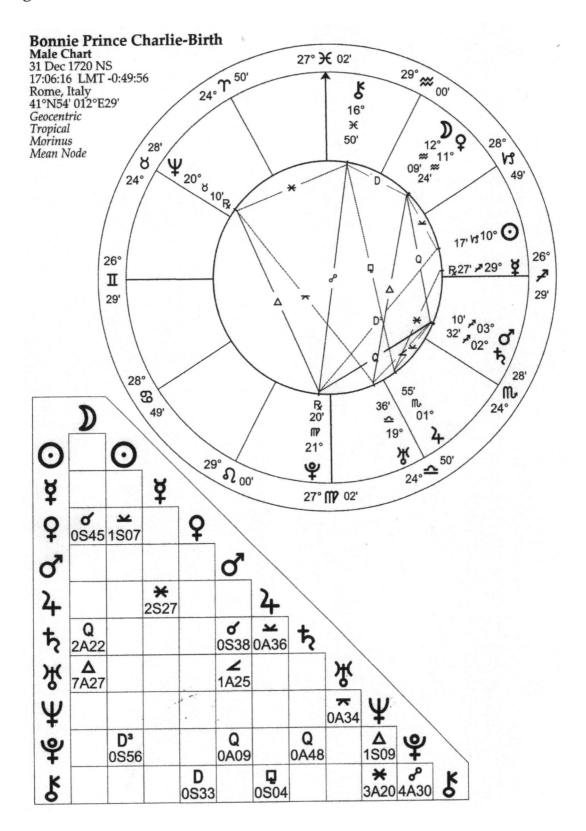

Appendix 3

Lines of Tudor and Stuart Descent

Now that we have examined the individual Character Portraits of England's Tudor, Stuart and Protectorate rulers, we can look at the Tudor and Stuart rulers as separate groups. To bolster the Tudor group to six we have included Prince Arthur Tudor, whose natal charts are given in Appendix 2 (A and B). Similarly, we have bolstered the Stuart group to nine by including Prince Henry Frederick, James the Old Pretender and Bonnie Prince Charlie. Their natal charts are also to be found in Appendix 2 [(I and J), (M and N) and (O and P)]. In both groups we have included two queens, because, as they are the direct daughters of a King of either group, they will carry 50% of their father's genetic make-up in theirs, just like sons.

Previously, we saw that there are three main indicators for interpreting any chart; namely the positions of the Sun, Moon and Morin Point. Thus there are 36 main indicators for the 12 Tudor natal charts. We found that that there were no substantially significant distributions for these among the signs or the Houses for the Tudor group, but the most occupied sign was 6 for Cancer, and the least was 0 for Scorpio. Similarly, there are 54 main indicators for the 18 charts of the 9 members of the Stuart group. Whereas we found nothing significant for these among the 12 Houses, we did find a significant occupancy of them in the sign Leo. The expected number of them contained in each sign would be 4.5 (i.e. 54 divided by 12) so that χ^2 for the sign Leo in the Stuart case is 20 [i.e. $(14-4.5)^2$ divided by 4.5]. Hence, we could suggest that the sign of the Stuarts is Leo.

We have also looked at all of the planets (excepting Chiron) by means of harmonic analysis using the 'Jigsaw 2' computer program. This can show number harmonics (i.e. closely related to aspects) that are important for family groups. Having made allowances for duplicates* (i.e. counting each duplicate as a single item of data rather than twice), we found that, of the first twelve harmonics (there were too many vacancies in the harmonics for those higher than twelve due to insufficient data for both the Tudors and the Stuarts) for the Tudors, the 2nd harmonic had a χ^2 value of 12.4 and the 7th harmonic (containing one vacant position) had a χ^2 value of 10.5. These results, like those of the Plantagenet kings group, suggest that the Tudors existed in a world of conflict, and also of transformation. For the Stuarts, the 9th harmonic (1 vacant) had a χ^2 value of 16.7 indicating that the right partner would improve their situation considerably and that the 3rd harmonic (χ^2 =8.1) indicates favourable conditions. In addition, the 10th harmonic (1 vacant, χ^2 = 13.3) and the 5th harmonic (χ^2 = 9.3) suggest support for an interpretation of good intelligence.

If we consider all of the planets for each group separately and plot their occupancy as polar graphs in 18 or 24 equal Morinus sectors for the Tudors and Stuarts respectively around the circle of the ecliptic, as we did previously for the Plantagenet kings group, then we obtain similar graphs of low significance for the occupancies of the sectors around the ecliptic. However, if, instead, we set the <u>Moon's</u> position as the origin in all of the Epoch and Birth charts for each of the members of the Plantagenet kings group, for the Tudor rulers group and for the Stuart rulers group, then results of a more substantial nature are obtained as illustrated in Graphs A, B and C, respectively. Notice that the 'P' values for all three graphs are around 10% or less, indicating good significance. For completeness, and similar to the 'Morin Point as Origin' graphs, those for the 'Sun's position as Origin' graphs (excluding Mercury and Venus that are always fairly close to the Sun) provide us with sectors whose occupancies are, again, of low significance.

For the 'Moon's position as Origin' graphs we see that the highest occupancy sectors occur in different parts of the graphs. Could these observations suggest differences between each of these families? In any case, the results support the idea that the Moon is the planet mainly responsible for controlling human reproduction as far as the Solar System is concerned. Importantly, they may also be starting to suggest that we are indeed 'Members of the Solar System' even though we are, naturally, Earthlings first.

----

*Duplicates occur mainly when a) we have retrograde motion, b) when we consider outer planets and c) when looking at low number harmonics because the allowed 'orbs' are larger, or d) with combin—ations of these.

Using The Moon's Position As The Origin In Every Chart, Graph A Shows The Occupancy Of All [300] Of The Rest Of The Planets In Equal [10°] Sectors [1 → 36] Around The Ecliptic In The 30 Natal [i.e. Epoch And Birth] Charts Of The Fourteen Plantagenet Kings And One Plantagenet Prince.

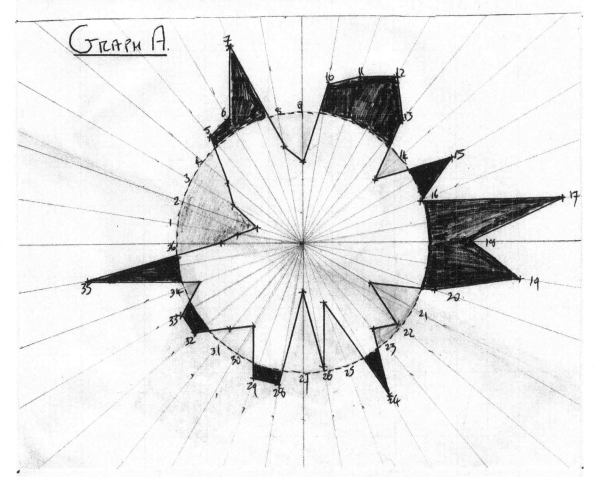

Graph A.

- - - - - - Expected Value Per Sector Is <u>8·33</u>
<u>Scale</u>: 1cm ≡ 2 Items Of Data ≡ 2 Planets Per Sector
$\sum \chi^2 = 45·3$ (D=35) P ⩲ 10%. χ^2 For Sector 17 is 9·0.

SETTING THE MOON'S POSITION AS THE ORIGIN IN EVERY CHART, GRAPH B SHOWS THE OCCUPANCY OF ALL [120] OF THE REST OF THE PLANETS IN EQUAL [20°] SECTORS [1> 18] AROUND THE ECLIPTIC IN THE 12 NATAL CHARTS OF THE FIVE TUDOR MONARCHS AND ONE TUDOR PRINCE.

GRAPH B

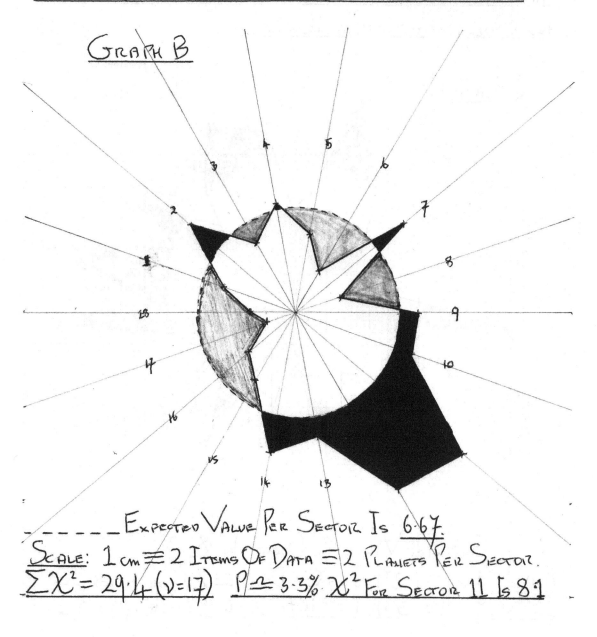

- - - - - - - EXPECTED VALUE PER SECTOR IS 6·67.

SCALE: 1 cm ≡ 2 ITEMS OF DATA ≡ 2 PLANETS PER SECTOR.

$\sum \chi^2 = 29.4 \, (\nu=17)$ P ≅ 3·3% χ^2 FOR SECTOR 11 IS 8·1

Setting The Moon's Position As The Origin In Every Chart, Graph C Shows The Occupancy Of All [180] Of The Rest Of The Planets In Equal [15°] Sectors [1→24] Around The Ecliptic In The 18 Natal Charts Of 6 Stuart Monarchs, One Prince And Two Pretenders.

Graph C.

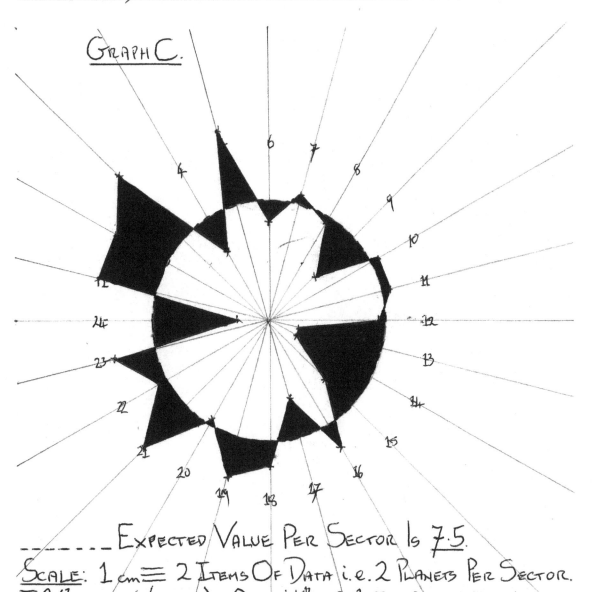

- - - - - - - - Expected Value Per Sector Is 7.5.

Scale: 1 cm ≡ 2 Items Of Data i.e. 2 Planets Per Sector.

$\sum \chi^2 = 30.6 \, (\nu=23)$ $P \simeq 11\%$ χ^2 For Sector 3 Is 4.0